Jay   Senior was born in Rotherham and still lives
the   with her husband and youngest son. She managed
Ris y Business, a youth work programme working with
vict ns of child sexual exploitation, for fourteen years.
Du   ng that time she repeatedly alerted the authorities
to   e growing number of girls being groomed and
abu   d. When she was hounded out of her position, she
to   job managing Swinton Lock, a charity that pro-
vi   ctivities for children, and in 2013 was asked by
M   rah Champion to take on a role supporting the
vic   f sexual abuse in Rotherham. In 2015 she won
the   *Housekeeping* Woman of the Year Outstand-
ing   ement Award.

Broken and Betrayed

The true story of the Rotherham abuse scandal

from the woman who fought to expose it

Jayne Senior

PAN BOOKS

First published 2016 by Pan Books
an imprint of Pan Macmillan
20 New Wharf Road, London N1 9RR
Associated companies throughout the world
www.panmacmillan.com

ISBN 978-1-5098-0162-6

a..nce

Pan M:...bility for,
any...book.

A CIP ca..sh Library.

Typeset by Ellipsis Digital Limited, Glasgow
Printed and bound by CPI Group (UK) Ltd, Croydon, CR0 4YY

Visit **www.panmacmillan.com** to read more about all our books
and to buy them. You will also find features, author interviews and
news of any author events, and you can sign up for e-newsletters
so that you're always first to hear about our new releases.

*This book is dedicated to Paul, Lee, Ben, Samuel,
my sister Susan and all my family. I always knew I
had your love and support. And to Mum, Dad,
Phil, Barbara and Joanne – I will always miss you.
And to all the survivors, and their families,
who have been through so much. It has
been a privilege to work with you.*

Prologue

I sat in my car outside the broken and peeling front door which led to Debbie's tiny flat. She was twenty-one now, and still the same angry, abused, vulnerable mess she'd been when I'd first met her at the age of sixteen. She was always late going anywhere, and as I waited, impatiently tapping my fingers on the steering wheel and repeatedly pressing 'redial' on my phone, I began to wonder whether I'd even got the right address. After all, we'd moved her no less than twenty-five times in five years . . .

She was a girl who fell out with everyone – landlords, B & B owners, pimps, punters, social services, the police. Anyone who'd ever dealt with her got the rough edge of her tongue, even me. You only needed to say the slightest thing and she'd flip, blasting you with a mouthful of vicious abuse. Then she'd suddenly stop and burst into tears. She was that kind of girl.

After my tenth call, the front door opened and out she came. We were due to go shopping to buy her a new bed. As she walked down the scruffy, can-strewn path I examined the outfit she'd chosen for the trip – a black baby-doll nightie, completely see-through, with feather trim. She had nothing underneath but a G-string, and on her feet a pair of tottering high heels. The outfit was completed with a battered carrier bag she swung from her left wrist.

As she got in the car I looked at her, raising my eyebrows.

'Fuck off,' she said.

'Good morning to you too, Debbie,' I said brightly. 'You look nice . . .'

'Fuck off.'

'Just the thing for going bed shopping,' I said. 'You couldn't have chosen better.'

The night before, we'd had some trivial argument on the phone that ended with her telling me where to go and that she never wanted to see me again. This was normal. Of course, I never did what she wanted, which is why she was trying so hard to shock me with her appearance. It was like water off a duck's back. Besides, I cared about her too much to be bothered by a protest like this.

From the age of four or five Debbie was being sexually assaulted by her alcoholic mother's various boyfriends. When she was seven she was taken into care just before Christmas after a neighbour spotted her standing outside her Rotherham home in the snow, barefoot. Her mum and stepfather had decided to punish her for some minor thing by turning her out in the bitter cold.

When the neighbour saw her she was crying to be let back in.

At fourteen she met a man who got her into drugs, then began forcing her out on the streets to finance both his habit and hers. She was about sixteen when I first met her through the work I was doing with Risky Business, an organization set up to protect and help girls who were being sexually abused. Debbie was working the streets of Sheffield, fiery and damaged and full of bitterness for everything that had happened to her.

'I'll never forgive social services for putting me in care,' she told me during that first meeting. 'What the fuck's a few beatings off your mam and dad compared to my life now?'

We found her a flat in Rotherham in the hope it would break the link to Sheffield. For a while she was doing well. Then she fell in with a pimp and his drug-addicted entourage. They came over one night and, for twelve hours, forced her to give them oral sex while they took crack and heroin. When they'd left, she called me in a terrible state. I went over to find her flat completely trashed, blood up the walls and drug paraphernalia everywhere.

We moved her again and again. She got involved with a known abuser who roped her into a terrible scam. She was small and thin, and when he had sex with her this man made her wear children's underwear, which he would then sell on to paedophiles as the real thing. She

3

knew it was wrong but she was too scared of him to refuse. We moved her again but danger and abuse followed her round like a dark shadow.

She got to know some of the other abused girls we were working with, along with their so-called 'boyfriends' – in reality, the men who were raping and abusing them, and trafficking them all over the north of England. One of these girls told me she'd been offered £200 by an abuser to lure Debbie into a lonely spot high on the moors, where she would be videotaped being raped and then murdered. The girl had no reason to believe this wasn't a genuine request, so I reported it to social services and the police before going to warn Debbie.

At this stage, I believe she had a complete nervous breakdown. She decided to change her life and she tried very hard to stay on the straight and narrow. But she was a wreck. Soon after, I was walking through a park with her when an Asian man came up to me and asked me the time. Before I could answer, Debbie let fly a tirade of abuse.

'Fuck off, you dirty pervert!' she screamed. 'I saw you looking at her tits! Fuck off or I'll do you!'

The man backed away slowly, palms raised upwards, shaking his head. Later, I took Debbie to a McDonald's for a burger. She insisted that we both had to sit facing the wall to ensure that no one could see her eating, so paranoid was she by this stage.

She moved again, into a dingy B & B. A couple of days into her stay, her seedy landlord said he would only make her breakfast if she gave him oral sex. She could hardly stay in such circumstances and so we had yet another housing crisis on our hands. When I went to pick her up, dirty and dishevelled, she was still complaining of feeling hungry.

'Don't worry,' I said, 'when we get to the office I'll make you some toast.'

'Toast?!' she screamed. 'Fookin' toast?! Why does everyone always mek me fookin' toast? Can't I have something better than bloody toast for a change?!'

I stopped the car at the side of the road.

'What you doin'?' she said.

'Here's a quid,' I said, handing her a coin that was lodged in the ashtray. 'Get out and go and get your own breakfast. I've had enough.'

She climbed out of the car and stood at the side of the road, a great pout all over her face.

'Where'm I gonna go?'

'I dunno,' I said, 'but I'm not being spoken to like that.' And with that I shut the door.

She started to cry, then tapped on the window.

'I'm sorry,' she said. 'Please don't leave me.'

So she got back in and we went to seek out yet another place to lay her head for the night . . .

Now here we were, a few months later, off to buy her a bed, her looking like something from a trucker's dirty magazine and me trying to keep my cool. I never mentioned the outfit again, which infuriated her even more. Finally, we got to the bed store at the edge of town.

'Right,' I said, 'let's go and have a look. You coming?'

She looked at me, then pulled her nightie round her. It was midday. Lots of people about; normal people, dressed in normal everyday clothing.

'Come on,' I said, 'I haven't got all day.'

'Oh, fuck off,' she replied, before pulling a top and a pair of jeans from her carrier bag. Then she smiled at me.

'I'm sorry, Jayne,' she said.

1

In the mid 1960s, when I was born, Rotherham was a prosperous place. The industries which had kept this part of South Yorkshire going since Victorian times were still producing enough steel and coal to ensure full employment in the town. It wasn't and isn't the prettiest place on earth; it was a town where work was hard and industry heavy, but the community was warm, caring and tight-knit. Families were the same and ours was no exception.

My parents, Joan Hazel Johnson, known as Hazel, and Arthur William, only ever called 'Johnny' Johnson, were in their late thirties when I arrived – unusual for then when many, if not most, couples had married, settled down and had their families by their mid twenties. Actually, that was my parents' story too. They'd met during the war and married quickly, as couples did then. Originally from Middlesbrough, my dad was an RAF Flight Engineer and was stationed at RAF Binbrook for the duration. Dad joined the air force in December 1941, aged just seventeen, and flew with 460 Australian Squadron Bomber Command in Avro Lancasters, in particular

'G' for George, which is now preserved in the Australian War Memorial Museum in Canberra, Australia. He was shot down over Caen, France, on his twenty-second mission but returned to England safely and carried on to complete thirty-one operations. He was then transferred to the RAF Transport Command at the end of the war, making regular flights to Singapore. He flew in the 1948 Berlin Airlift from start to finish, completing 294 missions. In October 1950 he was discharged as medically unfit from air crew duties after completing an amazing 1,754 flying hours.

By a long way, I was the baby of the family. My eldest sister, Barbara, was a full eighteen years older than me, my brother, Phil, was twelve and my other sister, Susan, was six when I was born. Phil, bless him, was probably fed up with girls and when Mum fell pregnant with me he'd desperately hoped he'd be getting a brother. No such luck. When Barbara picked him up from school on the day I was born he apparently took the news very grumpily. Perhaps to make up for his disappointment, my dad told him he was allowed to choose my name and so he picked Elizabeth.

Now I'd have been quite happy with that as it's a name you can do a lot with. Unfortunately my dad wasn't so pleased, so it was relegated to my middle name. Eventually they settled on Jayne and even today I'd have preferred Elizabeth!

Although he was hostile at first, Phil always looked

out for me when I was a toddler and would defend me against Susan, who was understandably jealous that I'd pushed her out of her rightful place as the youngest in the family. As the only boy he had a bedroom all to himself so he'd invite me in and sneak me a piece of chewing gum, which I'd chew for all it was worth until Mum or Dad shouted up to see what I was doing, and I'd have to spit it out. 'Our Boot' was his nickname for me – believe it or not, it's a term of endearment where we're from . . .

Sue had a much-loved doll named Tressy, and to make its hair grow you'd turn a key in its back. One day, for a bit of fun, I grew Tressy's hair to full length and promptly cut it all off. As payback, Sue cut my entire fringe off! Sue also had a black doll that she adored. I remember Mum washing it and putting it in the oven to dry but she forgot about it and when we opened the oven door it was just a pool of goo and a pair of eyeballs. I thought that was so funny but Sue was devastated.

As she got older, Sue picked up with a boyfriend called Willie, to whom she is still married. I took an instant dislike to him for no other reason than when he stayed at weekends I had to get out of my bed and let him sleep in it. By this time both Phil and Barbara had left home and I had been given Phil's bedroom. On the night of Sue and Willie's engagement, they were going out for a meal with both sets of parents. Sue had spent a fortune on a new outfit, but I got in first and put it on and went to the local youth club in it. My irate dad came looking for me but didn't find me – I was hidden in the DJ booth by my friends.

When I look back I realize I must have tested my parents' patience. One day, a group of mothers on our street organized a jumble sale to raise money. I was told I could go along and was given a little bit of cash by Dad. I came home about an hour later and I had bought every single item back that Mum had donated.

I grew up in Kimberworth, a suburb of Rotherham about two miles from the town and overlooking the giant steelworks. The neighbourhood was a quiet one, made up of private semi-detached houses and older terraces. It was a working-class area with a strong sense of pride and community; everyone knew everyone and all the kids who played on my road felt perfectly safe, even in the woods at the back of the houses where we spent many happy hours. When we were about thirteen one of my friends, Gail, was flashed at in these woods but we were so confident on our home territory – and naive too – that we trooped into the woods to look for the man who'd done the flashing. We weren't scared, just curious. In the summer holidays I would spend weeks with my nanny and granddad, George and Nellie, in Middlesbrough. She was kind and lovely and he was grumpy – a typical northern couple from that generation. We'd drive up to the north-east and all the way there I'd hug my precious cassette recorder, listening to tapes of Elvis Presley. To this day I'm a huge fan of Elvis, particularly his later stuff, and I even like his films – which must prove that I'm a true fan!

Nanny had a false eye and I was the only one that would happily take it out and clean it for her. After she died Granddad used to come and stay. He'd no hair and I used to play a trick on him which he never found funny – he'd fall asleep in the chair and I would smack him on top of his head, which made his teeth fly out.

When he visited I'd come home from school at lunchtime just to give him his dinner. He was always complaining about me playing my music, so one day I put the Muppets theme tune on repeat and went back to school. When I got home he passed me my favourite Elvis record, which had somehow ended up in four pieces. 'Sorry, Jayne,' he said, 'I accidentally sat on it.'

In Middlesbrough I obtained a nickname – 'No-Change Jayne'– which was given to me by my granddad after one particularly memorable incident. A van that sold anything and everything used to visit their street often and one summer's afternoon, as I played out in the garden, Granddad appeared with a five-pound note in his hand.

'Jayne,' he said, 'tek this and go fetch me twenty Woodbines from the van, would you, pet? An' if they don't have Woodbines, just get me owt.'

I took the five-pound note – a big sum in the early

1970s – and went up to the van. These were the days when children were served cigarettes without question, so it wasn't unusual for an eight-year-old to request Woodbines.

'I'm sorry, love,' said the van man, 'I don't have any Woodbines today. D'youse want anything else?'

I paused. Granddad had said get anything. Ten minutes later I arrived back at their house with my purchases.

'What the 'ell's this?!' he yelled when he saw what I'd bought. 'Sweets! Chocolates! And two pairs of flamin' tights! Warrama gonna do wi' them?!'

What could I say? He'd asked me to get anything, so I'd chosen whatever I'd wanted. And, worst of all, I'd spent every last penny. 'No-Change Jayne . . .' He never called me anything else until the day he died. When I left Middlesbrough after my long summer visits I'd always come home with a slight north-east twang that resembled my dad's.

Spending other people's money aside, I had the happiest of childhoods. I felt secure and, most importantly, was loved unconditionally. We were a close family, all looking out for each other. When I think about my childhood now, and compare it with the experiences of so many of the abused girls I've worked with over sixteen years, I feel very, very lucky indeed. I was close to both my parents, who in turn were close to each other.

Dad grew all his own vegetables in the back garden

of our house, so I'd help him in the garden and watch as he built and fixed things in his garage. He was an engineer by trade, working at the Guest and Chrimes foundry in the town, and perhaps I took after him, because I wasn't much of a girly girl; I was always keen on practical tasks. I loved animals too and kept mice and hamsters in the shed out the back. When they died I'd make their coffins and bury them with great ceremony in the garden. As I got older, and the hamsters became a bit embarrassing, I turned the shed into a Bay City Rollers club and wouldn't let my friends in until they pledged allegiance to the Rollers and could sing all their songs. We had a special dance that I can still do – but I won't!

Like most kids I knew round our way, I went to the local comprehensive school, Old Hall, now renamed Winterhill and still going today. I suppose I was a mediocre student; not a bad kid but occasionally prone to episodes of naughtiness. It was a strict school and every morning in assembly we had to read from the Bible. I got a bit tired of this, so one day I glued it to the prayer stand, much to the anger of the deputy head, who was deeply religious. I had really good friendships with a trio of girls – Amanda, Grace and Tracey. One day I was babysitting for our Barbara and Amanda was with me. Why Grace and Tracey weren't with us, and why the two of us weren't in school at all, I cannot recall, but Amanda and I decided to ring the deputy head and pretend to be Marjorie Proops, the newspaper agony aunt, and offer her some advice on men. After about thirty seconds she said, 'Jayne Johnson, is that you?'

Perhaps all this was born out of frustration, because in my third year I was the only girl to choose wood-work and metalwork as two of my options for O levels. Immediately my parents were summoned to be told I couldn't pick these as they were 'boys' subjects'. In a more progressive time my mum and dad would've pointed out how stupid this was and demanded I be allowed to study practical subjects, but even in the mid 1970s Rotherham could hardly be classed as a liberal town. People followed traditional paths all their lives. Mum and Dad had a close but old-fashioned relation-ship, in which he decorated and did the garden while she cleaned and cooked. Mum was a nurse at Rother-ham General Hospital and went part-time when she started a family. She loved it, and was very good at it, but people knew their place – especially women – so I had to choose typing and shorthand instead. Unsurpris-ingly, I hated both subjects and did not want to work in an office, but that was the path I seemed destined for, like it or not.

I left school with dismal results and had to go to night school to catch up with my shorthand. Mum and Dad were good friends with a couple up the road, Stan and Iris, whom we always referred to as 'auntie and uncle', as you often did with your parents' friends back then. Auntie Iris was the office manager of a sewing factory in Rotherham called Two Steeples and, after a word from my mum, she pulled strings to get me a job there. At the time, the Conservative government of Margaret Thatcher had just expanded the Youth Opportunities Programme, also known as the YOP scheme, which had been introduced in the late 1970s. I was the perfect candidate for such a scheme and so, with reluctance, I started working there.

I hated it. My job switched between reception and keeping a tally of the workers' hours so they would be paid correctly. I was frightened to death of the factory girls; they seemed tough, uncompromising and very clannish. Day after day I got the bus to work, wishing I was back in my dad's garage, fixing things and getting my hands dirty. After six months the scheme finished and I was taken on full-time. Everyone was pleased apart from me, but after a while I became used to the place. I started to get to know a few of the factory girls and was less intimidated by them, though woe betide me if their wages were wrong. It seemed I'd be there forever, or at least until I got married and had children.

By this stage I was seeing Paul Senior, a lad of my age from a nearby council estate. We met at a local youth club while we were still at school. When I say 'met', it was hardly love at first sight. There was some rivalry between my school and the one Paul attended, Kimber-worth, and sometimes the lads would kick off for just that reason. One night we were all up at the local youth club. I was playing table tennis with Paul's mate as we had a few friends in common. As sometimes happens with fifteen-year-old boys, a fight broke out and some-how Paul became involved. I'm not one to avoid trouble, as we'll see, so I waded into the fight in an attempt to break it up, and did so by jumping on Paul's back and hitting him over the head with a table-tennis bat. We were both slung out into the freezing winter's night by the youth workers, the doors banged closed behind us.

'Thanks a lot!' I said. 'Now we've been chucked out and it's all your fault!'

'It weren't me,' he said, shoving his hands into his jacket pockets, 'it were your lot started it. You shouldn't've got involved.'

'Well, tough, I did,' I said. 'What are we gonna do now?'

'Dunno,' said Paul. 'Better go for a walk to keep warm. You comin'?'

Well, I didn't have much choice, did I? Off we went into the night, and we've been together ever since. I can't say I fancied him at that point, though. Instead I had eyes for his mate, Andy Blakesley, the lad I was playing table tennis with when the fight broke out. As I got to know Paul I liked him because he wasn't one of the crowd. I don't mean he was a loner – he had plenty of mates – but he did things his own way. He was a lad off a council estate and he wasn't a follower. He didn't smoke, didn't really drink, didn't get into much trouble. He was a laid-back lad and not out to impress anyone. When he left school he was taken on a YOP scheme at the local steelworks and he's never worked anywhere else.

Mum and Dad really liked Paul when I brought him home to meet them. They and Paul had a lot of respect for each other and they were happy that he seemed a nice lad with a steady job. By this time, my sisters and brother had all left home and were married, and in due course that was what I'd do as well. There was no reason to suspect that my future wouldn't play out like those of the family and friends I'd grown up with in Kimberworth. And yet events were about to take a turn down a very dark road indeed.

It was December 1981. I was seventeen, and still working at Two Steeples. That winter was particularly cold and as my dad picked me up from work, which he occasionally did on his way home, it had started to snow heavily. It seemed to take ages to reach Hungerhill Road, the street in Kimberworth where we lived. We trudged up the drive through the settling snow and into the house. It was dark and quiet – unusually so. There was no familiar teatime smell of cooking either. You know that odd feeling you get when you think something's wrong? This was one of those moments.

'Mum!' I shouted. 'Where are you?'

'I'm up here,' said a low voice from the bedroom. 'I'm not feeling very well.'

We took our shoes off and went upstairs, Dad first. We found Mum lying on the bed, looking terrible. She'd been Christmas shopping and had started to feel unwell. Dad was a first-aider at work and knew something was badly wrong. He belted downstairs and rang 999. On a good day, an ambulance would've been with us within fifteen minutes. But this wasn't a good day. We waited and waited, but the doorbell remained silent as, outside, the flakes of snow became thicker.

Dad rang 999 again. 'The ambulance is on its way. Hungerhill Road, Whiston, isn't it?'

'No!' Dad shouted. 'It's Hungerhill Road, Kimberworth! You've gone to the wrong place!'

They must have turned the ambulance round and sent it in the right direction, but by the time the crew arrived it was too late. Just a few minutes previously I'd asked Mum if she needed anything.

'Will you hold me, Johnny?' she said to my dad. Then she died in his arms of a massive heart attack.

They put her in the ambulance anyway, my dad got into the back and it sped off to hospital. I stood alone on the pavement in the gathering snow, watching the blue light flicker into the distance. I felt like I'd been hit over the head with a hammer. I had no idea what I'd do next, but what I did do I will regret forever.

I charged back into the house, picked up the phone and dialled my sister's number. 'You'll have to come quick, Sue,' I said, 'I think our mum's dead.' What a way to announce the death of a parent. I was only seventeen, and obviously in shock after seeing my mum die suddenly, but still . . . That moment will always haunt me.

After I put the phone down I ran up the street to a neighbour, Gwen, one of my mum's best friends. I blurted everything out in a flood of tears and sobs, and from that moment everything became a blur of activity: phone calls, doors being knocked, people rushing into the house. It seemed like the whole street was out, despite the weather. Susan, Barbara and Phil all arrived, then Dad came home, his world completely fallen to pieces in the space of an hour or two.

We all felt the same way. Dad and I had left the house that morning with a packed lunch and a kiss, Mum waving goodbye to us as we closed the front door. Within fifteen minutes of us arriving home – no Mum. She was fifty-five, just five years older than I am now. Even today, I can't quite comprehend how suddenly and dramatically she was taken from us. A deep darkness descended on me as I realized that my life, and the lives of my siblings, would never be the same again.

For Dad, Mum's death meant complete shutdown. Just before she passed away he'd promised to remove the dingy wood panelling on the walls and replace everything with bright new wallpaper. They'd taken all the ornaments down and Dad had begun the work. After her death, we looked at bare walls for three years until Dad decided he should probably finish what he'd started.

Of course, I was left alone with him, and being a traditional sort of man he expected that I'd just slip into Mum's role. He meant no harm, he just thought it would be that way. So if I hadn't ironed his shorts or dusted the mantelpiece he'd be grumpy. I remember when I first tried to make a pan of stew, never having cooked a thing in my life. Mum had always done all that. I bought some meat and vegetables and threw them into a heavy-bottomed frying pan. I waited until the meat was almost black and then served it up on Dad's plate – the fact that you couldn't possibly chew any of it without breaking your jaw was irrelevant. For some reason, Dad just expected me to know how to do it.

When she was alive, Dad had given Mum housekeeping money which she'd top up with her wages. Out of my £40 a week I paid £20 board, but Dad only gave me the same as he'd given Mum, so I used what was left of my wages to pay the milkman, the window cleaner and the paperboy, along with other bits and pieces. I had nothing left at the end of the week, but Dad still expected me to shop at Asda. He'd sit in the car while I pushed the trolley miserably around the aisles, wondering what I was going to do with all this stuff.

Something had to give. Eventually I told my older sister what was going on at home and she was shocked. Immediately she took Dad down to Asda and made him do the shopping from the weekly budget we were trying to get by on. When he got to the till it dawned on him that we simply didn't have enough money to pay for it all. That was Lesson One. Lesson Two was about cooking and ironing. Barbara taught Dad and me to do both and from that moment things became a bit easier. I think now that I was pretending I could do it all as a way of coping with my grief. Even so, those lessons were very timely – for by now I had a secret, and was terrified of telling Dad my news.

2

I was pregnant. I couldn't believe it. I was in complete shock and fear, wondering how I'd tell Dad and what his reaction would be. This was the early 1980s, but the shame and scandal of young girls having babies out of wedlock still loomed as large in working-class homes as ever it had done. After all that had happened, I felt I'd failed Dad and completely let him down.

I was only a kid; seventeen, frightened and out of my depth. But I wasn't alone. Thank God I had my siblings. I went round to see Barbara and sobbed in her kitchen as I blurted out the news.

'Well,' she said, with the experience of a married woman in her thirties, 'you won't be the first and you'll definitely not be the last. It's not the end of the world, Jayne.'

Those were the kind of comforting words I wanted to hear. I hadn't meant to get pregnant, but I do believe things happen for a reason and at that time, still reeling from the shock of Mum's death, I was in a very dark place. Perhaps I needed something or someone to love. In the meantime, though, there was Dad to consider.

'Leave it to me,' Barbara said. 'I'll talk to him. It'll be all right.'

A day or so later she came round. It was the moment of truth, so I sprinted upstairs while Barbara gently steered Dad to the end of the garden. Peeping through the curtains at my bedroom window, I watched as Barbara put her arm round Dad's shoulder. I could tell by his sagging shoulders that he was crying. After a while they returned to the kitchen.

'Jayne!' he shouted. 'Come down . . . I think you've got something to tell me.'

Full of dread, I plodded down the stairs and into the kitchen. Without a word Dad just opened his arms and gave me a huge bear hug. I cried and said I was sorry. There wasn't much he could say in return: I'd been daft and got caught. But as Barbara said, I wouldn't be the first or the last . . .

Paul came round that night. He was only a young lad but he was actually really pleased at the news that he was to become a dad. It was me who was in shock; I was so scared I felt physically sick. Even if he'd wanted to, Paul wasn't the sort of lad who would ever shirk his responsibilities and when Dad asked him if he was going to marry me – almost the first words he uttered as Paul walked through the door – the answer was a definite 'yes'. But I had other ideas. I didn't want to get married, not without my mum being present. Of course, that was impossible, so I vowed never to get married.

To me, it was black and white; shame or no shame, I wouldn't go through with it.

Paul's family were good about it. His biological father had abandoned the family when Paul's mother was pregnant with him and his brother was only two months old. Paul never got to meet his real dad. They were perhaps more used to the ups and downs of life than our family, at least until Mum died. However, we weren't moving in together, not immediately anyway. Throughout my pregnancy and for several months after the baby was born I continued to live at home, working and looking after the house. Paul could only stay over at weekends and even then he had to sleep in the spare bedroom. It's only thirty-and-a-bit years ago but it seems like Victorian times compared to now.

The baby was born and he was a fine, healthy boy whom we named Lee. And, yes, I was right – he was the thing I needed in my life to make me feel a whole person again. I've met many, many teenage mums during my career and in almost all cases the one thing they have in common is the need for something to love and care for. It was the same when I had our Lee. Having a child and being determined to give them the life they didn't have – or that was taken away from them – seems to give young girls a kind of hope for a better future. There are exceptions, of course, but as I've said, things happen for a reason.

Paul would come over when his shift was finished,

looking after the baby while I got a few hours' sleep. When I brought Lee home for the first time, Dad's reaction was muted, to say the least. He hadn't discussed my pregnancy, not even towards the end when I was really big, and although there was a new arrival in the house Dad was almost pretending not to notice. A couple of days after I came home I was washing the pots in the kitchen when Lee started crying in his cot upstairs. Dad was also upstairs.

'Jayne!' he shouted. 'You might want to come upstairs. Babby's awake. He'll want feeding.'

'I'll just be a minute,' I yelled back. 'I'm finishing off down here.'

As I dried the last plate, Lee's cries subsided. I went upstairs. Dad was in the bedroom. He'd picked Lee out of the cot and was rocking him, soothing him with quiet words. I stood for a moment and watched. Something in Dad's attitude had shifted. He'd accepted the situation and embraced Lee as a member of the family. From that moment on, right to the day my father died, there was a unique bond between him and his grandson.

Still, Dad sensed that Paul and I needed a home of our own now that we were a family. A Rotherham Borough councillor lived down the road and was a friend of Dad's, so Dad suggested I go to see him about finding a place. And just a few months later I was leaving Kimberworth, where I'd spent all my life, and moving into a council house in the Rockingham area of Rotherham – a place I'd never even heard of.

Being a young mum isn't easy at the best of times. Back then, there was still the traditional thinking that once you had your baby you finished work and stayed at home to keep house. There was little to no childcare in those days either. You just got on with it. Luckily I had a supportive family to keep an eye on me. I spent a lot of time with our Barbara and her two children, Steven and Joanne. Just under three years separated Joanne and Lee, and our families did a lot together. I was an auntie from a young age so at least I was used to little kids, and I would regularly have our Joanne over to sleep. In return, Barbara would take Lee if we wanted a night off. For a little extra money I did some cleaning with a friend but as Paul worked shifts it seemed difficult to think about any kind of steady employment. Besides, there wasn't much I could do without Lee because he was a very clingy child. He'd go to Barbara's without fuss, but anywhere else he was like my shadow. When he was a bit older we'd go to the local playgroup and if I even went to the loo he'd be there at the back of me. As he got to about three or four I started a job in the local shop, just selling papers and milk, that sort of thing. It got me out of the house for a few hours at a weekend and back into a bit of work for a little extra cash.

Paul didn't give up on asking me to marry him but,

although he was persistent, I still said 'no'. No Mum, no marriage. But around three years after Lee was born, Paul took me to a restaurant one night and got down on one knee in the middle of the place. Well, who could refuse an offer made like that?! The truth was, we were considering having another child and although I've never been old-fashioned, morally speaking, I didn't want two babies when I wasn't married. So finally I agreed, but I wanted to do it at St Thomas's Church in Kimberworth, where Mum is buried.

Financially we didn't have a lot but we saved up for a year and the family stepped in to help. Dad paid for the reception at a nearby venue while Barbara made all the bridesmaids' dresses, including her own. We paid off everything gradually and by Saturday, 16 May 1987, we were ready for the big day. It was a lovely occasion, as all family gatherings should be. As a wedding present, my cousin Tony, who lives in Germany, offered to pay for us to go on honeymoon over there. We jumped at that, but we'd no spending money, so it was a choice between paying for someone to video the wedding or go on honeymoon. We chose the latter and had a wonderful time. It was hard to leave our Lee, and I felt many pangs of regret as we handed over our four-year-old to Barbara, but I have to say that we had a fabulous holiday. We visited vineyards and castles all over Bavaria and really enjoyed ourselves.

The following May we had our Ben, a little brother

for Lee. He was an easy baby but a lively one too and, like me, never sat still. He was always busy and we rarely had a minute's peace. It became a joke that anyone who came round for coffee didn't bring biscuits; instead they collected bits of old radios, video recorders and other fiddly things being thrown out to give to Ben and keep him occupied. The bits would be all over the garden, half buried in the soil, but activities like that kept him busy for hours as a toddler. I was happy being a mum to two small boys but, as anyone with young children knows, you sometimes wonder where your life's disappeared to and that can get you down. One afternoon, when Ben was about eighteen months old, I was having such thoughts and had become quite tearful. Coincidentally my brother-in-law Glynn called in to give me something from Barbara. He noticed I was a bit quiet and asked me what the matter was.

'It's nothing really,' I said, 'I'm just having one of those days when you wonder what it's all about. I think I could do with getting out a bit more, that's all.'

Glynn was a teacher. Perhaps he knew instinctively that I'd work well around kids.

'Look,' he said, 'I know this fella called Rob McLaren. He's a leader at Greasbrough Youth Club. I know him quite well. I'll have a word – then you could go to meet him, see if there's any voluntary going.'

Working with kids? I was already working with two and that was hard enough! But there was something about this idea that attracted me. I'd been around children so long that I felt comfortable and natural in their presence. Also, doing a couple of early evenings at the council-run youth club meant I'd be able to take Lee and Ben along too, and not rely on babysitters. I took up Glynn's suggestion and went to see Rob McLaren, who said I could start with the junior club on Friday nights: eighty kids aged between six and eleven, and a right collection of little tinkers.

I loved it. They made me laugh, they caused me frustration, they made me think and sometimes they made me cry. Through them, I felt I was doing something worthwhile and as time progressed I found we were exploring the deeper issues that affected their lives, but in a way which didn't feel questioning or intrusive. It was busy and often manic, but I really enjoyed it. They always called me 'Miss', even when I insisted they called me Jayne. 'Miss,' they'd say, 'how much are them 5p crisps?' I loved them all, even the naughty ones. Especially the naughty ones.

Not long after I started I was offered a paid part-time job as the club's coffee-bar worker. Seeing as we didn't actually sell coffee, the job title was grander than the reality. I sold pop, crisps and sweets, and after the coffee bar was shut I joined the kids in the disco or organized wild games which helped to run off their energy. This was at a time when the Youth Service attracted solid investment and quite quickly a job came up as a team leader. Again, it was working in the club but taking more responsibility for opening and closing times and the financial side of things. Also, it was working with eleven- to fourteen-year-olds – quite a different set of challenges to face. I applied and got it, and this is when I really began to understand the needs of this vulnerable age group. They didn't want to play hide-and-seek or queue up to buy toffees from the coffee bar; some were drinking, others sniffing glue, and we had to spend time working on these issues as well as all the usual teen-age stuff. Again, I enjoyed it despite the many tricky moments, and more work followed. I picked up a job working ten hours a week on youth club administration, which fitted in well with being a mum to two kids and a husband who worked shifts.

I remember one young boy who was really aggressive. No one could get through to him and it took months of him swearing at me before he realized I wasn't going away. He then did a full disclosure of the most horrendous abuse at home and I was devastated at what I heard. It was my first insight into the grim world of child abuse and exploitation, and all I wanted to do was grab him, take him home and let him live with me.

Another example was a young woman who came to the youth club really drunk and began to take her clothes off. It seemed like extreme behaviour at the time, but it was only in 2015 that I found out she was terribly abused. I spent hours with this girl trying to help her build her self-esteem, but at that time she never told me what was really at the heart of her troubles. Back then – and it's really not that long ago – kids very often couldn't or wouldn't say what was bothering them. There was shame and fear in disclosing deeply personal things. Thank God that's all changed now.

Next, I moved into work with the seniors, an age group which ran from fourteen to twenty-five. The irony was that I wasn't even twenty-five myself! In theory I could've been working with people older than me but I don't recall anyone of that age attending the youth club. This group had a different set of challenges again, but I seemed to be a good listener and the young people picked up on that. I still have that quality; only a couple of weeks ago I got talking to someone I'd never met in my life and within a few minutes she was telling me all about the domestic violence she'd suffered. After twenty minutes she stopped and stared at me, shocked.

'Why have I just told you all that?' she said. 'I don't know you at all.'

She looked at me again.

'I know why,' she said. 'You've just got one of those faces people tell things to.'

Perhaps it's true. It's also true that I have a lot of empathy for people, and I'm almost always on the side of the underdog. I was like that as a child. I remember being with a girl at senior school and it's fair to say that the poor thing didn't have much going for her. She was overweight and wore skirts down to her ankles (in the days when everyone else's was just below their bum) and cheap, blue-framed National Health glasses. She was bullied terribly. Although I wasn't one of her tormentors, I didn't do anything to stop it until one day I walked into a geography lesson to witness her surrounded by the all-girl bullying gang.

In horror, I watched as the ringleader – a very tough local lass – grabbed her victim, picked her up and threw her onto the classroom floor. The poor girl hit a desk and slid underneath it, sobbing. I just saw red and had an almighty scrap with the leader of the bullies. I wasn't a big girl and was never violent. I'd just had enough of seeing someone persecuted so horribly. Years later – just about the time I started in youth work – I saw the victim on a bus as I travelled into Rotherham, our Ben on my knee. We got chatting and she remembered that I'd stuck up for her. I'll never forget what she said to me.

'I had a terrible time at school,' she said, 'but my home life was even worse. Our dad was an alcoholic and he spent every penny me mum ever had in the pub. That's why I had to wear second-hand clothes, even to school. I didn't mix wi' anyone cos I didn't want no one to find out what were goin' on.'

That poor child. She had no friends because she was ashamed of herself, so no one could reach out to help her. Instead, she was picked on because she was different. *If only kids could see past appearances*, I thought, and I vowed to make sure that my youth club lot never took anything at face value.

I was becoming well established at the youth club and although I couldn't quite see a career developing I was keen to take advantage of the opportunities that seemed to be around. I applied for another role within the senior youth group and during the interview I was told I could have the job as long as I was prepared to train for formal qualifications in youth work. Further Development Training, as it was called, would involve studying one night a week and four residential weekends away over the course of a year. If I was to do it, it would involve juggling childcare with Paul and finding a babysitter. As ever, and like he's always been, Paul was supportive.

'I've got a job, Jayne,' he said, 'and that's that. This could be a career for you, so go for it.'

So I applied and began the year's training, which I found fascinating. I passed the qualification and went on to complete a TRIM course, which sounds like an exercise class but actually stood for Training In Management. At that time – and it's hard to believe now – the council's Youth Service had its own training centre, complete with crèche facilities, meals, drinks – you name it, there was money for it. Quite a lot of that training was done by a woman called Linda Bailey, a strong, strident character with very feminist views. She intimidated me at first and I didn't know what to make of her and her politics. But the more I listened, the more I learned, and the more I realized just how non-existent any of this had been during my days at school. We'd never been taught anything about women's rights, the struggle for gender and racial equality or anything else that wasn't the standard view of history at the time. Linda encouraged us to think for ourselves and express opinions that might have shocked the previous generation of working-class Rotherham people. We learned about Sojourner Truth, the Black American abolitionist and women's rights campaigner – not the usual fare we'd been served up in dull history lessons at school.

I went on other courses – self-defence for women, basic car mechanics – subjects I could take back into my youth work and pass on. At that time I began working with a girls' group and I would try to get them interested in subjects I'd heard Linda speak about, such as body image and the right to say 'no'. One such training session was based around a woman who had been involved in what was then known as 'child prostitution'. Today, I hate the word 'prostitution' in connection with any form of child abuse but back then 'child prostitute' was a term in common currency.

A few of us had gathered in a room in the council's Blenheim Centre one summer afternoon to hear the woman, named Fiona, deliver the talk. She began by detailing her descent into prostitution at the age of fifteen. As I listened I felt the horror of it crawl up my spine ... this was an ordinary girl who had become involved in the most awful abuse and, far from being rescued by anyone, she ended up selling her body to strangers on the streets. She hadn't had a bad childhood but was bullied at school and decided to run away. As she sat in a bus station in Bradford, thinking about her future, a man came along and started talking to her. She thought he was wonderful and her saviour, but in fact he was to lure her into abuse and pimp her to anyone who would pay him.

As I listened I thought back to my own childhood. Before my mum died, I'd had the best upbringing anyone could've wanted. And yet we'd had our arguments and there'd been times I'd stormed off and sat in a huff on the kerb at the end of the road. Supposing on one of those occasions some bloke had come up to me and said nice things? Like all children, I was vulnerable at that age. I thought about the girls in my group and some of the daft things they did. They were ordinary girls; some had issues but all kids come with vulnerabilities of one sort or another, especially teenagers.

I was utterly shocked and appalled that someone so young could become involved in something so horrific. I realized how sheltered I'd been as a child; what I knew about sexual exploitation could be written on the back

of a postage stamp and I probably associated 'prostitution' with hardened women in their twenties and
beyond who walked the streets of nearby Sheffield. I
had never imagined it could happen to the youngest and
most vulnerable members of society.

3

Fiona's story wasn't the only part of the training day that shocked me to the core. After she'd sat down, the woman she'd arrived with stood up. Her name was Irene Ivison and she lived in Sheffield. She began to tell the story of her daughter, also called Fiona, who'd been a normal teenage girl until she became involved in an abusive relationship at the age of fourteen. Irene fought and fought to claw back her daughter from the clutches of her so-called 'boyfriend' – a man in his mid to late twenties – battling with the police and social services to get something done.

What Irene didn't know at the time was that Fiona was being pimped into sexual exploitation by her 'boy-friend'. Tragically, she only found this out when, at the age of just seventeen, Fiona was murdered by a 'punter' and her body discovered in a Doncaster car park one freezing morning in December 1993. Her head had been bashed several times against the concrete floor. It was the end of a short life that had held so much prom-ise, but finished in terrible squalor.

By campaigning to alert people to child sexual

exploitation (CSE) Irene had found a way to go on. As I listened – the mother of two young kids I'd do anything to defend, as well as a wife, an auntie and a daughter – I asked myself over and over again, 'How can this possibly be right?' A young girl that no one in authority seemed to be able to help, even though her mother had reported her truanting from school, hanging around with older men and becoming involved in drugs. It seemed an appalling waste of life. I was angry not only at the abusers, but the system too. It seemed that hundreds, if not thousands, of young girls – by legal definition, children – were getting criminal records as prostitutes and being forced back onto the street to pay their fines, yet nothing ever seemed to happen to those who bought them. Who were they? Well, they were just like anyone else – husbands, uncles, fathers. Ordinary men, possibly with daughters at home of the same age as those they were exploiting. The whole thing disgusted me.

I went back to my girls' group determined that I would give them all the confidence they needed never to get involved in situations that would put them in such danger. We learned about self-defence and self-esteem, sexual, physical and mental health, when to say 'no' and when to say 'yes'. We learned not to be a group of tough girls, but ones who had confidence to be who they wanted to be. To understand their emotions as well as their bodies . . .

It was an exhilarating time, a period when women were really beginning to make an impact in so many areas. I'd introduce debates and play devil's advocate just to get them really fired up and opinionated. I wanted them to get past the idea that when a man stands up for himself he's regarded as confident, yet when a woman does the same she's labelled as a bitch. Working to empower young girls, I was reminded of Election Day in 1979. I was fourteen, and went with my dad to the polling station.

'Who are you voting for, Dad?' I asked, expecting the obvious answer from a working man who'd spent all his adult life in this most Labour of northern English towns.

'I think,' he said, answering carefully, 'I'll vote for that Maggie Thatcher. Perhaps as men, we're getting it wrong. The country's in a bit of a mess. Maybe if we give a woman a chance, we'll see a better Britain.'

And he did vote for her, though I imagine he regretted it for the rest of his life. She did little for Rotherham other than oversee the closure of steel mills and coal mines, putting thousands out of work. Even so, his words stuck with me. And not always in a good way, as we'll see much later in my story.

Another job opportunity came up within Rotherham Borough Council, this time doing detached youth work. This was aimed at young people who shunned youth clubs and preferred hanging about in their own areas.

We would find out who they were and where they were, and go out to them. This was at a time when any group of young people hanging about together were immediately labelled as a 'gang', even if they were doing nothing wrong. Such 'gangs' were being blamed by the media for all sorts of things and it was our job to break down barriers between ourselves as youth workers and young people who might just adopt the poses and behaviours they were already being blamed for.

I got the job and Rob McLaren became my manager, the same guy who'd taken me into the Youth Service in the first place. I would share the role with a woman called Andrea, and we would be based in the Oak Hill Flats area of Rotherham. The estate had been built in the early 1970s and like so many similar developments it had quickly descended into a place with a reputation for crime, violence, drug-taking and the like. It wasn't the nicest area to travel to on a dark winter's night but there were kids there who needed us – we hoped.

We travelled there in an old minibus that had been given to us especially for outreach work. It wasn't roadworthy enough to drive young people around in, but kids could sit in the back when it was stationary. We get a lot of rain in this part of the country so the back of the bus was a natural shelter for those we were working with. I remember one particularly cold and wet night we decided to treat the kids, so we baked a whole load of potatoes, wrapped them in foil, grated some cheese, made flasks of hot chocolate and took it all with us for the kids to share. We met with a group of lads who were lovable scallywags – they were blamed for everything, even if they hadn't done it. Their circumstances were difficult – parents in prison or unemployed, temptations with drugs, lack of opportunities – and yet they shared so much with us and were open and honest young boys.

As we all sat in the van chatting, we became aware of a flashing blue light approaching. Nothing unusual in this part of town, but the speed at which the lights were coming towards us made us sit up in shock. Within seconds we were surrounded by vans, police officers and snarling, barking dogs. Flashlights were shone right into our eyes. What the hell was going on?!

'Get out of the van!' a voice yelled from the darkness. 'The lot of yer!'

Bewildered, we got out. The officer in charge came forward.

'What have you got in there?' he demanded, pointing to the van's interior.

'Jacket potatoes,' I said. 'Why?'

The sound of muffled laughter could be heard from among the police ranks. The kids were sniggering too. Only Andrea and I seemed oblivious to what was going on.

'We've had reports you're dealing drugs,' the head man said, 'so we're gonna search your van.'

With that, an officer with a dog came forward. It

seemed extremely eager to carry out the 'sniffer' part of its job. The officer unwrapped one of the foil parcels, returned to his boss and whispered something in his ear.

'All right,' he said, 'seems like we've been misinformed. You're not dealing drugs after all. Someone on the estate reported seeing two women giving kids stuff in silver foil from their van.'

At that, everyone cracked up laughing. After a few formalities most of the cops and their dogs cleared off back to the station, leaving just a handful chatting to us and the lads.

And, for the first time, a little bit of ice had been broken between the police and the youngsters on this estate. The lads saw the police not as heavy-handed enforcers but local blokes just doing their job. The police realized that the lads weren't troublemakers but ordinary boys looking for something to do. And from that moment onward, we began to establish some kind of relationship between the police and young people living in Oak Hill.

Perception is a funny thing. I remember when Lee was a baby and I was walking down the road one night, him in the pram. I was catching the bus home after visiting Barbara and as I waited I could see a group of young punks approaching. They looked horrendous – spiky hair, ripped clothes, earrings, nose-rings, you name it. I felt fear rising from the pit of my stomach. A young mum with a baby stood no chance against these thugs.

They arrived at the bus stop, pushing and shoving, spitting and swearing. I could see the bus coming a few yards away in the distance. If I could just get on without being assaulted, I'd be safe. Then the leader, a big lad for his age, turned to me.

'Oi,' he said, 'does tha want me to carry t'pram or babby on t'bus?'

The bus pulled up and the door hissed open.

'Well?' said the lad, pointing to the door. 'Which is it?'

'Oh, the pram please,' I said in a high-pitched voice. 'Ta very much.'

'S'all right,' he replied, and with that I lifted Lee into my arms while the young punk heaved the pram on board. I sat down in shock. Where I'd seen rapists and murderers, the reality was just four lads on a night out, and thoughtful lads at that. It taught me never to judge a book by its cover.

So we had some laughs on that project. We went on trips, took them bowling, played rounders, badminton – whatever they wanted. They were always entertaining, even when they were naughty. On one occasion we were coming towards the end of a particular project and they presented us with gifts: chocolates, flowers and wine. We weren't supposed to accept presents but they told us they'd all chipped in to give us something in thanks. So we had a barbecue as planned, inviting local residents and the police. Everyone was having a great time, when across the field came the local shopkeeper. Oh, the kids had brought us presents all right . . . they'd just not paid for them! After a bit of negotiation, the shopkeeper and the police let it go. Little scallies . . .

And yet, youth work was – and is – so rewarding. Not financially, of course, but in terms of what you get and what you can give. You can cross barriers with young people that professionals in the field can't. You're not their social worker or teacher or their probation person; you can't make them do anything they don't want to do, but you can offer them choices. You can say, 'If you want me to go away I will, but before I do let's have a biscuit and a quick chat.' And before long they're sitting down and really talking to you because you've given them the choice. Of course, I've never not reported something that was serious or when a child is at risk, but there are times when you can respect what a child is telling you. For example, if a young person has been smoking you don't need to ring their parents to inform them. Instead, you could do some preventative work around it. You're a positive role model in the sense that you're a listening ear and one that has a certain amount of discretion.

And so my work went on, the challenges ever-varied but never less than interesting. Paul and I juggled child-care as best we could; luckily his shift patterns meant there was almost always someone around to pick the boys up from school, get them fed, oversee homework – all the usual stuff. Paul was a fabulous role model for Lee and Ben. He'd had a poor upbringing and an absent father, and right from the start he was determined he would be the best dad he possibly could. I'm strong-willed but, in a way, lacked some of the motherly skills my mum's death robbed me of. I'm not a very good cook and was never one for washing or ironing. So it was largely down to Paul, and shouts of 'Dad, what's for tea?' or 'Dad, can you iron me a shirt?' were nothing unusual in our house.

We disciplined them in different ways too. I was the one who said 'no' and meant it. With Paul, there was a little more leeway. Yet if I shouted at them they didn't bat an eyelid whereas if Paul did they'd sit up and listen – perhaps because he didn't do it as often as me! However, even in the trickiest circumstances he never smacked them. He has a big belief that you do not inflict physical harm on children, no matter what they've done wrong. You can time them out, take away their spending money, hide their electronic devices, but you never hit them, and he's stuck to that rigidly. Like all lads, as they became a little older they developed a mouthy side and they'd push it a little further with me, especially when their dad wasn't in. I remember our Lee coming in one evening and me telling him off for being late. He called me something under his breath and I saw red, chasing him upstairs. He ran into the bathroom and banged the door shut, locking it behind him. Now, I'm not a violent person but I wasn't having any name-calling so I kicked at the door – and it literally flew off its hinges. Our Lee was speechless, and he still laughs about it today – 'Mother did a kung-fu kick!'

Most of the time they were good lads, albeit boisterous and with a fair amount of sibling rivalry as they grew up. As a rule, they didn't bring trouble home. There was, however, one time when I could've swung for our Ben. He was about fifteen, and there'd already been a couple of occasions when he'd come home drunk and I'd had to pour coffee down him, trying to get him to be sick. I was terrified he'd swallow his tongue or choke on his own vomit. One night he'd been staying over at friends', as kids of that age very often do. Or so he said . . . That evening I got a call at about 11 p.m. from Rotherham police. Could I come to the station, the officer said, as they'd found Ben in the town centre, drunk out of his mind and claiming to have had his drink 'spiked' with something.

Well, I was furious enough that he'd been lying to me about where he was, and the little bugger had instead been going out into town. Paul was on nights, but being a mum, and despite the hour, I had to do something. I got my coat on, went to the station and saw the desk sergeant, who I knew, to be told that Ben was fine and was now asleep in a cell. The little sod. Something had to happen to make sure he never did this again.

'Can you keep him for the night?' I asked the custody sergeant.

'You what?' said the sergeant, sounding shocked.

'I said, can you keep him locked up for the night? I'm not being funny, but this getting drunk is becoming a regular thing and now he's trying his luck in the pubs. If he's being found sprawled out in the town centre he's putting himself at risk. So can you keep him here?'

'I see what you're saying,' said the sergeant, 'but it's Friday night. If we get busy, you'll have to come and pick him up.'

'That's fine,' I said. 'Just give me a ring if you need me.'

And with that, I left our Ben in a police cell to sleep it off. In the morning the sergeant phoned again.

'Mrs Senior, could you please pick up Ben now?' he said. 'He woke up after you left and has been crying for you all night.'

So I went down to fetch him. He looked dreadful. They'd treated him well, giving him a drink and breakfast, but his expression showed it was an experience he wouldn't repeat again so quickly.

'Mum, it was horrible!' he wailed. 'All these blokes were coming in and yelling at the coppers and there was a woman screaming at what she'd do to them if she got out of her cell. I were right scared!'

And I never told him the truth. From that day to this, he never knew it was his mum teaching him a lesson. When I told my friends, a few of them were horrified. Others said, 'Bloody good idea.' And he never did do it again. Sorry, Ben – but I think it was worth it!

Being a mum to two boys meant I had a bit of a steep learning curve when it came to teenage girls. I remember my first overnight stay – a camping trip – with a group of young women. We were camping in the middle of the woods and had booked rope climbing and stream scrambling as suitable activities to keep the group entertained. Meanwhile, the girls had all turned up sporting high heels and make-up. When we got to the site, out of three tents we had just enough poles for one, causing a few hours' head-scratching as we figured out what to do. Eventually, we managed to persuade a group of scouts camping nearby to help us with the tent and show us how to light a fire. We attempted to cook a basic meal once the fire was hot enough but that ended in disaster, so we trooped off to the nearest town and a Chinese takeaway. The girls were much happier after that, and so was I.

Anyway, I digress. In July 1999 there was a barbecue at the International Centre in Rotherham, a Borough Council-run building which housed various organizations including the Youth Service. It had training facilities, meeting rooms and offices, and a wide variety of groups would use the place. The Detached Youth Work project was based here, in the former caretaker's house, and the barbecue was being held in what was the garden. Many of my colleagues, past and present, were there, including Rob McLaren, who had brought me into youth work all those years previously. As we were chatting, he asked me if I'd applied for the job.

'What job?' I said.

'It's coordinator with Risky Business,' he said.

I confessed that I hadn't heard of Risky Business. Rob explained it was a local project that had been running for about two years which worked with young women and girls in danger of being sexually exploited on the streets.

'I thought of you when I saw the ad. It's right up your street,' Rob said.

It certainly was, particularly after the training I'd had with Fiona and Irene, which had really touched a nerve.

'Oh,' said Rob, 'you'd have to get a move on if you're going to apply. Closing date's today.'

Great, just my luck. But as chance would have it there was someone at the barbecue who could get hold of an application form for me. I read it over quickly. The job was for seven hours a week only; it would fit in with the detached youth work and the shifts I was doing at a hostel for homeless young people. It looked like a good opportunity so I filled it in and handed it back for consideration.

I thought no more of it, probably because at the time Paul's uncle Terry was dying of cancer and we were trying to help him as best we could while dealing with the grief. Paul and the boys were particularly close to him so the family was having an especially tough time. Eventually Terry was admitted to hospital, having collapsed in a local garage, so we started to spend days and nights there, waiting for the inevitable. We didn't want him to be alone when he died.

During all this I was told I'd been successful in getting an interview for the Risky Business job and was given a date, which coincided with my 'shift' watching over Uncle Terry at the hospital. It was a warm, sunny afternoon and Terry was motionless in the bed – large doses of morphine were now being given regularly to ease his pain. A Macmillan nurse came into the room and we started chatting. I said I had a job interview in thirty minutes' time, but wasn't going to go.

'Why not?' she said.

'Oh, I can't leave Terry,' I said, 'it wouldn't be right.'

'Now, come on, Jayne,' she said, 'don't be daft. Is this a job you want to do?'

'Yes,' I said.

'Well then, you'd better go to the interview. Terry could be here another day, or a week, or a month. No one knows. And if this is something you want to do, then you should do it. Anyway, I can wait around until you or your husband gets back.'

I thought about it. If I got my skates on now I could make the interview. There was also Ben's school sports day. I could get to that too. I hated missing any of my kids' school events and always made an effort to get there.

'Well, if you're sure . . .' I said.

'Go on,' she said, 'and don't worry.'

I dashed to the interview, which seemed to go well, and then to the sports day. As I shouted our Ben on, my phone rang. It was the Macmillan nurse.

'I'm so sorry to have to tell you this, Jayne,' she said, 'but it's Terry. I'm afraid he's just passed away.'

How guilty did I feel then? I'd only left him for an hour or so, and neither Paul nor I had been there for his last moments. I rang Paul in tears and explained what had happened. As ever, he was understanding.

'You've done your best, Jayne,' he said. 'No one could've predicted when he'd go.'

Paul said he'd go round to Terry's house to secure the place. In a state of shock I arrived home with Ben. I'd rung a friend, Maxine, and she'd promised to collect both boys so Paul and I could have an hour or so to ourselves while we took in what had happened. The friend arrived and took Lee and Ben off. I sat on the settee, waiting for Paul to return. Then my phone rang. It was Rotherham Borough Council's number.

'Hello, Mrs Senior,' said a friendly voice, 'I'm just

ringing to let you know that, following a successful interview this afternoon, we'd like to offer you the coordinator's job at Risky Business.'

'Oh,' I said, almost too numb to speak. '. . . Thanks.'

The poor woman on the phone must have been shocked. I could've shown a bit more enthusiasm. But she wasn't to know.

'Well,' she said, 'perhaps you'd like to come in next week for a look round? Get a feel for the place.'

'OK,' I replied, 'I will. I'd better go now.'

And so, in the middle of a family tragedy, I'd just been offered the position that would eventually change my life forever. We never know when those moments will occur. Perhaps it's as well we don't . . .

4

The Risky Business job – which, even on day one, didn't come with a description – actually started a few weeks earlier than the September date I'd been given. Kerry Byrne, who would be my manager, passed on a referral from social services involving a girl called Alison, who was then fourteen and living in a children's home. Alison was already having some support from a youth worker called Cassie, and so it was agreed that we would take on Alison and keep Cassie for some sessional hours with Risky Business.

It was known that Alison was hanging around with older men and kept disappearing from the home, leading to suspicions that she was at risk from sexual abuse. Various people had tried to get her to talk, but nothing was working. So Cassie and I went to visit her in the home. 'Yes, she knows you're coming,' I was told, 'but she won't see you. She'll be hiding in the bathroom . . .'

We arrived and were shown her empty room. The manager of the home pointed to the locked bathroom door a few feet down the corridor. 'Alison,' he said, 'your visitors are here.'

He turned to me. 'Good luck,' he said, 'and if you need me I'll be in the office.'

I tapped on the door.

'Alison . . . ?'

Silence. I tapped again, calling her name several times.

'Are you going to open the door, Alison?' I asked.

'No. Go away.'

Well, at least she'd spoken. It was a start. I asked her how she was.

'All right. Why?'

I didn't mention sexual abuse or how everyone was worried about her. I didn't mention the danger we all felt she was in. Instead, I talked about this and that, dropping in a few easy questions. After ten minutes of this the door handle turned and, through the narrowest gap, I could just about see a young, pretty but nervous face peeking out from behind a clump of blonde hair.

'I'll go away if you want me to, Alison,' I said, 'but can I just ask that you give me twenty minutes to talk to you? Then I promise I'll go away, and if you don't want to see me again, that's fine.'

'Who are you?' she asked.

'I'm a youth worker. Not police or social services. Just a youth worker.'

The door opened a little wider. 'Hm. All right then. Just twenty minutes. But I'm not coming out. You'll have to sit in here.'

That was fine by me. We sat on the bathroom floor for twenty minutes, then I left. And each time I went back, she trusted me just that little bit more with her story.

Alison was involved with an older man of Pakistani heritage from Sheffield who was pimping her to other abusers. For a long time she could see nothing wrong with what was going on.

'But he's a really nice bloke!' she said as I tried to point out that men of thirty don't usually have fourteen-year-old 'girlfriends'. 'He's got a sports car and he takes me out in it, and we go out for meals and everyone's dead jealous of me.'

'What about the other stuff?' I said. 'You know . . . when he makes you do things that aren't nice? And when he makes you see his friends?'

'Yeah but that's my choice. Honestly, I'm fine wi' it.'

'And what would you think if he was asking your little sister to do the same stuff?'

'No way! I wouldn't let her. I'd kill anyone who went near her!'

'So why is it all right that you're doing those things?'

I was trying hard not to tell her she had been groomed and exploited. I didn't want to put words in her mouth. Instead, I was trying to steer her in a direction where she'd eventually come to her own conclusions. And as time went on, she would indeed discover the truth for herself, and to her cost.

Meanwhile, my early days with Risky Business were about getting to grips with an organization that had a brief to help vulnerable girls, but little else. To give it some context, in 1997 a small grant of £1,500 was given to the Youth Service to do some initial research around vulnerable young women working on the streets. The research identified twenty-one young people in Rotherham who had disclosed they were involved in 'child prostitution' and the workers were struggling to find support for them. Part of the grant was to deliver some work with a group of young people who lived in a local hostel and were deemed high risk. A project called 'Girl Power' was set up on a once-a-week basis and at the end of the grant the group worked together to find a suitable name so that a new grant could be applied for. They chose 'Risky Business' and the job I got was part of this new initiative.

We had a dingy office in the International Centre in Kimberworth Park, a former secure unit for young people that had been converted into offices. There was just me and Cassie on the project and in later years we'd have a 'revolving door' of staff members, depending on whether we could get funding to employ them. At its peak there were ten people working for Risky Business, most of them part-time. Those first few days were spent finding out what the project was about and who we might be working with, though there were very few referrals to get to grips with.

However, we had some clues about where we might start looking for girls who needed our help. From the early 1990s a number of children's home managers established a group known as the 'taxi driver group'. Their remit was to discuss the number of incidents of taxis turning up at children's homes and taking away vulnerable young people. The care home managers who set up this group had all experienced the same thing – numerous taxis driven by Asian males arriving, picking up young girls and disappearing. The staff felt power-less to do anything, although several attempted to follow the taxis in their own cars. Even though they reported these incidents to the police, nothing was done. Eventually they set up their own group to moni-tor the situation as it was felt the girls were somehow being abused or pimped – though at this stage no one could prove anything.

As I've mentioned, 'child prostitution' is a term I hate because it implies that a choice is being made by the child themselves. As we'll see as this book pro-gresses, 'choice' is a highly contentious issue, but my argument is that, under the age of eighteen, there is no such thing as 'choice'. The law states that young people can consent to a sexual relationship at the age of sixteen, which is fine if it is consensual. However, the Children's Act states that a child is a child until their eighteenth birthday. So it seems to be an anomaly that a child aged between sixteen and eighteen who is involved in prostitution and forced to have sex with multiple males is somehow consenting.

Anyway, 'child prostitution' was the term back then, and the 'Business' part of the organization's name implied a transaction of some kind, so that's how we referred to it – at least at the beginning.

The vast majority of the girls coming to Risky Business at that time were working the streets of Sheffield, six miles from Rotherham, and putting themselves in terrible danger.

Risky Business had several main aims: to provide a resource for young people in Rotherham at risk of sexual exploitation; to deliver preventative work in schools and other youth settings; to work with other agencies to raise awareness of the project; and to meet the health and social needs of children at risk from school exclusion. To begin with, Cassie and I decided to sit down with the different agencies supporting young people around Rotherham and talk about what we wanted to do. The first was the Youth Offending Team and after Cassie and I had met them, and had talked about working with young women, attempting to improve self-esteem and introducing group work, we could have had a caseload each. So we designed a referral form for agencies to fill in whenever they had someone on their books whom they thought would benefit from Risky Business's intervention.

However, we quickly found out that going through the agencies was not necessarily the best approach. Not all young people have youth workers or social workers, particularly those who want to keep off the radar for their own reasons. This became apparent when we began work with one young woman, a referral, who then said, 'Can I bring a friend?' So in the end Risky Business became an organization that worked mainly by word of mouth, and the only one to which young people could self-refer.

The focus, as I've said, was mainly on girls being abused in Sheffield. The police in that city had noticed that a lot of the younger girls they were arresting on the streets were travelling from Rotherham, perhaps because there wasn't an established 'red light' area in our town. The girls were pretty much all fourteen and upwards, a fair few were in care and some had drug problems. They were being abused in cars, B & Bs, cheap hotels and in backstreets. They described the various pimps they were involved with – some of whom turned out to be the same man, or group of men – and some of the incidents they'd been involved with.

Anne was one of the first I met and I'll never forget her story. One evening, as I sat at home watching TV, I received a call from Sheffield Children's Hospital. They told me they'd admitted a badly injured young girl but, although they'd rung round numerous children's organizations, no one was available to help her. Anne lived in a children's home and just wanted someone with her as she was so frightened. Sadly, no one other than Risky Business responded – it was considered that now she was in hospital she was safe from any more harm. I knew she just wanted a little human contact and to see someone who cared about her. The hospital couldn't give me many more details, but it appeared she had been working on the streets and was a drug user.

I put on my shoes and coat, as I would do so many times over the next fourteen years, and drove over to the hospital. Anne looked like a little pale doll lying there in bed, frightened and uncomprehending. She was sedated, so I went back the next day to find a social worker present. She struck me as unsympathetic and unhappy about being there. I sat by Anne's bed and held her hand, then gently coaxed out the story of what had happened to her. Anne was around fifteen years old, from Rotherham, and had been working on the streets in Sheffield. She'd eventually been picked up by her pimp in his flashy car, where she told him the news she'd been dreading to speak about all night: that she was pregnant by an unknown punter.

'I knew it'd be bad,' she said, struggling to speak through lips swollen by numerous punches, 'but I didn't think he'd do all this. I think he were tryin' to kill me or summat . . .'

Furious, this man had driven her to an isolated and dark industrial estate where he beat her unconscious with a claw hammer in order to give her a termination. Then he abandoned her to her fate. Ironically, it was her drug addiction that saved her life. When she came round, the craving for drugs kicked in before she even knew where she was or what had happened. This need was stronger than the pain she was in, so she crawled towards a row of houses and knocked on the door. When the householder finally answered, he found the bloody heap of a teenager on his doorstep, begging for drugs. The police said that if she'd crawled off in another direction she'd have died of her injuries.

A number of the girls on our books knew Anne and when I next visited her in hospital they gave me little gifts to pass on to her. We were holding a crafts project for the girls at the time. Activities like this meant that the girls would relax and let their guard down, and it was during those times they'd often speak about what was happening to them. They'd made her some soap and bought her sweets in the shape of love hearts. They'd also signed a card, which included an interesting comment from one of the girls. 'Don't worry,' it read, 'we'll get the bastard if we see him! XXX.' For my troubles, I had a complaint made against me by the social worker who'd been at Anne's bedside, saying on the basis of that meeting that I was 'too informal' with our clients. Social workers in general tended to regard our approach as 'too friendly'. Nothing happened subsequently, but it was a sign of the tricky times ahead.

The girls were obviously concerned and angry at what had happened to Anne, not least because there had been a handful of similar violent attacks in the area. Sheffield police, who were investigating, asked if they could meet some of our girls. Now, these girls weren't exactly best pals with the police but they agreed to help, and one of them, Carla, said she'd been subjected to a nasty incident quite recently. She was a stunningly attractive girl – mature, open and honest – and would tell me anything I asked of her. When she spoke to the police about Anne, she did so eloquently, as she always wanted to help everyone. I remember her one day saying she had been on the streets and a car had pulled up. A man wound down his window and asked her if she knew where he could get hold of a twelve-year-old. In response she kicked his car and called him a dirty pervert. His request had horrified her, and yet when I said, 'But you are only fourteen yourself,' she looked at me and replied, 'Yes, but I'm not a child . . .'

Carla said she'd met a punter who'd taken her to a petrol station and made her buy a Kit Kat, which he wanted because of its silver-foil wrapping that he could use to smoke crack cocaine from. He'd then driven her somewhere quiet and violently forced her to have oral sex with him. As this was going on – and there is no polite way of saying this – he literally shit himself.

'Then he got very paranoid that he'd dropped drugs

in my hair,' she told police, 'so he started to rip my hair out and bang my head around. I thought he were gonna kill me.'

Her interview was full and frank, and it tied in with several accounts of a punter matching the description – and with the same bizarre toilet behaviour – who'd been violent with other girls. Sheffield Vice Squad made an arrest, a man was charged and eventually Carla was called to be a witness in his trial at Sheffield Crown Court.

I was delighted. This was early on in the project and we'd worked so well with Sheffield Vice Squad; they were always helpful and generally sympathetic to the girls' plight. They knew the girls we were dealing with weren't hardened older women on the streets of Sheffield.

I accompanied Carla to the trial and was impressed by the evidence against this guy. Someone had remembered seeing him around the petrol station at the given date and time, which she knew because she'd just won some money on the Lottery. I was very hopeful that we'd get a conviction and have one less violent punter – or punter of any description – on the streets.

As we sat outside the courtroom, waiting for Carla to be called, a young girl walked past us. She stopped and asked if she could buy a cigarette off me. I didn't have any, and told her that, so she asked Carla.

'Course you can,' Carla said, 'but I've only got roll-ups. Is that all right? Don't worry, you don't owe us any money. Just help yourself.'

Carla gave the girl some papers and tobacco and off she went for a smoke outside. Some while later Carla was called in. Although I could sit near the press bench in support I wasn't allowed to speak on her behalf.

And the defending barrister gave her hell. Her alleged attacker was dressed up to the nines and looked like butter wouldn't melt in his mouth. And while Carla was an intelligent, lovely girl, the jury didn't see that. Instead, the barrister cross-examined her so harshly that she became defensive.

'I put it to you,' he said, 'that as a prostitute, you have put your head together with other prostitutes and cried rape because you wanted drugs, which my client refused to supply you with.'

'No,' she screamed across the courtroom, and I winced as I saw rolling eyes among the jury members.

Then the barrister asked her if she'd ever met a particular girl from Sheffield, who had also been attacked and was a witness in the case. He asked Carla if this girl was a friend of hers. In all honesty, Carla had never heard this girl's name, and said so.

'So,' said the barrister slowly, 'you would swear on oath that you don't know XXX, have never had a conversation with her, never even met her?'

'Course I would,' Carla replied.

'In that case,' said the barrister, 'can you tell the court why you were having a conversation with XXX outside this courtroom not twenty minutes ago? And why you handed her tobacco and papers in such a friendly manner?'

Carla spluttered and tried to explain what had happened, but it was too late – she was skewered. The barrister, or one of his staff, had spotted the interaction. There was a short recess while the police, through the CPS barrister, asked if I could take the stand to explain what had happened from a witness's point of view, but it was disallowed. And in due course – probably inevitably – the accused man was acquitted and walked free. The police were furious. They'd considered it an open-and-shut case, but all the way through the defence had used the word 'prostitute' again and again, making sure that the jury didn't see vulnerable children, just hardened street-walkers on drugs and on the make.

I was shocked; shocked that a barrister could operate this way and shocked that a jury would choose to ignore such compelling evidence. But I was also naive; I'd never been in court before and had no idea what a bear-pit it could be, particularly for victims and witnesses. This feeling that the system was stacked against victims, especially those seen to be less than perfect in society's eyes, would be borne out time and time again during the life of Risky Business . . .

*

The self-referral system meant that the number of girls we had on our books quickly escalated from a handful to over seventy in just a few months. There was no way that my seven hours a week could stretch to helping all these people and by Christmas I was full-time. We were identifying indicators that highlighted when a young person might be vulnerable to CSE (child sexual exploitation) – truanting regularly from school, not coming home on time, hanging around with other girls known to be at risk, accepting lifts from taxi drivers and older men, having the same 'boyfriend' as other girls we knew were being groomed or abused – and acting upon those with the cooperation of schools, youth groups, care homes and other organizations that worked with young people.

Like Alison, these girls would often be very defensive when we first made contact with them, to the point of aggression. I remember approaching one girl, Charlie, who had been the subject of several conversations I'd had with other girls connected with the project. They all claimed she was at risk, so with the permission of her school I asked to see her one afternoon.

There was no returning my smile as she entered the office allocated by the school for our meeting. She positioned her chair so she could look out of the window, not at me. Charlie's opening line was a classic: 'Don't fuckin' ask me owt, cost I'm not gonna fuckin' tell you, so fuck off!'

The only way from there was up. 'OK,' I replied, 'if you won't tell me owt and I can't speak to you, how can I ask you if you want to leave school for an hour and have a Coke in McDonald's?'

She paused, twiddling her long brown hair. 'Well, I might do that,' she said.

We got into my car. 'This is going to be an awkward journey,' I said, 'so I'll tell you what, I'll make a deal with you – you speak to me for this one hour and if you don't want to see me again, I'll go away and never come back. It's your choice and I'll not pressure you.'

'Deal,' she muttered.

She kept her side of the bargain, albeit she was still defensive and reluctant to give anything away. Some years later she would play a significant role in bringing her abusers to justice. At the beginning, though, I had to take tiptoe steps with her, week in, week out, just to get the barest details.

We listened, we believed and we never judged. We gave girls a choice to see us and if we made a promise to do something, we did it. Most of all we laughed and tried to lighten the atmosphere, introducing our girls to the things that teenage girls should be doing. We organized activities, played games and talked about music. We just kept chipping away until we found the inner child, working to their pace and their agenda, and no one else's.

I remember taking a group of girls on a trip to Butlins.

I thought it would be nice for them to get away, and spend some time in a fun family environment. It didn't go quite as planned. A few of the girls had babies who cried relentlessly, stopping us from sleeping and annoying other guests. On our first night, the girls sneakily helped themselves to other guests' drinks in the bar, resulting in some truly outrageous drunken behaviour including fighting with other holidaymakers. The final straw for the management came when some of the girls were caught shoplifting in the camp's gift-shop – looking for presents to take home. Not only were we asked to leave, but our names and photographs were taken, for Butlins' records, and we were all banned for life. We were escorted off the premises, a Butlins security van in front of us, the police behind. Worse still, Rotherham Council were told they could never go there again. I think I was in a state of shock as I drove the girls home, then returned to the office. I'd just parked the minivan and got out when I bumped into an officer in the youth service, a nice lady who was a bit away with the fairies.

'Peace and love, Jayne,' she beamed at me. 'Peace and love.'

I leaned against the minivan and just laughed hysterically.

Eventually I packed in my other youth work jobs to concentrate on Risky Business, but I kept on the night-shifts at the homeless hostel because so many of Risky Business's clients were living there and being around meant I could offer some extra help. My family was always supportive in the choices I made about my job, especially Paul. It was obvious to anyone who knew me that I loved what I was doing and every time there was an emergency at work, Paul was – and still is – the type of person to say, 'just go and help out.' That said, it was a relief to eventually take up just one full-time post after juggling part-time jobs and various shifts for so long.

One Saturday I was on a shift at the hostel and I got talking to a girl who'd just moved in. Katy was working on the streets in Sheffield after being placed there by someone she regarded as a boyfriend, but who was actually one of the most notorious pimps in the city. She had been thrown out of her home by her strict Roman Catholic father when he found out what she'd been doing for a living. In fact, alongside the beatings she was getting on the streets, her father was also giving her what for. She told me she only had the clothes she stood up in and was too scared to retrieve the rest from her dad's.

The following morning I rang the police and they accompanied Katy and me to her dad's. She collected her clothes safely and we returned to the hostel. Then, suddenly, she moved out and I didn't hear from her again for two weeks until one night she rang in a state of absolute hysteria. It turned out she'd moved back home because her father had apologized. All was going well until she'd received a call from a man in Sheffield who was her pimp; a violent man well known to the police. This man had threatened her that he would be coming over in an hour to take her away and do God knows what with her. She was almost screaming down the phone, so I dropped everything and dashed round to her house.

When I arrived she virtually flung herself through my car window in her panic to get away. We drove round for a while, then parked up. I wasn't sure what we should do, so I phoned Rotherham police. I explained the story, hoping they'd be sympathetic. They weren't.

'I'm sorry, love,' said the officer on the other end, 'there's not a lot we can do. She's sixteen and if she doesn't want to go she doesn't have to.'

'Yes, but that's the point,' I said. 'This fella is coming round to get her and there's nothing she can do about it. He'll kidnap her.'

'Well, has he arrived yet?'

'No, but he's due here any minute.'

'But you're not at the house?'

'No.'

'As I say, there's not a lot we can do if there's no trouble so far,' said the officer.

I rang Rotherham social services. Exactly the same answer. Then I tried my contact at Sheffield Vice Squad, an officer I'll call 'Bob'. They'd been so good to us so far.

'The problem is,' Bob said, 'that we can't be seen to cross jurisdictions into Rotherham force area. But if you were ringing me in Sheffield, then I might be able to help.'

So we drove down the Parkway, which links Rotherham and Sheffield, and once I'd passed the 'Welcome to Sheffield' sign I pulled up in a lay-by and rang Bob again.

'Right,' he said, 'stay where you are, we'll come to get you.'

They were as good as their word, and after interviewing Katy they took her on a tour of the red-light area of Sheffield. Feeling secure, she pointed out addresses of pimps and places where drug dealers went, and in general provided some very useful information. Vice Squad officers rang Rotherham social services to see if they'd change their mind and do something to help Katy in terms of a bed for the night, but it was still no dice. So out of their own money they paid for her to stay in a nice B & B for the evening while something could be sorted out. I was starting to see a marked difference between the way Sheffield police and their colleagues in Rotherham treated 'difficult' young girls like Katy.

Social services never did pick this case up and eventually Katy left Rotherham and went to live in West Yorkshire. The last I heard she was married with two children.

5

From my earliest involvement, Risky Business always had monthly steering group meetings made up of like-minded people who supported the work we were doing and saw it as valid and worthy of time and effort. Most were in management roles across different agencies in the statutory and voluntary sectors. We'd have representatives from social services, health, education and the local police, along with workers in other agencies who had an interest in the protection of children. We shared information about issues around our work at these meetings, including policies, procedures, funding – all the issues that would come up as the work of Risky Business progressed.

Running alongside this was the 'key players' group, also monthly, which again included senior council managers and police officers, but this one concentrated on information about the girls, plus intelligence about pimps, punters and abusers that had been passed on to us and which we thought would be useful in helping to bring about arrests. Right from the start the police seemed very uncomfortable indeed about the information we were collecting and passing on, particularly when it involved ethnicity. We were told that passing on such information 'violated the human rights' of those we were accusing and that we must think very carefully about that, plus the 'lack of evidence' from our side. It seemed that from the beginning the rights of the girls not to be abused came way below those of their abusers.

By 2001 it was clear to both the steering group and key players group that there was a shift in the backgrounds of the girls being referred to us. The numbers of girls working on the streets of Sheffield were declining. Increasingly, it was girls who were being groomed by so-called 'boyfriends' (in fact, much older men) before being horrendously abused who were the focus of our attention. A number of these girls were referring to the same 'boyfriend' and the abuse was no longer taking place in Sheffield but Rotherham itself.

These girls were vulnerable; perhaps even more vulnerable than the girls who worked the streets. At least the latter group had some idea of the risks involved; those girls who classed the older men they were associating with as 'boyfriends' didn't see such dangers. In fact, they told us what a good time they were having with their 'boyfriends'. As I said above, we classed such girls as vulnerable because of the indicators they were presenting (truanting from school, coming home late, etc.) and the fact that other girls we were already working with had told us of their concerns. We weren't surprised that the girls didn't understand the grooming process. Not many people did, or still do to this day. The initial stages of grooming are not abusive; if they were, the abuser would never get to the next stage of his plan.

The age range of the girls we were now seeing had dropped too. At the beginning, the project's age range of young people we would work with was defined as fourteen to twenty-five. Within a year we dropped the lower age to thirteen and eventually it dropped to a starting age of just eleven. This was significant because the younger the girl is the more she is likely to be taken in by the grooming process. Our girls were talking about meeting men, travelling around in their fancy cars, being offered free drinks and soft drugs, being taken to McDonald's and treated to food. To them, they were living a life far removed from the day-to-day reality of school and home.

Such men were – and are – clever. They didn't always approach the girls themselves. In fact, they used boys – younger brothers, cousins or other family and friends – to carry out the initial pick-ups. These boys were often paid to do such work, and would also run errands for their seniors, including the delivery of drugs. The boys selected were of the same age as their potential victims and hung around shopping centres and parks, casually chatting up groups of girls who gathered there.

Gradually, the younger boy would introduce a girl, or a group of girls, to his older 'mates'. By this stage, a lot of information had been extracted from the girls: where they lived, which school they went to, what their parents did, what music and films they liked – the lot. Just recently, a woman I'd helped for years summed this up to me when she said: 'They knew every single thing about me – and all I knew about them was their nick-names.'

As an adult woman, this victim now knows that she has nothing in common with a twelve-year-old boy. But as a twelve-year-old child, she had been groomed so carefully that she didn't even consider there was any-thing wrong with a twenty-five-year-old man sharing her tastes in music and TV shows. If a child trusts you, they will tell you everything, and that's how grooming works. Once the abuser has this information, he has a great deal of power over his victim because he knows exactly what threats and actual acts of physical or psy-chological abuse will have the most impact.

In addition, at the age of twelve or thirteen there is that bit of enjoyment around doing something that pushes the barriers just a little, and yet not understand-ing that it is wrong. Girls might have a sneaky cigarette or go on a secret diet; all normal stuff that goes hand in hand with the path to adolescence and teenage-hood. As the same girl said to me: 'When I look back at getting involved [with the abusers] it was the worst time of my life, but also some of the best times too.'

Their abusers know this; they also know that when the abuse starts the girls won't immediately run off and call the police. Because they're in so deep, they just want their 'boyfriend' back; the same guy who they were having such fun with just a few weeks or months previously. The girl can't understand what has gone wrong, so time and again she goes back to him in order to locate the 'real' person she'd known.

Paula was referred to us at the age of fourteen because she was hanging around with various Asian taxi drivers who we heard were giving her cannabis and taking her out on trips, sometimes as far away as Birmingham. She was also truanting from school and was starting to get a reputation as a persistent shoplifter. Week after week we discussed her case with police and social services, but although her grooming and abuse appeared to escalate quickly, nothing was being done by the authorities to help. Her parents were extremely concerned, attending meetings with us, the police, social services and education (at one meeting with the latter, they were actually blamed for her not attending school) and doing everything they could to stop her from becoming more deeply involved. Her poor, desperate father even accosted one of the men she was hanging about with when he saw him in Asda.

'I go shooting,' he said to this man, 'and I've got a

shotgun. If you keep carrying on with my girl I'll use it on you.'

He related this story in a meeting at which police officers were present. They tore a strip off him, but still did nothing about his daughter's abusers.

One of these, Dawid, said he'd take her to London for the weekend. He became her 'special boyfriend' and by this time she'd stopped attending school altogether, spending most of her time with him before moving in with him. Quickly, this relationship turned violent and Dawid and his friends judged that because of her previously 'dirty' ways, she now had to convert to Islam. She was taken to a mosque, where she was stripped and bathed by around a dozen men. She was told that she must cover her hair and face, and must not smoke, drink or listen to music. However, Dawid deemed that it was OK for her to have anal sex with him and his friends.

Paula became pregnant by Dawid and, even though she was now carrying his child, he continued to be violent towards her. The abuse was psychological too; one night, Paula caught Dawid in bed with another girl, but far from apologizing, he made her listen in the next room as he finished having sex. Paula was now a virtual slave, cooking round the clock for Dawid and his friends while they watched gruesome jihadist videos and made Paula beg forgiveness from them.

This is an extreme example and it's by no means the

case that all the girls got into such deep trouble. But in almost all cases the pattern of friendship followed by sex followed by threats and violence was exactly the same.

So we were seeing a real pattern of sexual abuse developing in Rotherham, and all the time the same group of names was cropping up. And here is where it gets contentious because they were almost all Asian men. To be specific, we were able to narrow the abusers down to a small group of British Asian males, all related, and their many associates.

I've said before, and I will say now, that I don't think any of what has happened in Rotherham between white girls and Asian men is connected with religion. No religion on earth supports the view that sexually abusing children is a good thing, though we know that abuse has been carried out within various faiths. Neither do I think it is a racial issue. It doesn't matter if a perpetrator of abuse upon children is white, Asian, Afro-Caribbean, Chinese or so on: abuse is abuse, no matter who is carrying it out.

However, I do believe there are some cultural issues around abuse, and I also think this is exactly where those in authority have gone wrong; by not facing up to the fact that there are cultural issues at work here, and by actively turning away from the problem, a much wider scale of abuse has been created in Rotherham. The Jay Report of 2014, which we will come to in time, identified 1,400 victims of abuse in the town. I believe the actual figure to be significantly higher. And let's not forget the impact the abuse has had on families and friends of the victims.

I will state, quite categorically, that I believe there is an issue around respect for women, and particularly young white females, coming from some members of the Asian community in this country. I think that girls aged fourteen or fifteen are not always seen as children and, perhaps because of their own culture and customs, are deemed to be 'easy'. Saying all that, Risky Business has worked with young Asian Muslim girls who have been abused from within their own community, so it's certainly not an issue confined to white girls and Asian men. We once worked with a young Asian girl who was being abused within a youth group she was attending. The three men abusing her also brought their brothers, uncles and cousins along to have sex with her. When I asked her if she'd disclosed this to anyone else, she mentioned she'd told her youth worker (a man from within the Asian community), who apparently spoke to the young men involved and then asked the girl if she minded that they continued to attend the group. She agreed to this because she was scared of them. When we asked the youth worker why he'd placated the abusers he said that if the girl 'dressed more appropriately then she could avoid the majority of abuse that she was subjected to'.

Of course, let's not forget there are white men abusing and sexually exploiting young girls and boys too. Much of this grooming is done on the internet, with groups of men across the world sharing images and arranging meet-ups. Their behaviour may be more discreet than those in the Asian communities, but nonetheless they are abusing children just as badly.

Whatever the cultural aspects, I think that if in the early days the authorities had gone into Rotherham's Asian community and spoken about the abuse to community elders, imams and councillors, they would have been as appalled as we were. But allowing the abuse to continue unchecked was, I believe, a green light which indicated 'This is OK'.

I stated above that I believe it was some Asian men who had no respect for women. The emphasis is on 'some'. In the early days of Risky Business I worked with a Muslim man, married with children, who was absolutely appalled by what was happening. He regularly passed me information and intelligence, but wouldn't go to the police himself. He said that if the community was aware of what some of its men were doing they'd be disgusted. However, there would be others, he said, who believed the girls were 'asking for it' and were 'up for it'. He told us that a friend had been clearly informed by his father that white girls were there to 'practise on' before respectable marriage to an Asian woman. As far as I'm aware, that isn't in the Qur'an, so the argument for this being a cultural, rather than a religious, issue is a strong one.

Early on, we recognized there was some resistance in Rotherham to bringing up issues of sexual abuse relating to the Asian community, though of course we'd no idea of the scale of this until later on. We were starting to roll out an education programme in schools around abuse and so I contacted one school which had a high proportion of Asian boys and girls.

'Yes, we'd be interested in doing it,' said the head teacher, 'but do you think it would be sensible to remove the Asian girls before you speak?'

Why, I wondered? What would they hear that could possibly do them harm? It seemed wrong to shelter teenage girls of any background from the realities of life in modern Britain, so we got some money together and took a mixed group of Asian and white girls away for the weekend. The aim was to look at our prevention pack and see if it was fit for purpose; i.e. that it served both communities equally well. There was a little hesitation at first, but within two hours of settling into our hotel we had a group of fifteen girls with no religious, colour or cultural barriers between them. What united them was that they were all vulnerable and at risk because they were all so young.

The more we looked into the abuse, the more we realized that it appeared to be coordinated and well organized. There were the younger foot soldiers, picking up girls in shopping centres, bus stations, parks and outside schools. Girls being unwittingly groomed were bringing friends into their circle of 'boyfriends'. Then older men were becoming involved and the girls would be passed between them. Takeaways, B & Bs and hotels were being used for the abuse, and very often local taxi firms would be seen outside events for young people, waiting to pick up certain girls. There was a nightclub in Rotherham which held an under-eighteens' night once a month. No alcohol was served but it was a place young people could go to feel a bit grown up. Somehow or other, abusers attended too, even though most of them were well over eighteen – the whole place was like a meat market. Taxis sat outside, waiting to give lifts to young, excited girls who had just been charmed by handsome older men inside. Yes, it was a proper network, all right.

As an example of how quickly grooming can turn to abuse, the story of a fourteen-year-old girl called Lianna springs to mind. She came to our attention because she was seeing a man who was known to us as an abuser. Her mother was in a violently abusive relationship which Lianna found hard to endure, so she left, and when I met her she was living in a homeless hostel. I asked her about her 'boyfriend'.

'Oh, he's just lovely,' she said, a huge smile appearing across her painted lips. 'He takes me out everywhere, buys me stuff, fags and booze. And people are dead scared of him too.'

'Oh,' I said, 'why's that?'

She leaned forward. 'Guess what?' she said. 'The other night when we were out in his car, he opened the glovebox and showed me what was inside.'

'What did he show you, love?' I asked.

'A gun,' she replied. 'How about that?!'

'You know,' I said, trying to keep calm, 'that's all part of the way he's trying to control you. You'll find that one day you'll be very, very frightened knowing that he has a gun. And men who run around with guns in their cars are not nice people.'

'Nah,' she said, laughing, 'he's lovely. He'd never do owt to hurt me.'

A little over three weeks later I met her again, and I've never known anyone go from 'groomed' to 'abused' in such a short space of time. This time, there was no make-up or bright and breezy attitude. She sobbed hysterically and shook as she told me what had gone on.

'He was giving me cans of lager and a few cigs,' she said, 'and all that were fine. Then, one night when we were sitting in his car, he said I owed him two hundred quid for the booze and fags. He said he had drug dealers after him, and he owed them this money.'

Then she broke down into terrified sobs and it took a few moments before she could get her next sentence out.

'And now he says that if I don't get the money, he's gonna tell my mum!'

I tried to calm her down, but it was useless. In a whisper, she told me the rest of her story. As she spoke I could feel nausea rising up through my stomach and into my throat.

'He said his brother had the solution to it,' she said. 'He said he didn't like it, but his brother said that if I have sex with him, he'll pay the debt off cos he's got more money than his brother . . .'

So they'd taken Lianna to a flat above a shop – a place that had been mentioned to us before – and her abuser's brother had had sex with her, as planned. When it was finished, she got back into her abuser's car and he drove her home. As she opened the door, he grabbed her wrist.

'Now you only owe us £195,' he sneered. 'And if you don't pay it . . .' He tapped the glovebox, indicating what was inside it.

So now she was in a real predicament. How could she tell her mother that she owed all this money and could be in serious danger if she didn't pay? In addition, how could she explain that she'd tried to pay it off by having sex with a man much older than her? I encouraged her to talk to the police, which she did. Their advice was that she 'shouldn't hang around him any more'. Easier said than done, of course, so I also drew up a Child Protection referral, which went to social care to be assessed, and her mother was informed. The money was not paid, her mother refusing to give in to blackmail, but from then on Lianna lived in fear of her life.

This would not be the last time I'd hear stories of extortion and the payment of 'debt' with sex. It happened to another girl who did agree to make a statement to the police. The girl later became frightened and didn't want the investigation to go any further. She was then threatened that she might be charged for wasting police time. Not really what you want to hear from agencies meant to be protecting your child . . .

And yet, we were telling the police everything we heard. As I described at the start of this chapter, Risky Business had both a steering group and a key players group, attended by both senior police and social services representatives. At this latter meeting we would regularly share information and intelligence on those we believed were abusing young girls across Rotherham: names, nicknames, car registrations, taxi numbers, mobile phone numbers, takeaways, shops, relationships between abusers – you name it, if we'd been given it we shared it at the key players meeting. We were constantly told by senior police officers that it was 'hearsay'. 'Where's the evidence?' they'd always ask. 'Where's the evidence?'

Child sexual exploitation is a jigsaw in that everyone involved in protecting a child has different pieces of information to share. For example, if we shared a name it might be one known to police and also identified by housing as a person who'd been seen hanging around a children's home or hostel. We could then check with education to see if the same person had been parking outside local schools. So with all this input we could build a really good case for action and the possibility of arrests – or so we thought.

Our police representative was Inspector Anita McKenzie, who headed the Rotherham police district's community safety unit. She was a quietly spoken woman, approaching retirement, and at first I had faith in her because she was female and I thought she would have empathy for the girls whose abuse was being detailed in our reports, month after month after month.

I prepared a report to everyone present for every meeting that highlighted all our concerns, including abuser identification, hotspots, girls at risk and links between girls and abusers. At one meeting we even shared intelligence on a drug deal due to take place at a supermarket car park late one evening. The girl who'd told us had overheard her abuser arranging it on the phone – apparently, just under half a million pounds' worth of heroin was due to be handed over. Unfortunately our intelligence was not considered good enough to be evidence and no action was taken. We heard later that the drug deal had indeed taken place.

Very often I was concerned that the high level of

detail we shared at these meetings was not always properly minuted, only to be told that the minutes were only meant to be a summary. Most of the time, someone from social services came along and did the minutes. I always took my own minutes because more often than not I would give a detailed description of something that had happened, only to see it reduced to one line in the official minutes.

Eventually we had so much information collated that Anita suggested we do something formal with it. She proposed a system whereby we would share our intelligence with police officers, who would place it into something she described as 'Box Five' on the force's computer network. This, we were told, was a high-security program that would protect the identities of the girls involved in abuse and also those who were supplying the information. To me, this sounded like the ideal solution to the increasing number and variety of reports we were receiving. And, more importantly, that it would produce results in terms of arrests and convictions.

At the beginning, I can't claim that the way we were collating information was anything like official. We'd had no training in this; we simply wrote down what we were told and checked it against other sources of information. For example, I look back at one of my reports now and see that some information about a newsagent's had been passed to us. Four young women – two sixteen-year-olds and two aged just thirteen – were buying cheap cigarettes from this place and were being asked for sexual favours by the workers in the shop in return for free alcohol. Another young woman had offered to make a statement to police about this. Now, that's what we'd been told. If I could've visited the shop myself and made enquiries I would've done. But we weren't professional detectives, nor did we claim to be; we were just a group of people deeply concerned about a pattern of abuse in our town which seemed to grow on a daily basis.

With hindsight, perhaps our well-meaning approach at the beginning of Risky Business was part of the problem and the reason that Rotherham police refused to take us seriously. In their eyes, we were 'just youth workers', clueless amateurs who were presenting a whole lot of information to them without any evidence. But the point was – and still is today – that we weren't the police. Surely it is *their* job to obtain evidence based on what they are told. If a person sees a crime being committed in the street and has a good description of the offender, is he also expected to chase after him and apprehend him? Of course not. So why was it different for us?

Anita McKenzie was constantly telling me that the information we were collating was 'not strong enough to be evidence'. If I mentioned 'rape' or 'assault' to her when I was discussing one of our girls she'd always correct me with the words 'alleged rape' or 'alleged assault'.

I accepted that, but what I found puzzling was the seeming lack of will by the police to do anything about such allegations themselves, at least not for a number of years. As time went on, I'd visit projects around the north of England similar to ours and I'd think, *Our information is as good as – if not better than – theirs, and yet they're getting results and we aren't.* I simply couldn't understand it.

Still, we continued to supply the police and social services with information in the hope that somewhere along the line the abusers would be brought to justice. I see in the same bundle of files that two of the girls mentioned above in relation to the newsagent's had 'been giving oral sex to two Asian males aged sixteen and eighteen within the Clifton Park area of Rotherham'. I passed on the phone number of one of these males and his nickname, plus the fact that his number was linked to the sexual exploitation of another girl on our books. Where possible, we would provide a description of the alleged abuser and indicate his ethnicity. If he'd been white, I'd have said that. The fact that almost all those abusing girls were of Asian origin meant that in the vast majority of cases I put down 'Asian' as ethnic origin. I remember the intakes of breath when we mentioned ethnicity at steering group and key players meetings, accompanied by the occasional shaking of heads.

'Are you sure you should be mentioning this, Jayne?'

'Is ethnicity really relevant?'

'Jayne, don't you think it's a bit racist to say what their background is?'

No, I didn't. As I said, if they'd been white males I'd have mentioned it. Like the man in the street who witnesses a crime, I assumed the police would want to know as much detail about the criminal as possible, including ethnicity. Back then, I didn't think that was wrong. Others obviously felt differently . . .

6

Years ago, back when I was working in youth clubs, I often came across a very cute, very pretty nine-year-old who just lived to dance. Jessica was a sparky, lively, big-eyed child who showed me a new dance routine every week and was one of the kindest and most helpful children I'd ever met. She was a joy to be with, and everyone who worked with her said the same. Just six years later, I held this child in my arms as she sobbed and sobbed.

'No one knows what it's like!' she wept. 'They've got me, Jayne, they're doing all this stuff to me and I'll never get away from them. And no one even cares!'

I held her even tighter to me.

'I care,' I said. 'I'll always care about you. And I'll do everything I can to make it stop – I promise.'

The truth was, making Jessica feel safe would be a battle that lasted a long time. Her abuse began at fourteen, when she became involved with a twenty-five-year-old man, and although she went into foster care, after frequently going missing from home, the abuse continued unabated.

Far from being protected, the foster carer actually allowed her to go on seeing this man as long as she was in by 10 p.m. The abuser, who by the foster carer's account was a 'polite, well-mannered young man', was also invited home for tea. Incredible, really.

Eventually Jessica disappeared from foster care and was missing with her abuser again. Her father, who was devastated by what was going on, always made efforts to track her down whenever this happened and, inevitably, she'd be at a property owned by abusers in the town. One evening he set out to find her, having been told by police that 'it wasn't their problem'. He quickly located her and banged on the door of a terraced house, demanding that whoever was in should open up and give him his daughter back.

Unfortunately as he was shouting he used a racist comment towards the people inside. He shouldn't have said it, and it's unforgivable, but that's what happened. Neighbours heard the fracas and reported that someone was racially abusing people in their street. The police arrived pretty damned quickly, the door was opened and they went inside. By all accounts, Jessica was just getting out of bed with her abuser when the police came through the front door. So she hid under the bed while the man was caught pulling on his trousers. When they finally brought her out from under the bed she was intoxicated, semi-naked and clutching a police truncheon. She didn't come out quietly, apparently, which led to her being arrested and charged with disorderly behaviour, as was her father. And although the house was full of men, one of whom had just been in bed with a fourteen-year-old girl, not one of them was spoken to, arrested or charged with anything.

Jessica subsequently told me that when she was driving around with her abuser in his flashy car, he'd often play the 'race card' if stopped by police. 'You're only pulling me because I've got a brown face,' he'd say, and they'd back off. She also claimed that on several occasions officers known to this man would warn him to lie low because he was 'being looked at'.

Now, there is no doubt that Jessica was deeply troubled and could be a right handful, to put it mildly. But what she needed was understanding and support, not arresting and stigmatizing. Her father also needed that support. No parent, no matter how forceful, can stop his child being abused in this way without the backing of police and social services. It just isn't possible. Instead of arresting Jessica and her dad, wouldn't it have been better to collect evidence of abuse from a house that contained twenty men and a half-naked, underage girl? I'd have thought so, but this was the reality we were dealing with at the time and no amount of complaining seemed to do any good.

Along with a fear of treading on sensitive cultural issues, there seemed to be an attitude, particularly among some police officers, that the girls we worked with were 'difficult'; flaky, unreliable and damaged. 'Little slags', not to be trusted. In fact, nothing could be further from the truth. Yes, many of them had issues, but don't many young people?

Worse still, I believe there was a view that the abuse perpetrated on them was somehow 'consensual'. That they were hanging around with these guys and accepting lifts, drink and drugs, and really, they were just wasting police time. None of that, however, makes it OK to rape underage girls or pimp them out to other men.

In my view, and especially in the early days, the police were incredibly reluctant to get involved in what we were doing, for the reasons stated above, and also for the fear of being deemed 'racist'. And when they did get involved, their actions could be breathtakingly stupid, as Jessica's story shows.

Nationally, a somewhat different picture was emerging. The first faint rumblings of a nationwide problem with child sexual exploitation were beginning to be heard by government, though abusers and their ethnicity and cultural backgrounds were, for the time being, not an issue. Ironically, a lot of the worry back then was around the Catholic Church. A series of sensational cases in Ireland had blown the issue sky-high, and the repercussions were being felt in this country too. Scandals and rumours of abuse in UK children's homes had also prompted stirrings in Whitehall. In the middle of

2000, the Home Office decided to put money into a research project that would look at CSE across the country, with a view to finding out what was going on and how best to tackle it in terms of a national policy. The research would look at law and legislation, and how current legislation could be used in relation to information being supplied about abusers. The Home Office would fund a series of projects which looked at CSE in different regions and the University of Bedfordshire would evaluate the results.

When we heard about it we thought it would be an ideal vehicle for Risky Business to contribute to. Irene Ivison, whose daughter Fiona had been abused and murdered, and who had founded an organization called CROP (Coalition for the Removal of Pimping) in the wake of her daughter's death, got together with Kerry Byrne, my manager, and decided they would make a joint bid for the funding. We were the only bid that planned to look at the abusers and the current legislation available to deal with them. If we were successful Irene would be the appointed Home Office researcher in charge of collating information. However, the Home Office didn't want the bid to be 'single agency', so we had to put together a multi-agency bid which included social services, health representatives, the police, education representatives, etc. That week, I spoke to Irene and we were both feeling extremely positive about the bid. I thought that if what was happening in Rotherham came to national attention, something would be done about it. Irene was going in for a routine operation that Friday, 20 October, so I wished her all the best and got on with my daily life.

The following Monday I turned up to work as usual to find Kerry crying.

'You're not going to believe this, Jayne,' she said. 'It's Irene . . .'

'Why? What's happened?'

'Jayne, she's passed away. There were complications during her operation and she died.'

I dropped my bag on the floor in shock. 'I can't believe it,' I said. 'I was only speaking to her last week. Oh God, poor Irene . . .'

I was still struggling to come to terms with the awful news when, not long after this, Kerry said, 'We've got the bid. The Home Office one. I opened the letter this morning. It said we'd been successful.'

Unbelievable. For the first time, we had the chance of recognition for the growing problem of CSE in our town and yet we'd lost the one person who could lead the project and really make a difference. We were numb with sorrow over Irene's tragic loss – and yet we knew immediately we had to carry on. It was what Irene would've wanted. So an advert was drawn up asking for a researcher to work on the project. The interview panel picked Adele Weir, a Yorkshire lawyer specializing in family matters. She was very experienced and a warm, understanding and committed person. Further-more, a decision taken somewhere meant that she would be based in the Risky Business office while she compiled her report. Having her with us seemed more fitting, as opposed to placing her with social services or the police. This research would be overseen by Risky Business's steering group, and by our manager, Kerry Byrne, on a day-to-day basis.

Adele's job included researching and developing measures to disrupt the activities of the men targeting young women; to work with the Crown Prosecution Service (CPS) to look at how enhanced evidence gathering could be used in a court of law; to gather enhanced evidence; to produce a report on the pilot study outlining the development of ten young women's case studies and the targeting of six 'pimps'; to attend meetings as appropriate and to oversee the collation of data, including that currently held, and its input into an ICT system. The latter was developed by a friend of mine, Dave Bowman, who designed it for ease of use. While it wasn't networked to police or social services computers, it was as good as anything the police were using and in some instances better, as it cross-referenced and alerted us to patterns of abuse.

Adele began work with the thorough approach you'd expect from an experienced lawyer. She went through every file we had on all the girls referred to us, all the information we had on perpetrators of abuse, all the minutes from the key players and steering group meetings – we handed over everything to her so she could have a comprehensive picture.

In a statement Adele made to the Parliamentary Home Affairs Select Committee in 2014, she said that, 'from a very early stage I encountered a significant number of children who were believed to be either involved in child sexual exploitation or being targeted and groomed for child sexual exploitation. I also learned of a small number of suspected abusers who were well known to all significant services in Rotherham.'

She also said that right from the beginning she came across what she described as 'poor professional practice' in the police force, social services and education. She said there was 'widespread frustration' over responses to children involved in or vulnerable to CSE and the lack of action against abusers.

'I was able to observe and record several situations where children were left in situations of risk by those who were employed to protect them,' she said. 'I encountered numerous examples of child protection issues being disregarded, dismissed or minimized.'

Adele attended the key players meetings and shared the concerns she had. Like us, she noticed that while all the right noises were being made, nothing was actually being done. Unlike us, Adele knew what to do next. She asked for, and received, permission to create a mapping exercise which collated all the information she'd gathered about the abusers, because she'd been told by police that the evidence they'd been presented with so far – mainly from Risky Business – was 'anecdotal' and not strong enough. So using everything she'd gained from us (and from a homelessness project, drugs misuse services, health services, education, the Youth Service, confidential records and the police and social services), she cross-referenced and gathered all this information into one document, around ten pages long.

When I read it, I was astounded. It was a brilliant piece of work. It listed names, car registration numbers, links with people outside the area, links with businesses in Rotherham and relationships between abusers and girls. A senior detective couldn't have done any better if he or she had been given years to work on it. And it was born out of a genuine desire to protect children from a growing menace in Rotherham, and frustration that nothing was being done to help them.

Adele was absolutely shocked by what she was coming across. Which is no surprise, as day by day the abuse and the terror seemed to only get worse. Around this time we came into contact with a fourteen-year-old girl called Katrin who had wanted to break the cycle of sexual abuse and violence she'd become locked into. She was a quiet, almost mousy teenager who never said boo to anyone. Her difficulty – if it can be described that way – was that she had a figure to die for, which made her a real catch among the abuse gangs. One of these men took a shine to her, made her feel special, and for a while she became 'his'.

Now, the abusers enjoyed nothing better than making the various girls they were seeing jealous of each other, and because Katrin had a great figure she came in for some bullying and name-calling from other girls. When she was with her abuser she felt protected by him, but after a concerted attempt by her mother, who was forever going out looking for her at night, Katrin decided that she wanted no more to do with her abuser and his friends.

Stung by what he saw as disloyalty, her abuser decided to take violent revenge. The twist was that he wouldn't be carrying out the violence. Instead, he ordered a group of other girls to attack her. They were so brainwashed that they carried out his orders unthinkingly and, one night, gave Katrin a real going-over.

Some days later I went to see her at home. Her pretty face was swollen and bruised. I was furious that girls known to us could've done this to one of their own, but I also understood that they were all victims, and that their sense of right and wrong had been totally corrupted.

'So what are you going to do now, Katrin?' I asked. 'Give it all up or go back with him and wait until something like this happens again?'

Wearily, she turned to me. 'Jayne, I feel I've got two choices,' she said. 'I either sit around and wait while they kill me or I give evidence and take a risk. Either way, I'd prefer to be dead than live the life I'm living.'

They were brave words and, backed by her mum, she decided she would make a statement to police. But her abusers were clever, knowing how to press her buttons. Aware that she might be considering going to the police, they would phone her at home and ask how her little sister was, and how she was getting on. Her older brother was the victim of an unprovoked attack in the street – assailants unknown. In spite of all that, Katrin did want to speak to police so I arranged for a female officer to visit her. I was present at this visit and all seemed to be going well for a while. Fidgeting and biting her nails, Katrin talked while the officer made notes, appearing to take what she was saying very seriously. Then the officer looked up from her notepad.

'Now, Katrin,' she said, 'you know that if this goes further it's likely to end up in court?'

'I know,' Katrin said. 'That's all right.'

'Are you sure?' said the officer. 'I only ask because you know you'll be in court and they'll all be there, watching you when you give evidence. They'll know exactly who's told the police about them.'

Katrin blanched and suddenly looked very dejected. And despite my protestations of support for her in any legal proceedings, I knew there and then that she wouldn't take this any further or make a statement. Once again, it was 1–0 to the abusers.

What I didn't know then was that even though she didn't make a statement, Katrin's psychological torment was far from over. Some years later I bumped into her mum in town and we went for a coffee.

'There were things she didn't tell you, Jayne,' she said. 'She was so scared at what happened that she couldn't tell anyone for ages.'

'What things?' I asked, preparing not to be too shocked. Over the years I'd heard everything.

'She met [her abuser] again, you know,' her mum said, 'and he turned really nasty. He told her he was going to kill her.'

'Oh my God,' I said, 'that poor child . . .'

These men had done some bad things over the years, but what they put Katrin through was downright wicked. And to make matters worse, she is even today still in the clutches of her abuser, who stalks her and has a powerful hold over her. I work closely with one of the girls who attacked her, and she now says this incident preys on her mind constantly.

'I didn't know what I was doing,' she says. 'They had me under their complete control. If you ever see Katrin, please tell her how sorry I am . . .'

Shocking incidents like this aside, we had Adele's findings so far. Surely a document so comprehensive couldn't be ignored? We were confident that everyone would sit up, take notice and arrest the monsters out there on the streets. Adele handed in the document to

Inspector Anita McKenzie, of 'Box Five' fame, and we waited to see how quickly things would progress. Adele also sent letters in October 2001 regarding her report to the then Chief Constable of South Yorkshire Police, Mike Hedges, and to the District Commander in Rotherham, Christine Burbeary.

In the letter, Adele makes it very clear that she feels very little is being done by the police to tackle CSE in Rotherham. 'Although a great deal has been achieved,' she wrote, 'I still do not consider that enough has been done to protect children at risk and target their abusers. Resources in particular seem an issue of some contention.'

Adele goes on to say:

When I started in post I was made aware that the pilot had been developed through a period of consultation with services, including the police force. I therefore did not expect my work with the police to be so limited. The amount of information already being provided to the police by professionals would, I believe, warrant an investigation into this matter.

Furthermore, as part of my role, I have been visiting agencies, encouraging them to relay information to the police. Their responses have been identical – they have ceased passing on information as they perceive this to be a waste of time. Parents also have ceased to make missing person reports, a precursor to any child abduction investigation, as the police response is often so inappropriate.

This causes me a great deal of concern. Children are being left at risk and their abusers unapprehended.

Risky Business's steering committee had approved the content of the letters, and both CROP and our manager, Kerry Byrne, knew about them.

It went quiet. Too quiet, perhaps. There were no requests for further information, no arrests made, no nothing. We were puzzled. Why wasn't something being done? The answer is that something was being done, but not in the way we could ever have expected.

The following month Adele and I were called into a meeting with Christine Burbeary at Rotherham police station. Elated, we believed that she would want to discuss next steps and share with us a plan to make arrests and bring the child abusers to justice. That same morning, we were also called in to speak to a man called Phil Rogers, a Rotherham Borough Council employee who was assistant to Di Billups, the council's Director of Education. We'd no idea what this was about, but we'd no reason to believe it was for any reason other than a positive one. He was accompanying us to the meeting with Christine Burbeary, so he probably wanted a briefing ahead of our appointment.

At 8.30 a.m. we knocked on his door and went in. The big-built guy behind the desk barely looked up.

With a wave of his hand he motioned us to sit in a couple of chairs in front of him, then he pointed to a pile of paperwork.

'I've gotta get all this lot done,' he said, 'so fire away. I'm listening.'

So we talked away to the top of his head, describing everything we'd been up to, including the report. After about ten minutes Phil Rogers put down his pen and looked up.

'You know,' he said, 'I've got a daughter at university and she's forever getting leaflets on her car about being a lap dancer and all that.'

'What do you mean?' I said, totally confused.

'Well,' he said, 'there seems to be so much of it about, perhaps it's time we thought about legalizing it. Prostitution, you know? It might solve some of these problems you're talking about.'

For a moment I was dumbfounded. Then I spoke. 'Are you saying that child sexual abuse should be legalized, Phil?'

Now it was his turn to be shocked. 'Are you talking about children here?' he replied.

What the hell did he think we were talking about?! Adele and I looked at each other in disbelief. Had he really said that? And had he taken in anything of what we were saying? Our meeting finished in a kind of stunned silence as we all trooped out of his office and across the road to the police station.

Both Christine Burbeary and Anita McKenzie were present, along with a woman called Jackie Jenkinson, from social services. We were invited to sit down. On the desk lay a copy of Adele's report, along with the letter she'd sent. You could cut the atmosphere with a knife and suddenly I felt nervous. I could sense this wasn't going to be a strategy meeting or anything approaching a pat on the back.

We'd hardly sat down when Christine Burbeary tore into Adele with a ferocity I couldn't have predicted from someone so senior. She was wild with anger that Adele had contacted the Chief Constable by letter, yelling that she had gone over her head in doing so.

'This is not how I do business!' she shouted. 'You will not do this again!'

She accused Adele of making up stories and deliberately lying in her report. 'Intimidating' doesn't even begin to describe Christine Burbeary's behaviour that day. She just went to town on poor Adele while Anita McKenzie, Jackie Jenkinson and Phil Rogers sat there and said nothing.

Finally, after a tirade that lasted I don't know how long, she told Adele to 'get out'. As we stood up to leave, Christine turned to me – the first time she'd actually looked me in the eye during the whole meeting. She leaned over and touched the top of my arm.

'Jayne,' she said sweetly, 'if you're ever passing and

you fancy a coffee, give me a shout. My door's always open.'

The implication was clear: 'If you know what's best for you, you'll do what you're told.' To my mind it was an attempt to wield power and rub Adele's nose in it even further. The latter part certainly worked; Adele was distraught after that meeting. She couldn't believe she'd had such a terrible dressing-down over a document she knew to be the truth. I was open-mouthed. I wondered if I'd just walked out of a dream. Or, more accurately, a nightmare.

The following month Adele attended a meeting with a senior Rotherham Borough Council employee, Rod Norton, who also seemed to be very concerned that she had written to the Chief Constable. She was told she'd 'placed the project workers and the young people accessing the project at risk and consequently health and safety issues would have to be addressed, and full risk assessments undertaken on the project'. She was also told that when her final report to the Home Office was written, a senior council manager needed to see it first so that 'it could be managed'. An ominous statement, if ever there was one.

Some months went by. Then in April 2002, Adele was asked by the Home Office evaluators – the team based at the University of Bedfordshire – to submit some of her data and statistical information. This request was passed to Adele by Kerry Byrne, our manager at Risky

Business. So Adele sent off some of her findings to the evaluators, sending a copy to Kerry – who hit the roof. She rang Adele, telling her she was 'extremely upset' that the data had gone to the evaluators. As Adele said to the Home Affairs Select Committee in 2014: 'I did not understand her response because she had been involved from the start of the pilot in discussing the data, my findings, the case studies and attending various meetings with me. I had also had several supervision meetings with Kerry Byrne where I had expressed my frustration at the lack of progress and where we had discussed poor professional practice. I did not believe therefore that there were any surprises in the data that I had submitted.'

Kerry's 'upset' was a shock to Adele, and to me. What was the problem with sharing some interim information with the very team that was supposed to be monitoring it? Evidently there was a problem – and we were about to discover just how seriously those in authority were taking the information we'd gathered and the disclosures Adele had made.

7

The ongoing dispute about sharing information with the Home Office bothered us, but our work had to continue. The girls we were helping needed us, and no amount of wrangling over who submitted what, and whether they had permission or not, would prevent us carrying on.

The Thursday after Kerry told Adele of her 'upset' we went into work at the International Centre as usual. It was 18 April 2002. I parked up and walked towards the building, where I was met by the caretaker.

'Morning, Jayne,' he said. 'It's been a busy evening here.'

'How do you mean?' I said.

'Just that there's been a lot of traffic in and out of your office, that's all . . .'

In an evening? People did drop into the International Centre after normal working hours, but none of those visits would be connected to Risky Business. What was he talking about?

Puzzled, I went in and unlocked the office door. I spotted something on the floor – a plastic tag. I bent

109

down and picked it up. It had a little label on it – 'Home Office Case Studies', it said. Adele used these tags to separate her documents.

With a creeping sense of dread I unlocked my drawer and retrieved the keys to Adele's filing cabinet. As I did, Adele walked in.

'The caretaker's just made some funny comment,' she said. 'Something about this place being very busy yesterday evening?'

'He said the same to me,' I replied. Then I held up the plastic tag. 'I've found this on the floor. It's from your files.'

Adele took the tag from me and looked at it. Then she noticed the filing cabinet key in my hand.

'I think we'd better open it,' she said.

I unlocked the cabinet and pulled out Adele's drawer. Where there was once a space full of files, case studies and many other bits of information, now there was nothing. The drawer was completely empty. All that was left was this sad, solitary plastic tag.

'Oh my God,' said Adele. 'I don't believe it. I do not believe it. We've been burgled. Where the hell has everything gone?'

We looked around. There was no sign of a forced entry; no broken locks or windows. Whoever had removed the files could've only gained entry one way: by coming into the International Centre, disarming the alarm, moving through a key-coded and locked security door, unlocking the door to the part of the building where we were located, unlocking the door to the project office itself, unlocking a desk and finding the key to the filing cabinet.

We could barely speak. Adele suggested switching on our Apple Mac computer, as data was stored there too. It was password protected, but had been accessed. Documents had been deleted and minutes of a meeting created. Whoever had done it had been a bit amateurish because the time and date of the changes made was clearly shown. Adele read quickly through the documents.

'Jesus, Jayne,' she said, 'you won't believe this . . .'

I looked over her shoulder. The minutes showed that she'd apparently agreed to 'certain conditions' regarding the disclosure of information to the Home Office evaluators and that she had been told of the 'consequences' if she failed to abide by these conditions. She'd also 'agreed' not to send the data to the evaluators without line management approval.

Unfortunately Adele had not attended any such meetings, and was actually out of the country on holiday when one of the 'meetings' was said to have taken place.

'This is total crap,' she said, scanning the document. 'I don't know what's happened, Jayne – but I think we've been stitched up.'

For twenty minutes or so we sat at our desks, stunned into silence. Then our manager, Kerry Byrne, came in.

Immediately we asked her what had happened and where the files were. She seemed flustered, upset even; and yet it seemed she was trying to maintain a kind of professional demeanour in the face of an incident that would obviously prompt a lot of questions.

'I don't know anything about that,' she said, 'and anyway, it's irrelevant. There's other stuff happening. You've got a new manager, Christine Brodhurst-Brown. She'll be here in a bit to explain what's going on. That's all I can say.'

Half an hour later we were summoned into a staff meeting with Kerry and Christine. The latter was a Youth Service area manager at the time, a large lady who spoke her mind and wasn't always the most popular among council staff. However, in my dealings with her I found her to be generally a fair person, and at least she was to the point. That said, on this day all questions about the missing files and who might have removed them were swept aside as Kerry and Christine told us that key players meetings were effectively over. We were told we'd overstepped the mark by writing to senior police officers and that Risky Business would have to spend the next few days on 'lockdown' while Christine decided what she was going to do with us. Julie was not in the meeting but a number of other staff were. Cassie, Joanne, Sandra and I were then sent out and another meeting took place between Christine and Adele – after which she was threatened with suspension for gross misconduct, in that she submitted confidential data to the evaluators without express permission.

I was devastated. Adele had only the best interests of the victims at heart, and had no axe to grind against anyone. She just wanted certain things to happen which would stop the abuse of children. I told her that if I was questioned about her performance, I would be happy to say how good she was – even if I was threatened with suspension or sacking too.

Adele sought legal advice, of course, and while this was going on she found out that a decision had already been made to terminate her employment. There was talk of an industrial tribunal, but Adele, professional to the end, decided to negotiate a return to work so that she could conclude the project. After that, though, it seemed as if every effort was made to make Adele's job as difficult as possible. Council managers demanded to see everything first and there was a general distrust of Risky Business. Data, they said, needed to be 'managed'. Adele was told she was no longer allowed to attend strategy meetings, and although she complained about the missing files, the matter was never reported to the police. Neither did we get an explanation from council officers and, to this day, the mystery of who took those files and why has never been solved. Adele was also told she must never refer to 'Asian men' in her reports and for good measure was sent on a two-day ethnicity and diversity training course.

Worse was to come. Adele was given folders containing copies of the data she'd submitted. She noticed that comments and demands for information to be changed or removed had been made in the margins. She was told that these comments had been made by none other than Christine Burbeary from the police, Di Billups from education and Jackie Jenkinson from social services. There was a handwritten note from Christine Brodhurst-Brown attached to these documents saying: 'Please amend the work to anonymise individuals and institutions and only include facts and evidence that you are able to substantiate . . . please examine carefully the amendments and various criticisms concerning the response of various services . . . Also make amendments to the text based on the indicated changes.'

Adele was given a deadline to make these changes and was told to 'follow orders'. In notes she made after the meeting, she wrote: 'Said altering data – I have deep reservations – Looks like a cover-up – Overshadows good work. Told to just do it. Maybe some flexibility on deadline but not much. Told as line manager being made clear I had been given an instruction and that I was expected to follow it.'

Adele didn't make those amendments. Instead, she double-checked her work (which, as a good lawyer, she'd made copies of), sought legal advice and contacted the

Home Office evaluators. At first they were supportive. After that, they went deadly quiet and nothing more was heard from them again. The same went for the evaluators at the University of Bedfordshire. However, at the time of writing this book I managed to obtain a copy of the university's report about the various projects in the group, including Rotherham. It has this to say about Rotherham:

> There appear to have been some difficulties between the project and statutory organisations, such as the police and social services, which in turn have generated tensions between the project and the local authority. This has created a number of pressures within the team . . . at the time of writing it appears that these difficulties have prevented the research and development officer from carrying out her role effectively.
>
> Since its inception there have also been disputes in the project about where to locate the ICT database. This has unfortunately impeded the development of the database. At the time of writing, the database is housed in the premises used by Risky Business but the social services department has apparently refused to allow any of its data to be entered into it. The database, however, is running and it demonstrates the usefulness of this type of facility. It is, however, the view of development consultants and the evaluation team that it would be more appropriate from the

beginning of the project for the police to handle the intelligence that was available and for them to have developed the ICT database ... According to our sources, the police have been seriously hampered in doing the work they were expected to do for/with the project by a number of factors

- The lack of a vice squad or dedicated team
- Disbelief that Rotherham has a problem with sexual exploitation
- Judgmental moral attitudes towards the young women involved
- Lack of resources.

Interesting reading, especially when you consider it was written in 2002, twelve years before the full story of what happened in Rotherham finally made national news. The report concludes:

We have no indication that any of the men identified as involved in the exploitation of young girls are to be prosecuted, and in this aspect, the project has therefore been unable fully to achieve its aims. At the time of writing, the Home Office has chosen to 'stand down' the evaluation team [in Rotherham].

In spite of all the pressure to change her story, Adele continued to work for Rotherham Borough Council. But it wasn't easy. She felt harassed by senior council managers and police officers. Once, she was stopped by a police officer while driving her car and was told, in no uncertain terms, that 'people' knew where she lived. One day, I came out of work and bumped into a police officer I knew slightly as I headed for my car. He asked me how I was. Then he said: 'You know, you really need to make sure your tyres are in good nick, and your vehicle is insured. Just thought I'd let you know that . . .'

I got into my car and drove off, thinking that was a bloody silly thing to say to anyone. Of course, when I look back, I understand it much more clearly . . .

Finally, after months of pressure, Adele went off sick and eventually left. In a statement given much later on, she wrote this:

I left my employment with Rotherham Metropolitan Borough Council in the belief that I had raised concerns and provided evidence regarding young people who were believed to be involved in child sexual exploitation, and of the child protection concerns that I had, with managers of the highest level. I also believed I had provided sufficiently clear information regarding perpetrators to the police for there to be an investigation of the suspected abusers and their associates. I believed I had provided sufficient evidence of the issues regarding professional practice for this to be reviewed. I believed that because I had copied this data to the Home Office and the Home Office evaluators that Rotherham would be in a position where it would have to review and address the issues that I had raised. I now know . . . that this never happened.

During my final months at Rotherham Metropolitan Borough Council I was subjected to intense personal hostility and intimidation, not just from Rotherham Metropolitan Borough Council, but also South Yorkshire Police. There is no doubt in my mind that I was placed under pressure to change and present my findings in a way that presented services in Rotherham in a better light and diluted the findings of the pilot. I think that these requests were made by those identified in this summary in the belief that the data on which I based my research was no longer available to me; and that I would not be able to defend or prove my findings. Whatever the belief and reasons behind the actions of those managers at the time, action should have been taken to investigate the concerns that were being raised.

I am aware following my departure from Rotherham that there have been other investigations and reports which have validated and added to my findings. I find it personally and professionally a tragedy that Rotherham MBC did not avail itself of the opportunity it had to explore the information and evidence that I was providing to senior managers in key services in Rotherham in 2002.

I was heartbroken when she left. A good, honest, professional woman working with the best of intentions, and trying to make a difference to the lives of hundreds of abused young people, was hounded out of Rotherham Borough Council simply because they didn't want to hear the truth. It would make them look bad, and they'd have to do something about it – and that was not on the agenda. Our data was removed deliberately, I've no doubt about that. I've no reason to tell lies about the events of that day either. Unfortunately no one can give a satisfactory explanation about what happened because people are still denying they know anything about it.

Interestingly, the information that the powers-that-be seemed to be fighting so hard to play down was actually out in the public arena during the time Adele was employed at Rotherham Borough Council. She did an interview with Angus Stickler, of BBC Radio 5 Live, in which it was reported that, across Britain, 'child prostitution' (that loathsome term again) was 'spiralling out of control'. The radio station reported that: 'In Rotherham, for example, it appears there is a highly organized network of pimps involving up to eighty girls, again some as young as twelve. And there is evidence that they are being transported from Rotherham to private addresses in red-light districts as far afield as Bradford and Sheffield.'

So there we are. It was in the public arena as far back as 2001, and no doubt it was discussed at length when it came on the radio. Did anything happen as a result? Nothing, except a good person who was prepared to stand up and protect vulnerable children lost her job.

I can remember some of the girls we were trying to help at that time, whose case studies would have been in those very files that disappeared from our offices, taken by persons unknown. Girls like Julie, who was sixteen years old but had been assessed as functioning at the mental age of four and was living with a foster carer.

Julie had been working with another agency around learning life skills. One of the skills she had been taught was how to get on the bus independently so she could attend college in the town centre. Unfortunately it was at the bus station that she first met her abusers, who began taking her to a flat where she was locked in a room and raped by gangs of men. Julie was told they loved her and would marry her.

Numerous meetings were held but as Julie was describing the abuse as 'consensual' South Yorkshire Police informed us they could not act. Her foster carer would describe her as turning up home 'dripping sperm from every orifice' and needing to bathe her and tend to her wounds.

This abuse continued, with us constantly arguing she was unable to consent as she functioned as a four-year-old.

'Her birth certificate puts her at sixteen, Jayne, so she can consent,' Anita McKenzie actually said to me.

All Julie's abusers were known to us and their names had been passed to the police in connection with Julie and other girls. No action was taken against them.

Then there was Danielle, who lived with her parents, who both worked. Danielle had a good education and attendance record, but by the time she was fourteen the classic warning signs of abuse were present. She was going missing, not attending school, coming home drunk, hanging around with other girls known to be involved and meeting a new 'boyfriend' known to be a risk.

Her parents reported her missing on every occasion. However, they were actually told they were wasting police time as eventually she would come back.

Finally there was Jessica, who became involved with one of the most notorious abusers in Rotherham, and whose story I've touched upon earlier. This is more of Jessica's story, in her own words:

'I'm from Rotherham. I grew up here, and lived on an estate with my parents. I had a good upbringing and used to enjoy dancing and spending time at our caravan in Cleethorpes. When I was twelve I stopped dancing and started knocking about on the streets with other girls my age. One was called Clare. We'd grown up together. We were like sisters. It was just me and her at first and then we started getting involved with other kids, the same age as us. Then we were introduced to a group of older people.

'When I was twelve I met a guy called Craig first. He was about eighteen or nineteen. He was on heroin, a white guy. He was from the same area. He had a friend called Keith and I started going out with him. He also sold heroin for an Asian guy called XXX. I didn't go out with him but we kissed when I was drunk.

'Just after my fourteenth birthday I met YYY. We were hanging around some shops with a girl who knew both XXX and YYY and was already being abused. YYY pulled up in a car and he asked who I was. Then he asked my age and I lied and said I was sixteen. We went for a drive and he took us to a flat. About six Asian guys were there. We chilled there and that's when YYY said, 'You're not really sixteen,' and so I told him my real age. He drove me off in his car and we parked up and spoke for a bit. I was late – I was meant to be back for 10 p.m., so he drove me home. Then it started from there.

'I was impressed with YYY. He had designer clothes and a nice silver sports car. I thought he was right nice. He was funny. He would sit for hours just talking and always paid me compliments, telling me how intelligent and beautiful I was. Mum and Dad found out I was seeing him, and they kept grounding me. So YYY would get other people to ring my parents and make out I was going to a friend's house. So they thought I was safe.

'Then I started skipping school to see him. And I was running off; just for a few days at first, then it was weeks. I was just spending time with him. Because I knew my parents were looking for me I was locked in a house and he'd fetch me food. The police found me a few times in different houses and flats.

'I got pregnant when I was fourteen. I had an abortion because YYY would be pissed off – he would've been sent to prison. I got put into care when I was fifteen. I went to a few different places.

'YYY was getting away with all sorts. I didn't see him as a paedophile. I used to call him my bad boy . . .'

8

With Adele gone and Risky Business in trouble for sharing information with the 'wrong' people, our future looked decidedly uncertain. Nothing more was heard from the Home Office and the final year's funding we should have had for their CSE project vanished into thin air. Eventually, in July 2004, about a year after Adele left, the Home Office published 'Paying the Price', a consultation paper on prostitution, and although several of the projects which had been funded by the Home Office at the same time as us were mentioned, there was not a word about Risky Business. To this day, no one at the Home Office has officially ever said why they didn't continue the project, even in Adele's absence, or why they never even bothered to contact us again. Very strange . . .

Still, our work had to continue because our girls needed us. Referrals were continuously coming in and the catalogue of abuse grew day by day.

As an example, a referral might read something like this:

[Karen] is missing from home frequently, associating with older males. She has returned with a suspected broken nose, two black eyes, bruises and scratching. Her mum was told by police not to report her missing due to the frequency of this ... Karen is extremely sexualized in her language and behaviour ... drug paraphernalia has been found hidden in the house ... she has links to other women involved in sexual exploitation ... she is spending time associating with large gangs of young people and older men; some of these men are older Asian males ...

This girl was fourteen years old at the time.

Despite everything, we continued to compile intelligence against those we believed were responsible. I don't imagine I was very popular for doing so, but what choice did we have? I didn't know for sure what the police and the council's agenda was for acting the way they did (although I suppose I could've taken a wild guess) and until someone physically stopped me I would continue to collect information – car registrations, taxi numbers, drivers, vehicles seen around schools and parks, relationships between older men and younger girls, rumours of sexual activity, girls being harboured by family and friends of abusers. I noted everything and faithfully handed it in to the police, believing that at some stage something would be done.

*

At home, family life continued as normal. The boys were growing up quickly now and finding their own way in life. Ben was approaching school-leaving age while our Lee had done the one thing that every mother dreads, and joined the army. As a boy, he'd spent a lot of time with my dad and was very close to him. Dad loved telling Lee his war stories and throughout his childhood all he wanted to do was follow in Dad's footsteps and join the RAF. When the time came for him to make his career choice at school we had appointments to see all three of the armed services. Lee wasn't academic and he knew that to be a pilot you needed years of training and a degree. So that was out, and we passed on to the navy. The guy at the careers fair told us that if you joined the navy and picked a trade, that was the one you'd continue in for the rest of your career. We all thought that was a bit limiting, so the next and final choice was the army.

I'll take my hat off to him, the young soldier at the careers fair was a very good advert for recruitment. He was passionate about what he did, and our Lee could see that straight away. In his own way, Lee shared that passion, and as soon as he'd talked to the young soldier he knew which service he would be applying for. He left school, did his week's trial, passed easily and then went for his medical. He was in A1 condition, at least as far as we were concerned, and we thought he'd have no problem getting through. But we were wrong.

Lee opened the brown envelope on the day it arrived with the results of his medical, and just crumpled. He wasn't a crier but that morning he sobbed. He'd been failed.

'They're saying I've had psoriasis,' he said. 'I don't even know what that is. Why are they saying that?'

I read the letter. It explained that having a skin condition such as psoriasis was an instant 'fail' and they were sorry, but those were the rules. I couldn't believe it and I had to think back to understand what they were talking about. Then it became clear. Paul's uncle Terry had had psoriasis and when Lee was about two he developed a strange dry rash on his body. I took him to the doctor, who asked me if there was a skin condition in the family, so I told him about Terry. The doctor prescribed him Oilatum Cream, used to treat rashes or dry skin, and we thought that was the end of the matter. Lee did have dry skin, but it wasn't anything that bothered him unduly so I continued giving him the cream until he was old enough that he didn't want or need it any more.

Naturally, the army had to contact Lee's GP, who went back through his records and found a note that the rash he'd had when he was two 'could be psoriasis'. He was obliged to tell the medical examiner this, and they'd made their decision on this basis. I appealed, writing to tell the examining board that it was only suspected psoriasis and had never developed into the full condition. They told me that I'd continued to order

127

Oilatum for ten years or so, which seemed to indicate a serious skin condition. So began a battle, and the most difficult one a parent ever has to fight. I did not want Lee to go into the army, but neither did I want to see his dreams crushed, so I took up the case with anyone who would listen. I wrote to senior officers, army medical people, the Ministry of Defence; I badgered and badgered until in the end I received a call from a senior officer, who said he understood why I was making so much noise but there was nothing he could do personally. However, he referred me to one of the army's chief medical officers, who practised privately in London. Lee could have an appointment with her, he said, but at our own cost – and it would be a big one.

Well, you'll do anything for your kids, so we saved up and booked an appointment. On the day, I took Lee down to London and sat in a chair while this little woman with a very large magnifying glass examined his skin in minute detail. She was honest about her brief: she had to confirm that what Lee's doctor had written all those years ago was correct and that the decision to keep him out of the army would be upheld. She looked at his elbows, armpits, knees, behind his ears – all the areas that psoriasis can present itself. Finally, after what seemed an age, she put down the magnifying glass and sighed.

'Whoever thought this boy might have psoriasis was wrong,' she said. 'Lee, you've got dry skin, no doubt about that, but that doesn't stop you joining the army. So I'm going to overturn the MoD's decision.'

By the look on his face I think our Lee could've kissed her, but instead he grinned broadly as she stamped the word 'PASSED' onto a pile of documents next to her. Within weeks he was going for his basic training and, while I still had serious reservations, I was pleased for him. At the time people said to me, 'If you accept the army's decision he'll never have to go and fight.' But this was my child's dream. Even today he still laughs and says, 'Mum, it's all your fault I went in the army – cos you wouldn't let me play with guns when I was little!'

Sadly, Dad didn't live long enough to see Lee take up a military career. After Mum died he carried on and made something of a life for himself, but of course it was never the same for him and he missed her terribly. Being a close family, we rallied round and did his shopping, his cleaning and took him to the pub one night a week. About ten years after Mum died Dad started to go downhill and finally collapsed, requiring hospital treatment for Chronic Obstructive Pulmonary Disease (COPD). After a few days he wanted to come home – and was pulling out plugs and wires in a state of agitation – but he just wasn't fit, so he was sedated and we took turns sitting with him. One night I was there when he suddenly sat up and said he needed to get up, 'because Mum's here'! I tried to get him back into bed but, despite his frailty, he fought hard. I rang the emergency buzzer and the duty nurse came rushing down. She calmed him down for a while and although he was still shouting he seemed to respond to her. In the meantime I'd rung Sue, my sister, and told her Dad had taken a turn for the worse. The nurse could see I was stressed and she advised me to take a break.

'Just go for ten minutes,' she said, 'and we'll have him back to sleep. He'll be fine.'

So I went for a walk, just wandering the corridors looking for the hot drinks machine. Suddenly, a staff nurse appeared from nowhere, out of breath.

'Mrs Senior, you'd better come back,' she said, 'it's your dad!'

I ran back at full pelt and made it into the ward to find Sue cradling Dad. He'd just that second died in her arms. And it was strange, but I felt as though I had to be out of the room at that moment. I'd never really dealt with the way my mum had died so suddenly – I couldn't have coped with seeing both parents die in front of me.

While I'm sorry Dad didn't live to see Lee fulfil his boyhood dream of being in the military, I'm very pleased he didn't live long enough to witness what happened to my brother, Phil. As I've said, we were close growing up, despite the age difference. He was really into music and, as well as teaching, played in several local bands and wrote his own songs. He was a lovely, gentle, laid-back guy and when he got himself into a relationship and had two daughters we couldn't have been more pleased for him.

I don't know what it is, but as a family we've not had the best of luck – to put it mildly. All was going well for Phil until he began to get a lot of sore throats. He went to the doctor and following referral to a specialist was diagnosed with a rare cancer of the oesophagus. It was devastating news and it hit my dad particularly hard. He worried for all his children, as fathers do, and he fretted over Phil. However, after treatment and a series of operations Phil was given the all-clear, which was a big relief for all of us, especially Dad.

Then Dad died and very shortly afterwards Phil's cancer returned, and this time it was terminal. He told us he had about eighteen months to live but when I look back now I see that he was probably fibbing, perhaps to make us feel a little bit better. He also made the decision that he was going to refuse treatment. His daughters, Katie and Lucie, were in their mid teens and he didn't want them to feel responsible for feeding and changing him. It was a brave decision, typical of our Phil.

One afternoon we got a call from some friends in Birmingham whom we'd met previously on a holiday in Spain. Would we like to go over for the weekend? We said 'yes', as we got on with them very well. Just after, our Barbara rang to say that they were going over to

Castleton in Derbyshire for the day, and would be meeting Phil. Would we like to go with them?

'Oh,' I said, 'I'm stuck now. I've just promised that we'll be over in Birmingham on Saturday. Can we do it another time?'

Our Barbara said that would be fine, so we went to Birmingham and they went to Castleton. By all accounts they had a lovely lunch, and Phil seemed happy. But that evening he woke in the middle of the night, saying that he didn't feel well. He was rushed to hospital and died that night, aged just forty-four. And I will regret forever not seeing my brother for the last time at that lunch. It was only about three months after he'd told me his illness was terminal and I thought we had loads of time left with him. It was a terrible tragedy and the only positive thing I can say about it is that I'm glad my dad wasn't around to see one of his children die.

We were hit hard, all of us, and we thought that as a family we'd had more than our fair share of bad luck. Little did we know, but the worst was yet to come.

Around the period Adele was leaving work, I had a phone call from a woman called Dr Angie Heal. She explained that she was a strategic drugs analyst and had just been appointed by South Yorkshire Police to carry out research on drug use, dealing and related problems in the area. She said she'd met with various agencies in Rotherham and every time she'd visited or rung up, the name 'Risky Business' had been mentioned. Out of curiosity, she was keen to find out more about us and could we meet?

I was happy to meet anyone I thought might be useful to the project, so I agreed. Also, we had about six girls who were involved in hard drugs and were being exploited, so I thought that might be useful to share with her. However, there was one problem. Even though I was still collecting data, I had been specifically told not to share it and, as such, I had to ask Christine Brodhurst-Brown, my line manager, whether it would be OK to talk to a police researcher. Chris was always supportive and sometimes became as frustrated as me about how the information we shared was almost always ignored.

The request was granted, perhaps because Christine believed a police representative could be trusted with the information. So we met, and got on extremely well. Like Adele, Angie was an intelligent woman thoroughly committed to a task which she hoped would make for a better society. I gave her some background about the work of Risky Business and talked her through some of the cases we had ongoing at that time, including some connected with drugs and gun crime. Angie cross-referenced what I told her about abusers, CSE and drug crime and a considerable proportion of it fitted with her own research. Clearly, there were links between child abusers and drugs gangs across South Yorkshire, so she went back to her police line manager in Sheffield, an officer called Matt Jukes, and asked permission to widen her research to include CSE. The Sheffield police district was more up to speed with issues of CSE than Rotherham, as we'd seen in the early days of Risky Business, so it was agreed this was a good idea and Angie obtained the necessary permission.

At the time, Angie told me that when Matt Jukes heard about what we had in terms of names, car registrations, links to drug crime, etc., he found it hard to understand why the Rotherham police division didn't seem to be dealing with it.

'If we'd have been given that amount of good information in Sheffield,' he apparently said to Angie, 'we'd have launched an investigation.'

So Angie's work continued, widening to dovetail with our own. In 2003 she produced her first report, which went to very senior South Yorkshire police officers, as well as drug action agencies, local authorities and the central government for the north-east. She found that 'most' of those men in South Yorkshire involved in CSE were believed to be involved in drug dealing, and 'might be involved in rape, gun crime, violence, robbery and other serious criminal offences'. Angie noted that a 'significant' number of young people were being exploited in Rotherham, some of whom were subjected to violence, rape, gang rape and kidnapping. She recounted how police told her about one twelve-year-old who described being taken to a hotel by some men and being made to watch while her fourteen-year-old sister had sex with them. The police also spoke of a fourteen-year-old who was doused in petrol as a threat against reporting her abusers. On and on Angie's report went, detailing the kind of information we'd been sharing for a few years by then:

> Virtually all the referrals to Risky Business are young white women and girls. The age range recently has mostly been in the age 13 to 16 age group. Some asylum seekers, particularly Iraqi Kurds, are increasingly becoming boyfriends of the girls ... the girls involved in sexual exploitation in Rotherham appear to develop personal preferences for either Asian men or Iraqi Kurds. Some have become good at translating Arabic.

I wasn't shocked at the content. What surprised me most was that it shared so many of Adele's concerns, yet neither Risky Business nor Angie Heal got into trouble for writing it. And that still baffles me to this day. Did those people who read Adele's report and made it disappear or condemned it to the bin simply fail to read this one? Whatever the answer – and, as usual, no one seems to have come up with a satisfactory one – Angie Heal continued to work alongside us and, in fact, went on to write another similarly shocking report in 2006.

As we know, Adele's report and subsequent departure coincided with the end of the key players meetings, at which we'd share information with various agencies, plus the police and council officers. We had a period of about six months where we had no arena for sharing anything, until a decision was taken to set up a new discussion group. And so the Sexual Exploitation Forum (SEF) was born. This was a much smaller group than key players, comprising social services, children's services and police representatives, and while we were still able to share information within it, from the beginning I felt the potential for any action arising from it was minimal. Looking back at one set of SEF reports in my possession, I see that at one meeting we were discussing a fourteen-year-old girl with learning difficulties who was reportedly 'going with Asian men in taxis and performing oral sex'. Social services were working with her, but she hadn't been referred to Risky Business. The various 'action plans' agreed at each stage of the SEF's dealings with her state that her 'name be retained on the list for discussion and further information'. Eventually she was removed from this list, although I warned the SEF that she was still associating with a friend who had been abused and beaten by several men. This girl was missing a lot of school and was getting into serious trouble but, again, the action plan merely stated that her name should be brought 'back to the next Forum for discussion', despite me stating on the record that I was 'very concerned' about her.

We felt that the information we offered was being 'managed' carefully within the Forum and, in short, it seemed we weren't being taken particularly seriously. Perhaps there were other reasons too; reasons that included the ethnicity of the perpetrators and the sensitivity which that appeared to provoke. I didn't hold back from writing everything down. For example, I have in my files a full report about a particular group of Asian men who were involved with numerous girls around Rotherham and were known for their violent, controlling behaviour. In one paragraph I note that two girls have been physically assaulted and required hospital treatment. The police attended but refused to arrest the men for assault, instead focusing on the two girls' alleged use of racist language towards their attackers, who had actually complained to the police about it. Later the girls were approached by these men and warned off from making a statement to the police. And this was the same group of men who thought nothing of climbing through the bedroom window of a house in the town and threatening a seven-year-old boy whose sister they thought might have 'grassed' to the police about her abuse. And yet it seemed to be the girls who were treated as the real criminals . . .

9

To step back a few months for a moment, in early 2003 something happened which came as something of a shock, although not an unpleasant one. I discovered I was pregnant. Personally, I didn't want any more children – I was in a full-time job which demanded a lot of me both in and out of work – but Paul had always been keen. After the initial shock, though, I became used to the idea and we worked out a way of juggling a newborn with everything else in our lives.

Sadly, at fourteen weeks I lost it. We'd grown to like the idea of an addition to our family so we planned for another, and before long I discovered I was pregnant again, with the baby due in spring 2004. Ironically, I was expecting at the same time as several girls I was working with, including one who had moved to Sheffield. She'd got a job and was making a new life for herself, but she had no family. I remember visiting her one day, and during our conversation she went into labour. She had no partner, so I ended up taking her to hospital and stayed with her as the baby was delivered. She had a girl, and when everything had settled down and she'd recovered, I left the hospital and came home, getting in at 4 a.m.

'You're pregnant too, love,' Paul said. 'You should be looking after yourself.'

'I know,' I said, 'but I've got you. She has no one. I couldn't leave her.'

So our Samuel was born in the March and another big chapter in our lives had begun. Lee and Ben were delighted to have a baby brother. Being away in the army, Lee didn't see much of him, but Ben was still at school and he took to the changed arrangements with ease. He was at an age when I could ask him to mind Samuel while I pegged out the washing or had a bath. Samuel was a good baby – just as well, really, as he was shared between everyone in the house. Paul and I split the duties 50/50 and really enjoyed it. We've never been well off but by now we were a bit older and were more comfortable financially than when we had our first child.

Just before I went on maternity leave I had a training appraisal because I'd been put on a higher salary level, but had to prove that I was willing to undertake extra training. During the appraisal Christine Brodhurst-Brown asked me if I had any training needs. I told her that if possible I would like to go to university and do a degree in criminology.

Though I'd left school with very few qualifications I'd had plenty of experience of youth work in the years since. And having spent so long dealing with the police and other agencies, and fighting on behalf of so many victims of CSE, I felt I'd like to know more about the criminal justice system which seemed to put so many obstacles in our way. Christine said she'd look into my request and a couple of months after Samuel was born I received a phone call from her boss, who gave me the go-ahead to apply for the course at Sheffield Hallam University, to be funded by Rotherham Borough Council.

I was very excited indeed. I'd never dreamt I'd go to university one day and even as I called Sheffield Hallam to register my interest I imagined myself taking my place with all the other students enrolling that autumn. But, within minutes, those dreams were dashed. There was a waiting list, I was told, and if I chose to put my name down I'd be the seventy-third person in the queue. So not a huge chance of success, given there were only twenty-five places anyway. However, the lady on the phone asked me if I'd ever considered studying law. I hadn't, but I was open to the suggestion, so she sent me a prospectus and invited me to an upcoming open day. We went along, I met the tutor, liked him and found myself being talked into studying for a law degree which would start in October 2004.

Looking back, I don't know how I did it, even though it was part-time. I'd gone back to work for a few hours by October, but I didn't want to put Samuel into nursery for any longer than necessary. Luckily I could rely on my niece Joanne, Barbara's daughter, to give me a hand. She was studying childcare at college, and she was tremendous – patient, kind and a complete natural with children. My course wasn't easy and I often wished I had more time and space to really concentrate on the modules I was being taught. Still, being a working mum you have to learn to multi-task so I got on with it as best I could and, in fact, really enjoyed it all – except for land law, which I hated with a vengeance.

I particularly enjoyed it when practising lawyers came in to lecture us, as the practical application of the law fascinated me. I also enjoyed 'mooting', or taking part in mock trials as the prosecution or the defence. Every fortnight we would be given a case based loosely around a real-life event and the class would be divided into opposing teams. I found I was a natural at arguing my point – some might say that they knew this long before I did! – and would almost always be on the winning team. However, unlike most other students on the course, I hadn't decided to study law to become a lawyer. Which was just as well because on one occasion we were given a mock trial which closely resembled the events of a real case that involved the abuse and subsequent death of a child. I was put in charge of the team that was 'defending' the mother on charges of allowing the death of a child and, although it went against everything I believed in, the case was argued well and the 'judge' ruled in our favour. I was mortified; to be part of a team that could do this so well really upset me.

After the 'verdict' one of the course tutors took me to one side. 'Jayne,' she said, 'I just want to tell you this now and I hope you won't be offended. I need to tell you that if you are thinking about becoming a lawyer, then don't. You'll never make it.'

Well, I had no intention of practising law, but even so I was curious to know why she'd come to this decision.

'You'd get too involved,' she said, 'and as a lawyer you can't afford to do that. One day you could be defending a rapist and the next you could be locking another one up. You have to stay dispassionate, and I'm not sure you could be like that.'

I nodded. She was right. How could I not get involved when cases such as the one I'd just contested were so close to my heart?

'But I'll tell you one thing,' she added, 'you'd make a bloody good politician!'

I laughed, knowing by that she meant I had conviction, could argue my point and wouldn't shut up until someone listened!

Unsurprisingly, I was one of the oldest students on the course and most of the time I enjoyed the company of my younger colleagues. Occasionally I found them frustrating. I remember one lecture in which we were asked to give opinions about the issue of rape and consent.

One young lad, who was a real high-flyer and wanted to be a barrister, threw something in about women dressing provocatively, implying that consent was somehow part of this issue. Naturally, I flew in there with my counter-arguments and it went backwards and forwards between us. I was thinking, *Oh God, in a few years this guy could be dealing with women who have been raped and abused, just like the girls I deal with now*. I tried to make him see that rape was rape, but he didn't seem to have any empathy that way, making it clear that it should be taken into consideration what a woman looks like when she goes out for the night. I remember thinking, *There's no humanity test to become a lawyer, but perhaps there should be . . .*

I worked as hard as I could and eventually graduated. It was a very proud day for all of us. I never thought I'd get a degree, though I did have a Diploma in Youth and Community Work. I remember the day I collected my degree at a ceremony in Leeds. My family was always supportive and Ben in particular was keen to come with me. I was pleased, but less so on the morning of the ceremony when he came out of the bathroom having shaved his own head until it was almost bald. Teenagers . . . Anyway, having the degree and the training gave me more confidence to argue and challenge decisions if I thought they were made on legally shaky ground. It also taught me to 'read' – not literally, but to be able to look at large, complex documents and pick out the key points quickly before committing them to memory.

Unfortunately legal knowledge appeared to count for little when children were caught up in the criminal justice system. We became involved in a complicated case which started when Liz, a girl I'd been working with for some years, called me in a highly emotional state. She had something to tell me, she said, and could she meet me?

We met in a cafe just outside Rotherham and over a cup of tea she told me she'd been seeing a guy in Sheffield, who'd asked her if she could bring along another girl, Debbie (whom we met in the prologue), when they next got together as he 'wanted to make a snuff movie'. This man was a sexual predator involved in all sorts of things, but even though I thought I'd heard everything by this stage, snuff movies were a new one on me. The girl, who was sixteen, broke down and then confessed she'd done something 'really bad' but refused to tell me what it was. Immediately I called the police and asked if this allegation could be investigated because I considered there was a child – possibly two – at risk.

A few hours later I was called by the social worker of a twelve-year-old girl who was in care. Apparently, this girl had been asked to go to Sheffield with an older girl, who had 'met this bloke who'd asked her to stick pins through his nipples'. For this, he would pay them £20.

It turned out it was the 'snuff movie' man, said to be a club owner (among other things) in Sheffield. Again, we contacted the police, who acted by arresting the man – and the sixteen-year-old girl on suspicion of being an accessory. I was outraged because she was just as much a victim of this as anyone else.

There was a court case and I went along to do everything in my power to stop the man and the older girl being tried together. I argued with a barrister that the sixteen-year-old was a child and had no place in the dock.

'If she pleads guilty,' he said, 'she won't have to go through with the trial or sit in court.'

'And if that happens, how long would this offence stay on her record?' I asked.

'As it's a sexually related offence, it would be there all her life,' came the reply.

Well, there was no way she deserved that and the trial began. For the life of me, I couldn't understand why they should be put together as abusers. Luckily the prosecution decided to offer no evidence against the girl and she was free to go. The man was convicted, but only did a short term in prison before he was on the streets again. It was said he knew some influential people in Sheffield who had effected his early release. Whether that was true or not I don't know, but cases like this did make me wonder who was getting justice when it came to abusers and their young victims. Even now, Liz is still an emotional mess. Her children have been removed and she has numerous chronic health problems. Recently, she said to me, 'It's too late for me now, Jayne, but if there's anything I can do to help anyone else, I will.'

It wasn't just the police and the CPS who blundered into sensitive issues, making them a whole lot worse. We had continued to work with Alison, the young girl who had hidden in the bathroom the first time I'd gone to talk to her. She was still involved with an older man from Sheffield and he was pimping her to another abuser while pretending to be her 'boyfriend'. As I said before, at the time she could see nothing wrong with what was going on, and couldn't understand why we had a problem with him. We worked with her for a long time but just after she turned sixteen she became pregnant by her abuser. Although she was young she was adamant she would keep the baby – like most of the girls we ever dealt with who became pregnant, she just wanted someone to love, and to love her in return.

With the help of social services we managed to find her a house and she split up with her abuser. She was really trying to make a go of it as a single mum but, although we supported her as best we could, she began to fall behind on rent, electricity and gas. Plus, the baby was a poor sleeper and she was struggling through the nights. One day, after another sleepless night, she rang me begging for help. I said I'd do what I could, and I also rang social services. 'Sorry,' they said, 'we're not here to babysit.' They wouldn't even do a 'Safe and Well Check', even though this girl was a child herself.

There were several nights of this. Then, one evening, her abuser contacted her. Alison told him how tired she was, and how much she was struggling. The man offered to come round and babysit so she could get some sleep. I wish she'd told me at the time, but she didn't, and the man did what he promised. In the morning he fetched her some shopping and within a few weeks he was a regular fixture in the area. Then social services became involved and threats were made to remove the baby if Alison didn't break off the relationship with him. By now, though, she couldn't do that. He wanted access to the baby and was making some very nasty threats to Alison – that he would beat her up and kidnap the child – if he didn't get what he wanted. I tried to make it clear to social services that we were talking about two children at risk, not one, but that message never really hit home. Risky Business argued that Alison and her child should be moved to a mother and baby unit, where they would be safe from the abuser and Alison would be able to learn parenting skills in peace and comfort. Care proceedings began and I wrote to the judge outlining the mother and baby unit idea and asking if Alison could have another chance. If I'd thought her baby was at risk I'd have been the first to say so, but both children were in danger here; it made sense – at least to me – that they should stay together.

Sadly, Alison lost her case and an order was made that the baby should be removed and placed for adoption. I was called in and given a proper dressing-down by social services managers for using council-headed note-paper to write a letter disputing this. Well, so what's new? My main concern was for Alison. We put in a request for her to have one last contact with the baby, which was granted, borrowed a video camera and all went for a picnic in Clifton Park, Rotherham. It was a beautiful day and the baby was just about to walk and say his first words. Alison played with him, hugging and kissing him, pulling him close to her. We videoed him making noises and smiling, trying to get up on his feet. Then Alison recorded a long message for him to watch when he was grown up, explaining why she'd had to give him away. We were sobbing as we listened, and all the while a social worker hovered in the background, waiting to take the baby.

Alison wept and wept as she said her final goodbye to the child. She knew she had done wrong, she just didn't have the power to fix it. She needed help, and if she'd had that opportunity to live in a mum and baby unit who knows how she might have turned her life around?

We returned to the International Centre and made a DVD so that he – and she – could see what kind of relationship they'd had. I'd suggested she choose a song to put on the video, and she picked Puff Daddy's 'I'll be Missing You'. I played the video recently and I cried my eyes out; poor Alison was sat in Clifton Park with this little toddler and a picnic blanket with all the food, and Cassie and me with her. She was so young and she was telling him how much she loved him and how one day she would be able to explain that to him in person.

Even after the baby had gone, Alison found it difficult to break the relationship with her abuser until eventually we managed to find her a place in a different town, where she began a new life. I didn't see her for a long time and then a few years ago I bumped into her. How her life had changed! She was married and had two children, and they all knew about her past and the child she'd lost. She seemed happy and, at last, sorted out. At least Alison's story had a happy ending. Other girls weren't so lucky. Even when they tried to break away from their abusers and make a new life for themselves, they were constantly looking over their shoulders. Consider this letter from an abuser in his late twenties to his fourteen-year-old victim when he was on remand for sexual offences against her:

Hello baby,

Don't be scared about what is going on with us, OK? You don't have to be scared for my sake, if anything does happen then I will just take it as it comes. And if I get sent down then I am going to be asked to be put in Wakefield then you can come and visit me. I probably won't even get time, lol. Maybe community service, banned from owning a computer, banned from my job with children, have to sign the sex offenders register or see a professional person about what I was like, or I could get away scot free and your mum just gets done for wasting police time.

You have to stay strong and everything for me, yeah? And I want you to stop cutting as much as you do, whenever you feel the need to cut, write me a little letter explaining exactly how you feel at that time, yeah? . . .

I don't want you to spend loads on me just because it's Christmas time. If it were up to me I would just ask for a really lovey-dovey letter that gives me butterflies and makes me smile and that's it. Oh yeah, and I'd ask for a series of pics of you in red stockings/ tights, with a red bra that has fluffy thin straps, some matching pants with you in a Christmas hat while sucking on a sugar cane and in each pic you do different poses (each pose more striking than the previous one) and yeah . . . you also ditch the bra and pants but you leave your hat on!

The rest is too explicit and too sickening to print here. The girl's mother found this letter and passed it to us.

At this point the project was again in financial

trouble. Most of the money for staffing came from bids I submitted to the area's Single Regeneration Budget, plus the Neighbourhood Renewal Fund and Comic Relief. This time staff were due to lose their jobs, including me. I had been on a temporary contract since 1999 and had to secure my own salary from somewhere every year. A suggestion was made to me by a senior manager, George Simpson, that I could provide some training to elected members of Rotherham Borough Council, during which I could mention the lack of funding. I turned up at the town hall to be greeted by a very senior councillor who asked me if I had 'fetched any of the kids along' – these were children who had been horrifically damaged, not participants in a bloody freak show.

When I went into the room it was quite full. I had prepared a presentation but senior managers I'd sent it to beforehand for approval had done a lot of editing. I was told this was because my slides could 'end up in the public domain', so it would be better to provide case studies and explicit details as part of the spoken presentation, which would not be minuted.

I honestly believed this was an ideal opportunity to raise some council funds so I went to town on the information I had, even going into details around the abusers.

I remember one member actually becoming quite

upset about the content of my presentation. Later, I was pulled up for that by no less a person than Roger Stone, the leader of Rotherham Borough Council, and told to tone down my description of the abuse the children were enduring.

I was asked numerous questions at the end, especially about why no one was being arrested. I explained that the police constantly said it was due to 'a lack of evidence'. The councillors were in uproar at the time. I wonder now why they sat there and obviously listened, but never asked again how things were going for us. Perhaps we just dropped off their radar?

10

After months and months of submitting information to the police via 'Box Five', I was contacted by two officers who wanted to meet me. Finally, something had attracted their attention – but not for reasons of child exploitation.

Debbie, the girl we met in the prologue, had told me about a corrupt police officer she'd had dealings with. She was a drug addict, and this officer worked for the drugs squad. It seemed that he was raiding houses of known heroin dealers and confiscating their supplies but only handing part of this in. The rest he would give to Debbie. She could have a portion of it for personal use as long as she sold the remainder and handed him the profits.

I reported this as intelligence and within twenty-four hours was talking to the two officers in a quiet car park. It seemed they'd had suspicions about this rogue policeman for a while and had acted quickly when the information I'd passed on had been picked up by the police's Public Protection Unit.

The PPU, as it's known, deals with crimes of abuse,

CSE, hate crime, rape and sexual assault, among other things. Its aim is to protect victims and other members of the public who bring allegations against individuals and support them. It's a national police initiative and each force has its own PPU. It appeared that at least some of the intelligence we'd been submitting via 'Box Five', which included this allegation about a police officer, had been going to the PPU, and this particular piece of information had been picked up on the day after we sent it.

I must have expressed some surprise to Angie Heal about this because she told me she'd had a conversation with Sheffield detective inspector Matt Jukes in which he said he'd heard about information being passed to the PPU from Risky Business and wondered why Rotherham police hadn't done anything much about it. He couldn't assist personally, he added, because he was part of the Sheffield division. However, Matt was a supporter of ours and around this time he paid for me and one of my staff to attend a conference in London with two of his officers, based on sharing information in relation to hate crime and terrorism.

This had been prompted by us sharing some information with anti-terrorist police officers nationally, via a phone number broadcast on the radio that you could ring if you were concerned someone was acting strangely and might be plotting an act of terrorism. This was soon after the 7/7 bombings in London and we had certain suspicions about an abuser – the same man virtually enslaving Paula – who was also thought to be an extremist. Our information must have been passed on quickly to South Yorkshire Police, for that same afternoon one of Matt's staff came out to see us. They organized surveillance on this male and took all the phone numbers and addresses we had on file for him. We had a dossier of intelligence that was very worrying – this male was in possession of four passports and made numerous trips to Birmingham. He had told Paula he was in London on the day of the bombings and forced her to watch extremist videos denouncing Tony Blair and George Bush.

Meanwhile, our regular meetings with the Sexual Exploitation Forum were proving a frustrating experience. In the year or so since it had been set up nothing had happened in terms of prosecuting offenders – or if it had, I certainly wasn't made aware of it. As usual, I felt we were more of a hindrance than anything else, though what problems our general busybodying was causing, no one ever explained. Anyway, sometime late in 2005 it was decided by the police and the council's Children and Young People's Services that the Forum should limit the number of cases it was discussing. The police carried out an audit of eighty-seven files and proposed that a large number of children be removed from the Forum's monitoring process.

I was outraged. I couldn't believe that the same cases

we'd expressed so much concern over, researched carefully and tried to resolve were being scrapped in this way, for no apparent reason. Or if there were reasons, they seemed ridiculous to me. One girl – a very high-risk case – had had a baby and the case had been closed because 'no one knew where she was'. Didn't they think to knock on a few doors, ask questions, track her down? In response, I decided to challenge with my managers every single one of the cases they were proposing to ditch, but as usual landed in trouble for sticking my nose in.

For example, one girl was removed from the Forum because there were no 'sexual exploitation concerns'. 'Is the social worker aware of the concerns of the Forum?' I wrote. 'Has anyone spoken to [the girl] re. the self-harming, abuse, suicide attempts, threats made to rape her?'

In another case, a young boy had also been removed from the Forum because there were 'no concerns'. I countered the decision by asking: 'Is the social worker aware of the allegations of [the boy] having been made to watch pornographic videos and also watch his parents having sex, allegations of [the boy] sexually abusing his sister, a relationship with an older male, fantasies of indiscriminate behaviour towards children and women?'

In yet another case – again, 'no concerns' from social workers – I argued: 'Who is addressing the issues of [the girl] having sex with older boys and Asian males in the toilets at Meadowhall, the two rape allegations, under-age sex?'

And what happened as a result of all these challenges? Nothing, of course.

I was very unhappy that vulnerable girls were being treated this way but, as usual, Risky Business was seen as a group of uneducated youth workers causing problems. And I believe the police found the amount of information being passed to them simply too unwieldy to handle, along with an attitude that called into question the 'morals' of the girls themselves. No one ever said 'she asked for it', but there was a real feeling that a fair percentage of these girls were their own worst enemies and therefore weren't worth police time. Yes, some of them were challenging, but that didn't give anyone any excuse not to do something to help them. At the end of the day, they were children.

Next, we were invited to meet the new commander of the Rotherham policing area, replacing Christine Burbeary, who had retired. We had a call to tell us that the new commander would like to come and see us at our offices. 'Fine,' we said. We never turned down the opportunity to meet anyone, despite knowing that the many nice words always exchanged during a visit were hardly ever followed up.

So imagine our surprise when the new commander walked in . . . and it was none other than Matt Jukes.

Although he had been in the Sheffield police district we had felt he was an ally and someone who would take us seriously. Whether he was willing and able to really tackle the problem was another matter, but the day he visited he stopped for a long while and talked to us about many areas of our work. He was particularly interested in our intelligence gathering – given that he'd had experience of us passing information to the PPU – and he asked me if I'd come along to the police station at some stage to talk to him about this in greater depth.

So I did. Also at the meeting was an officer whom Matt had assigned to look after intelligence coming via the PPU. We'd chatted for about ten minutes or so when Matt leaned back in his chair and looked at me directly.

'Jayne,' he said, 'there's something I can't understand about the way you're submitting intelligence. I know that you are giving us it, but I can't find it anywhere on the Police National Computer. So exactly how are you submitting it to us?'

'Well,' I said, 'for ages we've been putting it into Box Five and—'

'Hang on . . . Box what?'

'Box Five. It's a file or something on your system. It's meant to protect our identities and those of the girls.'

Matt looked shocked. 'I've never heard as much crap in all my life,' he said. 'Who told you that?'

I said that it was Anita McKenzie.

'Well, I don't know what Box Five is or where it's

supposed to exist,' he said, 'but wherever it is, it's been of no help to us or you. Why didn't they tell you that you needed to put in intelligence sheets that referenced Risky Business? Then it might have flagged up some-where.'

I felt sick. All this time, it appeared that 'Box Five' was nothing more than a term for a digital wastepaper basket. All the time and effort we'd spent passing in-formation to the police, and not a scrap of it had gone anywhere, except for the information about the police officer and a drug-dealing allegation.

Matt promised to sort out the mess and said he would task an intelligence officer to talk to his team and make sure what we were submitting was being put on to the Police National Computer, where it could be cross-referenced and matched as potential evidence. Not for the first time did I walk out of a meeting think-ing, *What a mess has been created, but here is someone who will do something to sort it out.*

So, the result was that a new intelligence sheet was devised which was much more user-friendly, from our point of view. This would be sent to Matt's intelligence officer and also to a sergeant in charge of child abuse investigations up at Maltby PPU. I'd no reason to sus-pect that any of this would not happen; Matt was a very nice guy and, furthermore, he'd asked me to give some training to his whole team around issues of CSE. This, he said, would be mandatory.

And so, one grey morning, my manager Christine Brodhurst-Brown and I carried a stack of paper, flip charts and PowerPoint presentation equipment into the PPU at Maltby, where we were faced with a room full of reluctant-looking police officers of all ranks and from all relevant departments, including CID and the drugs squad. The place reeked of aftershave and instant coffee. The officers sat back, arms folded, as Matt introduced us, told them what a brilliant job we were doing and said that he wanted them to take on board what we would be telling them. You could see the look on their faces. It said, 'Hurry up, let's get this over with, we've got work to do.'

Hostility doesn't bother me that much – I'm used to it. So we just plunged in, explaining how grooming worked, what effect it had on victims, how they got sucked in, who we believed was behind the problems of CSE in Rotherham. And to illustrate what we were saying, I told them the story of Amy, a young girl we were working with at the time . . .

Amy first became known to Risky Business when she was twelve years old due to her friendship with other vulnerable young women known to us. At this time her 'boyfriend' was a twenty-four-year-old male who was known along with his brother for grooming and violence towards young women in Rotherham. Because she was young, naive and vulnerable, Amy then began grooming other young women on their behalf.

Amy lived with her mother and alcoholic father, and would constantly go missing and place herself at great risk from her abusers. Her mother didn't understand about her daughter's needs and couldn't provide any kind of a stable home for her. Reports had identified longstanding and chronic neglect and this affected Amy's self-esteem and confidence. She didn't attend school regularly and when she was at school she caused problems for staff, whom she threatened with violence, verbal aggression and abusive behaviour. Amy was also abusive to her fellow pupils and targeted the most vulnerable; this ensured she was unable to form lasting relationships or friendships. When she wasn't at school Amy would spend time at the house of a school friend who was also on the child protection register.

The poor girl was in and out of hospital regularly, the result of beatings that left her black and blue, and sexual assaults. Often she dragged herself there alone, as there was no one to come to her aid. On one occasion when Amy was missing from home she was found by the local police in the car of one of her abusers at the back of an unused building. However, no arrests were made. When speaking to us at Risky Business the following day Amy told us she had been sexually assaulted by two of his friends and that there were drugs in the boot of the vehicle.

On another occasion Amy was battered severely for offending her abusers in some small way and her whole family received threats and had to be moved to a safe house. At this time Amy tried to get away from these men only to find they would turn up at the family home and make threats towards her mother and siblings. The police were called out on numerous occasions when windows were broken. Within a period of six months Amy and her family had to move six times.

During this chaotic and vulnerable time in Amy's life she went to stay with an auntie. Far from being her protector, this woman was approached by her niece's abusers and was somehow persuaded – probably with cash – to take Amy abroad, where permission would be granted to marry a relative of one of the abusers, so that he would be able to apply for British citizenship. This was shocking, but it wasn't the first time I'd heard of it happening. Another woman known to me apparently 'sold' her sixteen-year-old daughter's hand in marriage to an Iraqi, via a deal set up on the internet. It was said the marriage went ahead and the mother earned almost £5,000 from the deal. Fortunately for Amy, as she was only thirteen or fourteen years old at the time child protection procedures could be put in place to ensure that she would not be allowed to leave the UK, and the 'sale' never went ahead.

In 2005 Rotherham Borough Council rehoused the family yet again. However, the men continued to call at the house for Amy, threatening her if she would not leave with them. At this stage Amy's mother made the unfortunate decision that the best way to protect her daughter was to allow the men to visit.

Amy then began telling us how they would come to the house with bags of shopping for the family and then take it in turns to force her into oral sex in the bedroom, sometimes with other young women present. They would leave her ten cigarettes, which Amy saw as a sign that they cared about her. During some of these visits Amy would also be given drugs to sell on their behalf. On one occasion the men jokingly told Amy that they had been stopped by the police as they had driven onto her estate, but luckily the car had not been searched.

Clearly, Amy was physically and mentally damaged. She attended education for only two hours a week and had groomed other women on her abusers' behalf. She had been trafficked all over the country, which was a common feature of the abuse being perpetrated in Rotherham. The abusers in our town had connections, mainly across the north of England, and local girls being abused in Rotherham were undergoing the same experiences in Leeds, Manchester, Liverpool, Doncaster, Barnsley and elsewhere. Also, girls from other towns would appear in Rotherham in the company of our home-grown abusers. Amy had spent so much time with her abusers that she had learned to speak Punjabi reasonably well, and it wasn't uncommon for us to talk to other girls who'd also picked up this language, even if it was just a smattering.

I told Amy's story to that roomful of police officers in front of me and by lunchtime they were all leaning forward, looking far less comfortable and unconcerned than they had been at 9 a.m. When we finished the training presentation and Matt asked if there were any questions, the place went mad.

'Why didn't we know about this?'

'Why haven't we got these names?'

'Why is there no full-scale investigation?'

'Who are you sharing the information with?'

To say they were angry is an understatement. There were possibly twenty-five or thirty police officers in there and not one of them appeared to know the scale of the problems we were having in Rotherham. And that made them furious. To me, it seemed clear that whatever we'd been sharing in the past hadn't been deemed serious enough to flag up, or just hadn't been given any examination at all. At the end of the question session Matt said that, as the new district commander, he had helped us to work out a new system of sharing intelligence which would be available at investigation level for everyone to see and enable them to do something.

At the end of the event I made a plea to the officers.

'There's nothing that would please me more than for you all to go out and arrest fifty people tomorrow for this,' I said. 'I know that's not realistic when you haven't got all the evidence you need. But is there anything you can arrest them for? Drugs, for instance? If you can catch them drug dealing, this will give you time to investigate anything else they're up to.'

It wasn't an off-the-cuff remark. I'd been thinking that it made sense to get the abusers for the more obvious stuff, charge them with those offences and keep them in custody. If they were on remand, I felt girls would then come forward, knowing they were safe from their abusers for the time being. I really wanted the police to take this approach seriously because I felt it was the only way to draw out the girls to make statements without fear of retribution, thereby giving the police the evidence they needed to charge their abusers. Whether this would happen or not, we just had to wait and see.

Nonetheless, we'd had a very positive outcome from that day's training and at last I felt the police in Rotherham were coming round to our way of thinking. We were delivering training in schools too, a rolling programme of preventative work to thirteen- and fourteen-year-old girls. This focused on personal safety and how to recognize grooming and the way it led to sexual exploitation. We included internet safety, self-confidence and human rights. They loved it, telling us they were now much more careful about who they talked to online and face-to-face, and wouldn't be afraid of reporting anything they felt uncomfortable about.

Around this time there was also better news for Risky Business from a management point of view. We were looking for a new chairperson and Christine Brodhurst-Brown suggested we ask a woman called Joyce Thacker, who was manager of Connexions South Yorkshire (a youth advisory service which is run nationally).

I hadn't heard of Joyce but she came highly recommended. She had helped to launch the 'Streets and Lanes' project, which had looked at issues of CSE in Bradford in the 1990s, and had a solid background in this area. She sounded an ideal chairperson for Risky Business so I went to see her. She listened carefully as I explained the various ups and downs of the previous few years, and the problems we'd had being taken seriously. She didn't commit herself there and then but asked to come and see us, which she did. And soon after that she made the decision to join us as chair.

Personally, I was delighted. I liked Joyce from the beginning. She was a warm, understanding person who always made a point of meeting our girls, never talking down to them or patronizing them in any way. She had empathy for them, and seemed very happy at the approach we were taking as an organization. She was one hundred per cent our ally and champion when she first came on board, which makes what happened with her much later on even more shocking . . .

Joyce understood what we were saying about not being taken seriously enough and decided that it would be useful to share our concerns and experiences at a conference in Rotherham in spring 2006, focusing specifically on CSE. This was called 'Every Child Matters, But Do They Know It?' and was held at the Marriott Hotel, Rotherham, on 24 March 2006.

People were invited from all over the country and from Rotherham there were senior councillors and our local MP, Denis MacShane. It was a full-day event, with speakers in the morning and workshops in the afternoon. Joyce made the opening speech and speakers included Sara Swann MBE, a leading UK expert in CSE. Angie Heal was there too. So it was a fabulous day, marred only by the appearance of our MP. Before the conference I was asked to prepare a briefing for him before he spoke, which I did in detail, including case studies, numbers, risks and abuser information. Joyce checked all this out before I sent it over to him.

However, on the day, Mr MacShane stood up and talked about a recent incident where a group of white and Asian youths had been involved in a fight, resulting in someone getting hurt.

'And so,' he said, 'if we could all just learn to get along and accept the ways of different cultures and to stop competing then we would have a lot more harmony between the different sections of our community . . .'

On and on he went, and I felt my anger rising like a tide. This conference wasn't anything to do with racism, it was all about the sexual exploitation of children. What was he saying? That if our girls just accepted the 'ways of different cultures' they might not feel they'd been abused? I wasn't the only one fed up with what I was hearing. I caught Joyce Thacker's eye from across the room and in response she shook her head. In later years, Mr MacShane would tell the BBC: 'I think there was a culture of not wanting to rock the multicultural community boat if I may put it like that.' He added that he had been guilty of 'doing too little' to help the Rotherham victims but said that no one had come to him directly with allegations of child abuse during his eighteen years as MP in the town.

Well, maybe that's true, but he was certainly at that conference and would have heard plenty about the subject, had he chosen to listen.

Joyce Thacker was a fabulous chair of Risky Business. She sided with us during difficult periods, she was there to talk to us, to help us write reports, to lobby for extra funding. She was a true friend of the project, which made it all the more sad when she told us she'd applied for the job of Assistant Head of Children's Services at Rotherham Borough Council. If she was successful she would have to step down as chair, as there would be a conflict of interest between the two roles. I was pleased for her, and even more happy that we would have a strong supporter at the top of the Children's Services tree, but on a personal level I was sorry to see her go. That said, I was delighted when, shortly after taking on her new role, she asked me to write a full report into the workings of Risky Business, an intensive document that would cover everything we'd done over the past. Joyce said she was hoping to secure extra funding for the project from Shaun Wright, the councillor in charge of Children's Services.

I did this, detailing every one of the sixty-seven referrals we had on our books that year. Looking back, I see that the majority were just fourteen and fifteen years old. We checked and re-checked all this information before submitting it and Shaun Wright gave us the green light to continue as we were. Later on, he would claim to the Parliamentary Home Affairs Select Committee that he'd put extra resources into Risky Business, which wasn't quite accurate. I was on a rolling temporary contract and each year money had to be found so that I could continue the role. In 2006 the council appeared to be having a particularly difficult time finding this money so Shaun Wright authorized a payment from the existing Youth Service budget. We didn't get any more staff but at least we had the financial support we needed to continue dealing with the increasing number of referrals the project was attracting.

I met Shaun Wright several times and there was at least one occasion – possibly more – when he visited Risky Business at the International Centre. In fact, he came to a barbecue there one afternoon and spent a long time talking to one of the girls, who told him of her experiences. This was a young woman who had been systematically abused throughout her life and was in care as a child before being targeted by a gang of Asian men. She was raped horrifically several times, was threatened, attacked, went missing from care, missing from home – the kind of thing we were hearing every day, but to those who hadn't heard such experiences before, it was truly shocking. And after she made him a cup of tea she related all this to Shaun Wright, who would later claim – again in front of the Parliamentary Home Affairs Select Committee – that he had no memory of this meeting ever taking place, nor could he remember 'anyone' raising the issue of CSE in Rotherham as being 'significant'.

11

By late 2006 Lee was settled in the army and had carried out tours of duty in Iraq and Afghanistan. As a mum, I hated every moment of him being in those places and, as anyone whose sons or daughters have fought in war zones will know, you dreaded the knock on the door in the middle of the night. But the army was his passion and his life. Who was I to question what he was doing?

Our Ben was training to be a plasterer and was getting on with his life in his usual happy-go-lucky way. Samuel was still only two around this time. He was a good little kid and no bother to us, but he still had his needs, and due to the intensity of my job and the irregular hours it demanded, sometimes I wasn't there to fulfil those needs. Luckily he had a super dad in Paul and a brilliant cousin in Joanne, my eldest sister Barbara's daughter.

Joanne was almost three years older than our Lee and as children they'd been very close, almost like brother and sister – and they fought like siblings too. Barbara and Joanne had been my lifeline in those days as a young mum. Joanne grew up into a very spirited, very sporty young woman who would light up a room the moment she entered it. She was loud, funny, kind-hearted, opinionated – sometimes a 'right cowbag', as we say in South Yorkshire. Her dad, my brother-in-law Glynn, used to say that she reminded him of me when I was little! You certainly couldn't ignore her and within our close family she was a real character. And she was fabulous with our Samuel. As I've mentioned, she was doing a college course in childcare when he was a baby and naturally she took to practising on poor Samuel. He was the guinea pig for all her observations about baby lifting its head up, forming its first sounds, taking its first steps. Joanne passed the course and went to work in a local nursery, a job she loved. Kids were her passion. She coached a local under-sevens' football team and had a massive crush on Steven Gerrard, the then Liverpool FC player.

Naturally, she wanted children of her own and when she was twenty-six she discovered she was pregnant. To say she was over the moon would be an understatement. She and her partner, David, started to plan for the big event in November 2006 and as a family we were delighted for her. During her pregnancy she'd come round to ours every Saturday night and we'd watch *The X Factor* while Paul cooked tea for us. Then, tired out, she'd stay over. It was lovely being able to look after my niece and her unborn child in this way, and I felt I was giving our Barbara something back for all the years she'd helped me with my kids.

That November, she went into labour as planned. I remember we were at Thoresby Market in Nottinghamshire, and we'd only just arrived when Barbara rang to tell me Joanne had gone into labour. So we turned round and headed back, as I wanted to be there for support. When we arrived home our Joanne was in the front room of her mum's, puffing and panting like you do. Our Barbara was going into the hospital with her so we had a cup of tea, kissed her and wished her luck, then headed home to wait for news.

Joanne had a successful labour until the very last moment, when the baby's heartbeat dropped and for safety reasons the doctors decided to carry out an emergency caesarean. Nothing particularly unusual about that; as far as we were concerned it was a routine operation. The person it gave least concern to was our Barbara, who'd been a nurse and knew it was nothing out of the ordinary these days. So Joanne gave birth to a healthy little boy whom she named Harrison, and the following day we all went in to offer our congratulations to the family and coo over the new arrival.

Joanne came home after a day or so and I went round with a whole load of 'boy' baby clothes I'd bought, plus our Samuel who was only two and a half but already dying to meet Harrison. Joanne was breastfeeding but she told me she was struggling with it a bit and didn't feel so well. I assumed she was tired after the birth and I suggested she expressed some milk and then went to bed, leaving David to stay up and feed Harrison. We got the breast pump out and were howling so hard with laughter trying to get this thing going that I'm surprised the whole street didn't hear it. Anyway, we finally managed to get enough out so that Joanne could have a nice bath before going to bed with a couple of painkillers. David looked a bit concerned, but I told him that everything would be all right. *It's early days*, I thought. *It's just how it is at the beginning.* Those of us who've been through it understand, and as I left I never gave it another thought. Joanne was a fit and healthy girl and, given a few days, would quickly bounce back from the trauma of giving birth.

At 11 a.m. the following day my phone rang. It was Barbara.

'I wonder if I can ask you a favour, Jayne?' she said. 'Glynn's gone fishing and our Joanne's not feeling so well and I think she needs checking over. Would you be able to drop us at the doctor's?'

Well, of course I would. I left Samuel with Paul, picked up Joanne and her mum, and took them for an emergency appointment. The doctor they saw wasn't happy at all and recommended that Joanne go back to the hospital for a proper check-up. He noted that her caesarean scar looked tender and red, and might be infected.

We took his advice and drove Joanne to Rotherham General District Hospital. A junior doctor from the ward she'd been on prodded around a bit before giving his diagnosis: Joanne had nothing more complicated than constipation, he said, and he would give her some suppositories to take home. Barbara argued that she was sure it wasn't that, but the doctor was adamant; she simply needed to empty her bowels.

They went home and tried the treatment but Joanne began to feel worse. Two days later they returned to the hospital and saw the same doctor, who again diagnosed constipation, without bothering to consult anyone else for a second opinion. Barbara was furious; she knew something was seriously wrong and she demanded Joanne be given a blood test and intravenous antibiotics. As a nurse, she knew what blood poisoning could do. The doctor insisted that Joanne went home but Barbara stood her ground. There was no way her daughter was leaving hospital a second time without a proper examination and tests. Her scar had become very painful, so much so that if it was even touched lightly she'd scream out loud. So several hours later tests were carried out, Joanne was given antibiotics and a decision was made to keep her in.

I visited her the following morning and she looked terrible. She had the baby with her and she was taken down to the Intensive Care Unit where the scar was due to be looked at. As we sat by her bed, waiting for something to happen, I noticed that her speech had become disjointed; she was rambling on, something about Christmas dinner, and what time it would be, and she wasn't making much sense.

'I don't think I can breathe,' she said, and within minutes she'd become delirious. The emergency team literally crashed through the door and she was rushed into theatre. A virulent infection had got a deep hold in her scar. They cleaned out the scar, which had become gangrenous, and gave her emergency antibiotics. But it was too little, too late. Joanne never regained consciousness and, although various things were tried, the infection spread to her lungs. On 14 January 2007, six weeks after being admitted, my beloved niece died in my arms, leaving a newborn baby without his mother and a family torn to pieces.

The fallout was horrendous. As a family we'd had more than our fair share of tragedies, but nothing compared to this. I thought I was going to tip right over the edge. I kept waking up hearing the phone ringing, and our Joanne's voice on the line. She'd been like a younger sister to me, or even a daughter. I'd had so many plans for what we'd do together when her baby was born. The age gap between my Samuel and her Harrison was the same as Lee and Joanne, so it would've been a nice bit of history repeating itself.

I don't know how we got through the funeral. Our Lee, who had been so close to her, was one of the pall-bearers and spoke at the service. He said he thought it was the hardest day of his life when the invasion of Iraq happened in 2003 and he knew he'd have to go to war, but he'd never imagined he'd have to do anything as difficult as speaking at his cousin's funeral.

It seemed so horribly unfair. She'd only had a baby, not been hit by a car or come off a motorbike. She was a fit, healthy, sporty twenty-seven-year-old. It was all so wrong. I took two weeks' compassionate leave from work and then decided I needed to go back in, to save my sanity. That first Monday back I pulled into the car park by the International Centre and sat crying for ten minutes before I could even open the door. I went into the office and the minute I sat down the phone rang. I froze. I couldn't answer it. How could I deal with anyone else's difficulties when I obviously wasn't coping with my own? In a terrible state I rang Christine Brodhurst-Brown, who told me to go home. In all, I took about five weeks off, spending time with Barbara, Harrison and our Samuel, just trying to hold a family together and barely coping. Every time Samuel asked me a question about Joanne or Harrison – what had happened, and what would be happening next? – I just burst into tears. I didn't give myself any time to mend and, to be honest, I've never properly healed. I've learned to control it, and to make it right for Samuel and Harrison, but the pain is as raw as it was on the day she died. I still have her Christmas presents from that year in my wardrobe, wrapped up for the new mum who would never receive them. One of them was a ticket to *The X-Factor Live* event, which took place a month after she died. I'd also got our Barbara a ticket and we went together, but there was no joy in it. All the time we kept thinking, *This isn't right, Joanne should be here.*

Barbara eventually went back to work part-time, ironically at the hospital where Joanne had died, which was very hard for her. And a couple of months after she returned she noticed she had a persistent cough. She went to the doctor and was referred for tests; it turned out she had lung cancer. The prognosis was five years. She knew she had to keep battling the disease for the sake of her grandson, and I believe that's what she did.

Sadly, she got rather less than those five precious years. About eighteen months after Joanne died I was delivering some training at a conference in Rotherham's Magna Centre when, during a break, I noticed I had a voice message on my mobile. I listened to it and it was Barbara.

'Eh up,' she said, 'it's only me. I'm just phoning to tell you that I'm not feeling that well, so our Sue is nipping me up to the hospital. There's nowt to panic about, I'm just out of breath, that's all.'

It sounded like nothing, so I didn't call her back, and after the break I continued with the training. As I was talking, a woman walked in and asked if there was 'anyone here called Jayne Senior?' I said it was me, and she announced that my husband was in reception and needed to see me. So we had a hasty five-minute break while I went to find out what Paul wanted. 'I'm sorry to do this, Jayne,' he said, 'but it's Barbara. She's up at the hospital and has taken a turn for the worse. I think we'd better go.'

We did, and within half an hour Barbara was dead. She was just sixty. There was only eighteen months between daughter and mother dying – the age of her grandson, who had now lost both his mum and his grandma. In my bleaker moments I've often wondered, as a family, exactly what we'd done wrong to deserve such pain. I've been asked many times if Barbara just gave up fighting, but I don't believe she did. She wanted to stay alive as long as possible for Harrison.

And when tragic events happen, there are often un-expected consequences. The impact of all this death and misery played out particularly badly on our Samuel. He started school some months after Barbara passed away and within a year or so a little member of his class died suddenly. Normally, you explain death away to children as something that happens to old people, but he'd seen it affect all generations and he became very anxious about the whole subject. On a daily basis he'd worry about us dying, his brothers dying, him dying. It was very difficult to know how to deal with it. In the end, I took him to CRUSE, the bereavement counselling service. We had a family appointment, and afterwards they spoke to Samuel on his own. Then they called me back.

'You have an intelligent, happy little boy,' the counsellor said, 'but his problem is that he's bottling things up because every time he mentions Joanne or Barbara, you end up crying. So he doesn't want to upset you, and this is what is causing him anxiety. You need to talk to him about those people who were close to you all.'

Wrapped up in my own grief, I hadn't seen it that way, but she was absolutely right. We went home, got out the big box of family pictures and trinkets, and lay on the bed. I told Samuel stories of when I was little and how I was with my big sisters, when Joanne was growing up, about our Lee and Ben. Samuel just sobbed and sobbed, yet he cried out his anxieties. In a way, it was like turning a corner for us because now we had a new rule: 'If it's in your head I can't help you; if it comes out of your mouth we can discuss it.' And that applied to us all. Every day, Samuel and I would share memories, with one listening while the other talked, and it worked incredibly well. Samuel's anxieties faded and to some extent the experience helped me too.

Of course, as a family we were left with a little boy whose mother had died in what we felt were negligent circumstances. An inquest in 2010 found that Joanne's death had been accidental. However, Nicola Mundy, the Rotherham coroner, said that the junior doctor had given 'insufficient regard' to his patient's complaints and notes provided by her GP. We decided to continue fighting the case and in 2014 the local NHS Trust finally admitted liability, settling out of court. It was a large sum, but no amount of money will ever bring back the mother Harrison never knew. It's in trust, and it can be used for his post-eighteen education, if he chooses to go to university, and to buy a property. Luckily Harrison has a wonderful dad and has grown up to be a grand little boy who would make his mother very proud. I sometimes take him to a park in Barnsley where Joanne and Lee played when they were little, and I'll admit that it's difficult for me. However, that doesn't mean to say I'd ever deny him going there. If I avoided all the places I went with our Joanne when she was a child, and all the places we'd planned to visit after she'd had her baby, Harrison would never go anywhere. He still asks questions about her, and wonders if I ever knew her. So we go over the whole story again until he's satisfied. At least we have some beautiful pictures of her holding him as a baby – even if it was only for six short days.

12

In 2006 Angie Heal had produced a new report for South Yorkshire Police into sexual exploitation in South Yorkshire which this time linked it with gun crime and violence. Again, her findings made for grim reading – but were those who were reading it actually taking any notice?

Angie noted that:

> The situation in Rotherham continues as it has done for a number of years ... the issue of sexual exploitation in the town remains significant.
>
> In relation to violence, verbal intimidation and threats are regularly used, as are physical beatings and rape ... Young women are regularly trafficked between different towns and cities, and some are told that they cannot return home unless they have sex with a number of different men.

Angie went on to say that it was believed the sexual exploitation in Rotherham was 'well-organized, with one or two networks of men thought to be behind the physical and sexual abuse of young women'. She described how younger men and boys were 'financially rewarded' for starting the grooming process of girls their age, before passing them on to older contacts.

'Some men in the town,' she wrote, 'are reported to see this lifestyle as a more viable career option than legitimate work, as they can easily attain cars, money, girls, power and respect.'

Then she said this:

It is believed by a number of workers in the town that one of the difficulties that prevents this issue being dealt with effectively is the ethnicity of the abusers. Whilst abusers and paedophiles come from a number of different ethnic groups in the town, the main gangs associated with organised sexual exploitation are Asian.

Angie noted that a rise in the number of reports of guns seen on men involved in CSE in Rotherham had become a feature since 2003, and she recommended that more emphasis should be placed on 'tackling the abusers, rather than the abused'.

So the big issues remained, and still we felt that not enough was being done to hunt down the abusers and nail successful prosecutions. However, as youth workers who'd toiled hard – and more often than not, unsuccessfully – to raise awareness of what we saw as a major problem of child sexual abuse in Rotherham, by 2007 we might have been forgiven for thinking that we'd turned something of a corner.

We had been asked to help train all newly recruited police officers in CSE, and three-day training courses were now being run for senior officers. We also delivered training to five schools, other youth workers, foster carers and magistrates. The magistrates even requested names of current abusers, which I gave them, and asked if I could start sharing information with them so if any of these males came before them for other crimes they could take into consideration the information I had provided. However, the police said 'no' to this as – again – we 'did not have sufficient evidence'.

Rotherham Borough Council appeared to support what we were doing, financially at least (I have a report from the previous year which agrees to extra funding on the grounds that we contributed successfully to a number of 'outcomes' regarding the health and well-being of children), and finally we seemed to have a workable method of submitting our intelligence and information to the local police. All we needed now were some arrests and prosecutions.

Our information was being submitted to Detective Sergeant Dave Walker, who worked within the PPU, the Public Protection Unit. At the time we were told not to submit what we had to the police's Safer Neighbourhood teams, which were dotted around Rotherham. We were told that the role of the PPU was to disseminate information and areas of investigation to the Safer Neighbourhood teams, so the PPU would take our intelligence and decide what needed to be shared. This was somewhat frustrating because it was the Safer Neighbourhood teams who really knew what was going on and might actually be able to keep tabs on some of the things we were reporting. I remember one incident in which some girls we were in touch with, who lived in a homeless hostel, told us that every time they went into Clifton Park, in the centre of the town, they came across a guy carrying an orange rucksack who invariably offered to sell them drugs.

I gave this bit of information to Dave Walker, who said: 'What exactly am I meant to do with that?'

'It's up to you what you do with it,' I said, 'but I think you should do something.'

Nothing was done, but the point is that if I'd been able to share this with the local Safer Neighbourhood team for the Clifton Park area, they'd have known exactly who it was. Similarly, if I'd said that a black car had been reported loitering outside a school, its occupants asking kids to get in, the PPU couldn't have done much with it – but the Safer Neighbourhood team might have nipped round there and had a word with the men inside.

So that was disappointing, but at least we were

Jayne Senior

establishing better links with the police and some progress was being made in this direction. And around the same time we were fortunate enough to meet a police officer who is, perhaps, one of the unsung heroes of this story and who played a pivotal role in the next major stage of Risky Business's fortunes.

We were part of a strategy meeting at Clifton School, just by Clifton Park, because we were concerned about some of the female pupils at this school and we thought we could link them to a group of men we believed were abusing them. Clifton Park was seen as a grooming location for local girls, and so we invited along Rupert Chang, the police sergeant in charge of the Safer Neighbourhood team for that area.

We had learned that girls gathering in Clifton Park were being plied with drink and drugs, and being abused in bushes behind the park's bandstand. Cars full of men were pulling up at all hours of the day and night; taxis too. There seemed to be all sorts going on and we felt the situation was escalating, with potentially around seventy girls involved. So this was serious stuff, prompting us to decide that a multi-agency approach was needed, which is why we invited the police.

On the day of the meeting Sergeant Chang sent his apologies. He couldn't make the meeting, he said, but would dispatch one of his junior officers to listen to what was being said. I wasn't happy. We felt that a lot

186

of nasty stuff was happening in and around the park which linked up to other things going on all across the town, and I was annoyed that the police couldn't be bothered to send someone more senior than a constable. But as it turned out, this young constable – whose name I've forgotten – was to do more for us and our girls in one night than any other officer had done in a decade. During the meeting we shared everything we had – nicknames, car registrations, phone numbers – and in turn listened to eye-witness reports from teachers and council employees who worked in the park. The young officer took out his pocket book and wrote everything down before going away and doing something he believed, as an officer of the law, was the right thing to do – he put the whole lot straight onto the Police National Computer.

A few days later I received a call from Sergeant Chang. It appeared there'd been some kind of investigation going on in Sheffield and the investigating officers had struggled to identify two of their main suspects. They'd drawn blanks, until they'd logged on to the PNC a few days previously and seen all the information I'd given – unwittingly – via this young officer. They then realized that two of these people were the men they were looking for, and they weren't happy, particularly when they saw a note attached that intelligence on the same men had been shared by me two years previously. I was summoned to Sheffield CID to explain myself.

I was met by four grumpy-looking officers. 'We've been looking at these guys for ages,' one of them said. 'If you had all the information, why the hell did you sit on it?'

'I didn't,' I replied. 'I shared it with you two years ago. There's a note on the computer to say that.'

'Then why haven't we seen it?' the officer demanded.

So I went through the whole 'Box Five' saga and their mouths opened in shock. 'Never heard of it,' one of them said, which confirmed Matt Jukes's view that 'Box Five' was 'crap'. Anyway, the officers were left in no doubt that I never sat on information and had been sharing it for years. It made me wonder, though, to what extent the PPU were cherry-picking through the information I provided, as I'd been sharing intelligence with Dave Walker ever since Matt Jukes asked me to and it was only through error that this particular bit had ended up on the PNC.

'I think I could do with meeting you, Jayne,' Sergeant Chang said after I returned from Sheffield, 'and then perhaps we can get some of this cleared up.'

So we arranged a date and one morning I dropped in on a team briefing being held in a small office on Sergeant Chang's patch, which covered a substantial part of the town centre – an area where there was a high proportion of incidents relating to CSE. I gave my usual spiel; describing how Risky Business started, what we did, who we worked with, the information we shared and with whom. And it was apparent that all the information I'd shared before, including the latest stuff being passed to Dave Walker, had completely passed this lot by. They'd absolutely no idea about any of it, which made me feel we were back at square one; back to the days of 'Box Five' and the police refusing to take a bunch of silly youth workers and their dysfunctional clients seriously. And yet Rupert Chang's team had their own separate concerns about vulnerable girls and alleged abusers and were passing these on up the chain of command.

I was astonished. So was Rupert Chang. He, like me, realized that if we'd pooled our resources, arrests might have been swiftly made. I went back to the office and asked Christine Brodhurst-Brown if I could share what we'd got directly with Rupert, and she agreed. So I brought over our intelligence one afternoon – several boxes of it. Rupert looked at the pile of paperwork beginning to tower over his desk and the expression on his face read: *Where the hell do I start with this?*

But, to his credit, Rupert did not waver in his determination to get to the bottom of what was going on around his patch. He didn't pass the buck or refer us on to some mysterious 'Box Five'-style black hole. He and two officers began work sifting through everything. I continued to pass on my information and intelligence to Dave Walker – but made sure Rupert received a copy too. I told Rupert about the orange rucksack-carrying suspected drug dealer in Clifton Park and we waited to see if the PPU ever passed the same bit of information on to Rupert and his Safer Neighbourhood team, but they never did. Which makes me believe that the PPU was just 'gatekeeping' everything I was sending them, deciding what was fit for purpose and what wasn't. Personally, I don't think any police officer in this country has the right to decide that, especially not when it comes to CSE. Very often, 'jigsaw evidence' is needed to build up a profile of a perpetrator or perpetrators which can then be considered legally sound. And if pieces of the jigsaw aren't being passed on to others working on it, it's never going to get finished.

Rupert and I decided to concentrate our efforts on Clifton Park, as the park itself had recently attracted a grant to generally tidy it up. This, we thought, was an opportunity to get people together and ask what kind of improvements they'd like to see. We realized that with its rabbit warren of paths and patches of dense undergrowth, Clifton Park was an ideal place for the sexual abuse of children away from prying eyes. We wanted to change things so that children and families could use the park and feel safe. We knew that those who used it regularly had complained to the council numerous times about broken bottles and condoms everywhere, young girls getting drunk, strange men hanging around and noise issues. Because it was something that affected the whole community I suggested that we needed to include those who worked in or used the park – the council employees, the children's ride operators, the dog walkers, the local schools – and enlist them as our eyes and ears. The best way we'd ever get hard evidence would be to encourage local people both to tell us what they were seeing and to recognize what they weren't.

For example, I did some training on those lines to a group of council-employed park keepers and grounds maintenance people and pointed out that where they might see a drunk, angry girl, I would recognize a frightened child being groomed and out of her depth. I taught them that if they were collecting condoms near certain clumps of bushes, perhaps they should keep a closer eye on the bushes themselves. Hearing this shocked them, I think, because previously they'd only perceived annoying teenagers. One woman, whose job it was to prune, went out the following day and apparently reduced one or two selected clumps of undergrowth to twigs! Suddenly, everyone could see right through those bushes.

I gave similar training to local dog walkers and the people who operated the park's children's rides. Risky Business's preventative team also went into the local schools and talked to pupils about passing on information confidentially. So we were building community links and encouraging people to keep an eye out for what was going on. Within weeks, we were beginning to receive excellent information that we could pass on to Rupert and his team. In turn, Rupert recruited the help of a force analyst who started to put together an 'Anacapa' chart – a piece of software which links hundreds of pieces of seemingly random evidence into an overall picture, helping police to build a case. As time went on, Rupert's analyst linked alleged perpetrators and their victims with phone numbers, descriptions, nicknames, car registration plates, taxi firms and takeaways. In fact, no less than three Anacapa charts were created, and they were incredibly comprehensive. Perhaps for the first time we had a clear picture of who was abusing who, and exactly how it was happening.

Then Rupert pulled a masterstroke by handing over everything we'd got to the PPU. In normal circumstances the PPU would task the Safer Neighbourhood teams with jobs based on information they'd received. But this was the other way round; in effect, Rupert had done their job for them, and evidenced everything we were saying. The PPU had no choice but to take this information seriously and so Operation Central was born.

Central was the first of three police operations – Central, Czar and Chard – involving CSE in Rotherham, and by far the most successful, as we will see. A meeting was held involving everyone connected to the operation, headed up by the PPU: ourselves, health, education, safeguarding and people from Rupert's team. In short, four girls – three of whom were already known to us, and another referred to us after coming to Rupert's attention – were eventually identified as being at immediate 'high risk'. Although I was never quite comfortable with the label, believing that risk is risk, the police liked to categorize risk. 'High risk' was when the girl was being abused regularly; 'medium' was being groomed and hanging around with 'high risk' girls; and 'low risk' applied to girls who were just starting to become involved with other girls already being groomed. It wasn't a perfect categorization but we used it anyway, to avoid confusion. Having contributed information and intelligence and looked at the web of interconnectivity thrown up by the Anacapa chart, we believed we had the best chance of successfully prosecuting these girls' alleged abusers.

These four girls at 'high risk' were young – two thirteen-year-olds, a fourteen-year-old and a sixteen-year-old. Abused, frightened, angry girls. Girls with stories that would make your hair curl. One of the girls, Charlie, who I mentioned in chapter 4, had previously been orally raped in the street, an act witnessed by her mother, who gave chase but couldn't catch up with her abuser. The day after – and I remember it was November – I was with Charlie trying to sort out the aftermath of the night before and encourage her to report what had happened.

'Do you know, it's nearly Christmas?' she said at one point. 'Why don't we go over to Meadowhall today and see Santa?'

I could've wept when I heard it. The day before, this little girl had been subjected to the most horrific sexual assault and all she wanted to do was go to see Father Christmas. It just gives you an insight into how vulnerable these children really are. I remember saying that of course we could go to see Santa. And we did. We queued up in front of the grotto at Meadowhall and she was as giddy and excited as any kid would be.

Then my phone rang. It was a police officer I knew.

'Are you with Charlie?' she said.

'Yes, why?'

'OK. Don't reply as though you know who I am. I'm just ringing to tell you that, for her own safety, we're removing her tonight.'

Evidently, the girl's abusers, or their associates, had got wind that something was up. If they got to these girls first, there was no way they would give evidence and the whole operation would fall down. We'd seen it in the past. Girls who had been prepared to make statements had suddenly gone missing, then would appear a day or two later in a state of shock. They'd been threatened with violence, torture, even death. Their abusers had promised that harm would come to their parents, brothers and sisters if they spoke out. And because they knew their abusers well, knew what kind of men they were, they had no reason to believe they wouldn't carry out their threats.

This time, however, the game had changed slightly. In the past, as I've stated, it's my opinion that the police generally looked down on our girls as 'little slags' who were responsible for everything that happened to them and whose abuse didn't seem to warrant much attention. No matter that they were twelve, thirteen, fourteen – there was an ingrained attitude that they were 'bringing it on themselves'.

But in the run-up to Operation Central, Rupert Chang and his team had gone to great lengths to build a rapport with the girls we felt were being exploited in and around Clifton Park. This tested the officers to the limits because many of those girls had had bad experiences with the police and weren't above giving them a mouthful of swear words whenever they felt like it. Rupert's team persevered, and within a short while the girls were greeting the officers by their first names.

So Charlie was removed and taken to a place of safety in Nottinghamshire. I went to see her the following day and she wasn't happy that she'd been rehoused somewhere right out in the sticks. While we were talking, an officer from the PPU turned up, presumably to ask her about the sexual assault. Charlie quickly told him where to get off.

'I'm not speaking to any police,' she said, her face set hard, 'unless it's Rupert, Paul or Matt.'

Paul and Matt were members of Rupert's team and it showed what an impact those officers had made, and how they'd earned the girls' trust. One of this team had regular contact with sixteen-year-old Heather. When the other girls were removed for their own safety she was left on her own, terrified that her abusers would get to her. If it hadn't been for Rupert's team I'm convinced we'd have lost her, but luckily they were fabulous – which is more than can be said for social services.

To put into context some of Heather's later experiences, her words below give an idea of her background and how she was groomed:

There was a lot of stuff that happened to me before the men came into my life. Mum's boyfriend would come into my bedroom and do stuff to me when I was a little girl. The first man who made me do anything with him, I was nine and it happened in the back of his car. Mum didn't know any of this so I kept quiet. Then Mum took an overdose, and she was so depressed social workers came to the house and told her if things didn't change they would take us kids into care. One day I came home from school and Mum was laid on the floor, she was rushed to hospital and I had to stay at home to look after my brother and he kept screaming. When we got to see Mum she said she wasn't going to be with us much longer. There were always different men in the house. She kept going out and leaving us at home.

When the Asian guys came along and offered

me rides in their cars and cigarettes I thought that someone did care about me. When I was twelve I started to hang around with another male who was older than me. The next thing is that his older cousin started texting me and asking me to meet up with them. These guys were well known and I thought the attention would make me popular. 'Z' kept saying he told the man how nice I was. They texted me late at night. One day me and my friend called a taxi to take us to Asda and 'Q' turned up. He started talking to us, he knew who I was. I asked how and he said through some mates and I gave him my number when he asked. I thought it was exciting that he knew who I was. Me and 'N' went to meet 'Q' one day and he said he was bringing his friend 'S', who he said was nice and kind and good-looking.

When they came to pick us up, 'S' said hello and he was good-looking. They took us for a drive some-where. I'd never seen him before and I remember he took us somewhere really quiet in the middle of nowhere. 'Q' stopped and asked me to get out of the car and we all talked for a bit. He gave me some alcohol and I went for a walk with 'S'. I said that 'Q' freaked me out sometimes, and he asked for my number. In my eyes I thought 'how lucky am I?' It happened so fast and I understand I was probably already being groomed but then it all seemed like fun and attention. I was only a little girl and I still can't understand why no one asked me why I was going off in cars or why I had an older boyfriend.

After that I went out with 'S' every night, sometimes he picked me up at 2 a.m. I was so proud I had a boyfriend who gave me all the attention. Even my friends at school were jealous. He would text me and ring me because he cared about me and wanted to make sure I was safe. 'S' had an amazing car, it had big speakers, I loved his car. It had leather seats. We just cruised and showed off. What other thirteen-year-olds have a nice boyfriend with a car? I cruised past all my mates at school, it made me feel powerful. I was head over heels with him, so when he asked me for sex I thought 'why not?' He used to say he loved me all the time. He would fetch me from the top of my street. I wanted to have him all to myself. He knew I went to school and he knew how old I was. School knew I was seeing him because one teacher was asking me why I went out with older Asian guys.

One night 'S' brought along a friend called 'A'. I struggle to understand how it happened all so quick. 'A' said he was waiting to pick me up. He took me and my friend to buy cider and got us drunk. Then other men kept coming up. I woke up somewhere and couldn't remember what had happened. Where was 'S'? After that, strangers started ringing my phone and told me that I had to meet them. Then my friend refused to come out and so it was just me. This guy turned up one night, called 'F'. He was really bad – I can't say what he did to me.

I was a mess but no one seemed to care. School knew I wasn't going very much, no one did anything. Someone at school must have known but they never did anything. No one got involved when all this was going on.

Heather was locked into the cycle of grooming and only found the courage to speak out with the help and encouragement of Rupert and his team. She was terrified that her abusers would find out where she was living. 'They'll shoot me if they catch me,' she said.

In spite of that, we had a battle on our hands trying to persuade social services to move her or give her anything at all. Eventually we found her a foster-care placement which unfortunately didn't work out, so just before Christmas we were again struggling to get her housed safely. A social worker called me and said that a hostel had been found in Nottingham, and could I take her?

I didn't know how bad this place was until my phone went at about 9 a.m. on New Year's Eve. It was Rupert Chang, telling me he'd received a call from Heather, who was in hysterics. The hostel she'd been placed in turned out to be near a red-light area and it was full of street workers. Nor was it twenty-four-hour staffed, so men were knocking on residents' doors, including

Heather's, looking for the prostitutes. Heather only had £20 to last her all over Christmas and had walked to the Job Centre to claim benefit. On the way back, she got a tap on her shoulder.

'Eh up, Heather, what you doin' here?'

It was a man linked to Heather's abusers. God knows what he was doing in that area, but he'd spotted her and no doubt he would tip off his mates – hence her hysterical phone call to Rupert.

'Right,' I said, 'I'm on my way down.'

I grabbed my coat and my car keys, leaving the family behind in my wake. As I pulled up outside the place I noticed a large group of Asian men gathered there, tinkering under the bonnet of a car. Others were sat on a nearby wall, just watching. No one said anything but there was an air of quiet menace about. I decided to park round the back and, after a quick chat with the hostel manager, went upstairs to see Heather. She was shaking with fear, and told me that she had to leave because the staff had done a risk assessment and decided she was putting the other residents in danger. She needed somewhere to go, immediately. I rang Rotherham social services and explained the situation to the out-of-hours team.

'Not much we can do, I'm afraid,' came the reply. 'She's sixteen.'

I asked to speak to the manager. Same response. So I

rang Christine Brodhurst-Brown, and said we had to do something about this girl. While Christine rang round, I contacted a friend, Tracey, who managed an organization called Safe At Last, for young people who go missing from home. I was hoping they'd be able to find emergency accommodation for Heather, which they did.

Then I received a call from a woman called Jill Holbert, a Locality Manager with Rotherham Borough Council's Children and Young Persons' Services. I did not get on with her at all, finding her cold, hard and abrasive. Behind her back she was known as 'Aveline' because her flowing hair and full figure reminded staff of the character in *Bread*, a BBC sitcom that ran in the 1980s.

'Jayne, I've heard about this business with Heather, and you trying to find her a place,' she said. 'Let me just tell you now that we're not in the business of babysitting sixteen-year-olds.'

'Under the Children's Act a sixteen-year-old is still a child,' I said. 'Besides, if we don't find somewhere soon for her, there's no way I can guarantee her safety. She's at real risk.'

'I do know the Act,' she replied, 'and I'm telling you that we don't have a budget for this. We've other priorities. There's a hostel by Clifton Park. She'll have to go there instead.'

Clifton Park was, of course, the very area in which

Heather was being abused. I couldn't send her back there. In the end, Christine Brodhurst-Brown advised me to take the place with Safe At Last.

'Just do it, Jayne,' she said, 'and we'll face the consequences later. If I have to fund it from my budget, I will.'

So we had a place, but the problem of the men hanging around outside remained. What were they capable of? I wasn't sure, but Heather looked frightened enough for me to take the perceived threat against her seriously. I rang Rupert and, after a long conversation, I took Heather and her bin bag of clothes down to my car and set off. What she didn't know was that I'd arranged to meet Rupert and one of his officers in a lay-by, so that she could be transferred safely to a police car. On the way up I needed to stop at a motorway services and because the poor kid was starving hungry I took her in and bought her a burger. As we came out I noticed a police car nearby. I caught the eye of the officer in the driver's seat and he just nodded before following me out of the services.

Two junctions on, I came off the road and found the lay-by where Rupert and his officer, Paul, were waiting. Heather got out of the car and just hugged him. Now she felt protected and safe, and was taken to the refuge without further incident.

All of which proves that the police, when enthusiastic and supportive, could be brilliant in these situations. If only they'd been like this much earlier, how many girls might we have saved from abuse? And as for social services, well, my battles with them had lasted a long time and would, sadly, get much worse as time went on.

13

Inevitably, I got into trouble for taking Heather to Safe At Last. Jill Holbert phoned me to have another go.

'Don't you think you're exaggerating the risks, Jayne?' she said.

Well, she was the Locality Manager for the area all the girls came from – perhaps she should've known the answer to that.

Heather knew she couldn't stay at Safe At Last for too long and after a day or so there she rang her social worker.

'I can't help you,' came the reply, 'I've got other kids to look after. You're an adult now.'

Anyway, we eventually found her a foster place right out of Rotherham, where she thrived. I will let Heather tell the rest of her story in a later chapter. For now, she was happy, and well away from the men who threatened her.

Luckily we managed to keep all four of the girls safe; their abusers were known to have links over a wide area including Nottingham, Hull and Barnsley, and, as we saw with Heather, just one chance meeting with them or their associates could potentially scupper the operation as well as putting the girls in danger.

25 March 2009 was designated as Operation Central 'Strike Day', the day the alleged abusers would be arrested. One of the most important first steps after arrests were made would be the identification parade at a police station – an event the girls dreaded for obvious reasons, even though it would take place behind darkened glass. Each of the girls would take turns in identifying the arrested men and, of course, the girls weren't allowed to speak to each other during this process. I asked if we could have some funding to ensure their comfort and safety on the day, and we worked with Rupert's team on a plan we thought was failsafe. I would allocate one Risky Business worker and one person from social services to each of the four girls and instead of driving around, waiting for turns to attend the parade (it was to be held in Sheffield), I asked that four budget hotel rooms be booked, so at least the girls could relax a bit before their ordeal.

No chance. Social services wouldn't fund it.

'Why?' I said. 'We're not asking to have the place overnight, just for an hour or two before the parade.'

But they wouldn't budge. So again Christine Brodhurst-Brown stepped in and authorized it from the Youth Service budget. We got our hotel rooms and I was assigned the Hilton, with Charlie in tow. A decision was made that, to minimize their distress and anxiety, we wouldn't tell any of the girls what was happening until the day of the parade. I turned up at Charlie's placement in Nottinghamshire just after 7 a.m. that day and when she met me at the door she burst into tears. She just knew. But I'd been working with her long enough for her to understand that, although she was frightened, she was also in a powerful position. She knew now that she had been groomed for sexual abuse, and that she'd had no choice in it.

Although we'd tried hard to make the identification parades as painless as possible for the girls, we were under no illusion that it would still be traumatic. A total of eight men were arrested. (There could, and perhaps should, have been many more. A lot of men abused these girls; nameless men, men with families, kids of the same age at home. Men still walking free today. Every single one should've been on trial, but for the lack of hard evidence against them. I hope and pray that one day this will change.) It was particularly difficult for Charlie as her mum was a witness too and, of course, they weren't allowed to see or speak to one another during this identification process. Charlie's mum was standing behind a door that led to the identification suite, waiting her turn to go in, and because the door was open slightly she heard the sound of her child crying with fear in another room, but could do nothing about it. When children are abused, their abusers never stop to consider what impact it has elsewhere . . .

Aside from that, the day went smoothly enough although, of course, as soon as they were arrested and charged the men knew exactly who would be giving evidence against them. The moment the girls were finished with the parade they had to return to their temporary addresses out of the area. During the period between the arrests and the trial, there were a couple of odd incidents that made us wonder whether the girls' whereabouts had been discovered. One involved Charlie, who was living somewhere quite remote – a place you wouldn't accidentally go to – and the manager of the hostel rang the local police to let them know about a couple of out-of-area taxis that had turned up and were lingering at the end of the road.

It was difficult for Charlie. She had a supportive family who loved and missed her. One weekend she came home to visit them and they went out for Sunday lunch. Not thinking, her mum posted a message on Facebook to say she was having a lovely time in a local pub with her daughter. Luckily this was spotted and taken down before anyone who might threaten Charlie or her family saw it and turned up. Her mum wasn't acting maliciously, she just didn't think. And why should she? She was just a parent sharing a nice afternoon with her daughter. Again, abusers never bother to consider how many lives they'll ruin.

Charlie's mum acknowledges that she made some mistakes in her parenting. In her early teens, long before

Operation Central, Charlie fell in with a group of abusers and missed a huge amount of school. She was also going missing for days on end, as her mother tried desperately to locate her. One evening her mother was informed that Charlie was missing again, but this time she knew where to look . . . This is her story, in her own words:

I just kept circling the field because I knew. I phoned up social services and said, 'I can see her in the field, she's with some Asian guys. Can you send the police?' So I took my kids home and then my friend came back with me. We walked on to the field and we saw one of the men making her give him oral sex. Then everything just went haywire. I shouted, 'Get off my daughter, you black bastard, she's only thirteen!' I shouldn't have said that, I know, but it just came out. They cleared off. We phoned the police and told them straight away. They still didn't come. It took an hour for them to arrive.

They eventually came in a dog van, and I thought, 'Surely they can't take her in there?' One officer said to her, 'If you go back to them men, everyone will think you're a little slapper.'

She was taken to the Nottingham area, in the middle of nowhere. She had to have a member of staff with her all the time. I wasn't allowed to know the address or the home number. They'd phone me. I couldn't see or speak to her for a full week.

They took my statement two days after they took her. A police officer came to my mum's and because I'd called the guy a black bastard she said I wouldn't be a credible witness. I didn't mean it like that, it just came out.

I wasn't allowed to talk or tell anyone what had happened. I was told that if I did they would take the other kids off me. I wasn't allowed to tell even family. When Charlie went to open up to me they stopped her. I was a witness. Then they said my statement wasn't good enough so they wanted another. They said I wasn't a credible witness.

After 'Strike Day' the alleged abusers of all four girls were charged and, to no one's surprise, bailed with conditions to appear in court at a later date. I didn't feel those conditions were enough to protect our girls, but at least they had been charged after all this time we'd spent pushing for something to happen. The girls were kept away from Rotherham and while we waited for a court date we carried on with our caseloads. The arrests certainly didn't succeed in acting as a deterrent. Below, from late 2009, is a referral form on a boy who had fallen in with a group of abusers who were using him to deal drugs and hook in young girls.

[An abuser] allegedly involved in a serious sexual assault on another child has made threats towards [the boy], stating he will hang him from a tree in Clifton Park. [The boy] allegedly has a drug debt owed to [an abuser]. Information received is that [the boy] is also dealing drugs around the Ferham area on behalf of adults of concern, including [the abuser].

[The boy] was allegedly assaulted over the theft of cannabis. His mother was informed they needed to pay £20.00 per day until the £1,000 was paid in full. This boy was just twelve years old.

Not long after this, my husband Paul, our Lee and Ben and two of my brothers-in-law went out for a Christmas drink. At about 11.30 p.m. they came out of the pub at the end of the road and saw a young girl walking up the street ahead of them. Then a van screeched to a halt and the Asian driver shouted, 'Get in, you bitch!' Paul approached the van and told him to 'do one'. They then walked the young girl home. I reported it immediately to the police, as I knew who the girl was, and on the Monday I rang her social worker. In response to my concern, she said: 'What were your husband and sons doing approaching a young female late at night?'

The 'young female' was an extremely vulnerable child who went on to be raped with a broken bottle and will never have a baby due to the damage caused. She is now back in touch with me and told me recently that the night Paul intervened she had just been gang-raped and had run off, wanting to get home to where she knew she would be safe and her mother would give her a hug and make everything better.

It was around this time that a new senior manager by the name of Howard Woolfenden came into the Children and Young Persons' department. Like everyone else before him, he wanted to take a look at the project and the database we kept. He seemed a nice chap and was impressed by the amount of information we had and how we kept it. He was very high up in the Safeguarding field so his opinion on that front mattered. Furthermore, he seemed committed to making sure we were funded properly, proving this by finding a few extra resources for us in the lead-up to the trial. We'd no reason not to have faith in him or to disbelieve anything he said. During Operation Central we also had a letter from Simon Perry, Director of Targeted Support Services at Rotherham Borough Council and Christine Brodhurst-Brown's boss. He thanked us for our contribution, saying that 'our input was critical to the success of the operation'. He added:

I know many staff worked long hours to support the youngsters through this very traumatic time. This was certainly the type of professional assistance these youngsters needed in order to manage the stress that will have been associated with the whole of the investigation.

On behalf of the service I would like to offer my appreciation and acknowledge the professional service offered by you and the team. The communication with the other parts of the service and other agencies was excellent and of great value in managing clear information flow and the subsequent interest from the Press.

Once more, thank you for your dedication and input.

Lovely words that now seem deeply ironic in the light of what would ultimately happen to Risky Business.

Between the Operation Central arrests and the trial itself, a 'Lessons Learned' review of the operation was commissioned by the Rotherham Local Safeguarding Children's Board (LSCB). This was to be headed by Malcolm Stevens, a senior social worker with many years' experience as an inspector and government adviser. The aim would be to see how we could build on the success of Operation Central in getting people to court, and how all the agencies involved could work together more effectively in the future. I met Malcolm and he was a lovely guy. He appeared to be impressed with what we were doing, and visited all the other players in this drama (apart from the girls, whom he was not allowed to meet as they hadn't yet been in court) to see how best to tackle the issues.

In his review, Malcolm noted that while it was 'not possible to say whether or not Rotherham has a problem of child sexual exploitation which is more significant than anywhere else', he did say that the facts of Operation Central and the circumstances outlined by the victims and Risky Business indicated 'child sexual exploitation at the top end of seriousness'. He also said that the twenty charges listed against the Operation Central defendants 'do not represent the full extent of child sexual exploitation in Rotherham'.

'From the evidence of these girls,' he wrote, 'and from other police and Risky Business intelligence there is cause to believe that many other girls are involved, similarly aged, and there are other perpetrators particularly aged between 30–40.'

However there was also this:

Although the alleged perpetrators are of Asian origin and the victims are white, this is the factuality of these cases alone; nothing more can be drawn from that. It is imperative that suggestions/allusions of a wider cultural phenomenon is avoided. The BNP in Rotherham is said to have made such assertions already, in public and on its website, and that is highly regrettable.

I would argue that it is the denial of such 'cultural phenomenon' and the failure to tackle this properly in a way that would bring in all members of the community that led to the British National Party (BNP) and the English Defence League (EDL) making political capital out of the situation.

That said, the review was very favourable to Risky Business and its working methods.

'What Risky Business has achieved is significant competence in specialist high-profile and complex CSE work,' Malcolm wrote. He also mentioned that we should not be the answer to issues of CSE, and that we needed to be part of a multi-agency approach which ensured that 'the traditions of supportive youth work can be sustained'. Risky Business would be the 'nucleus' of that team.

He mentioned that:

- we were 'well thought of' by young people
- we attended all strategy meetings and responded to action points
- we held 'highly relevant' training programmes
- we had good working relationships with the police
- we needed better offices.

I was perfectly happy with all that but it made what happened with Operation Czar harder to understand. This was a similar scenario to Central, in that girls were being abused in and around a public park, except this one was Ferham Park, in a predominantly Asian area of Rotherham. I'd met the Safer Neighbourhood team there and had got on well with the sergeant, Paul Newman, as I had with Rupert Chang. He was shocked at the information we'd been passing on about Ferham Park, which again leads me to believe that the PPU weren't doing what we'd hoped they would. In addition, people in the area had seen various goings-on and had rung the police independently, so it was looking hopeful that Czar would be as successful at bringing alleged perpetrators to court as Central had been.

The referrals and information around the girls involved in Operation Czar made for uncomfortable reading. One girl, aged fourteen, was being picked up in taxis, driven across Yorkshire and beyond and made to have sex with numerous Asian males. For this she was paid £10. Another hung around in Ferham Park, waiting for various males to pick her up and have sex with her. Once, when she refused, she was thrown in the canal as a threat. Yet another was seen getting into taxis and cars with different men and was being paid to have sex with them. She was threatened with having her throat slashed. This girl was thirteen at the time.

Anyway, Howard Woolfenden decided that he would put Jill Holbert, the Locality Manager mentioned above, in charge of the social care side of Operation Czar. This was the role Risky Business had performed in Central and by all measures it had worked very effectively. I was surprised because we'd worked with the Czar girls for quite a while and knew them well so there seemed no reason why we shouldn't continue our work through this operation. I've never had a satisfactory explanation for this decision. However, for whatever reason, it was decided that Risky Business wouldn't be part of this particular investigation. I argued against this and we went back and forwards for a few months, with Risky Business staying involved. But eventually, Jill Holbert put three social workers on the job. The same day some of the girls were introduced to these social workers, they were removed from their homes without warning. Naturally, the girls were furious and blamed us – because we were the ones they'd trusted in the first place.

Shortly after, Jill Holbert asked to meet me and Christine Brodhurst-Brown. She had a list of all the girls connected with Operation Czar and she told us, in no uncertain terms, that all these cases would be closed to Risky Business, 'because now they have a social worker'. I was furious, and protested loudly, but it was too late – the deal had been done. It was also suggested that we close down the cases relating to Central but I argued that one vigorously, given that the trial was so close, and managed to keep those girls on our books.

One of the Czar cases we were forced to close was that of Laura Wilson – and just a few weeks before the trial was to begin, in the autumn of 2010, one of our staff got a call from Laura's mother, Maggie, who told us that her daughter was missing. Now, at various times a good number of our girls would go 'missing', but usually for only a night or two. They tended to turn up, in whatever state, having spent time with their abusers or other men they'd been trafficked to. They'd come back looking rough and dirty, but at least they were back on the patch and we could do something for them. But when Laura went missing and stayed missing, alarm bells immediately rang. For a start, she was extra-vulnerable. And she'd just had a baby. Despite everything that had happened to her, she wasn't the sort to walk out on her child. For various reasons she'd wanted this baby badly.

As I said, we'd worked on and off with Laura for many years. As part of a tactic to threaten another girl, she'd been driven down the motorway by a group of men and watched as these men made the other girl drink something out of a bottle she believed was 'spiked'. Laura was just ten years old at the time and the family became embroiled in a horrendous situation. As time went on, threats were made against the family and Laura stopped going to school. Her social worker and the school who referred her said she was giving favours to men in the backrooms of takeaways in return for alcohol and there was even an incident when a gun was pointed at her.

In her mid teens she started to date an Asian boy a year older than her by the name of Ashtiaq Ashgar.

He was on our database of people we believed to be involved in CSE in that he was befriending and grooming girls of his age who would then be passed up to older men, and we mentioned him in our meetings as having links to other abusers. He came from a strict background and didn't tell his parents he was dating a white girl. Neither did he inform them that he drank alcohol, smoked cannabis and had relationships with several other girls alongside Laura. She, of course, was obsessed with him; she truly thought their relationship was solid and forever – the usual teenage stuff – so when she found out what had been going on behind her back, she hit the roof.

Laura never did anything by halves, so to take revenge on her boyfriend she slept with his married friend, Ishaq Hussein, who was twenty-two. The inevitable happened and Laura became pregnant, eventually giving birth to a girl at the age of just sixteen. She decided to keep the child and, against the odds, restarted her secret relationship with Ashtiaq Ashgar. However, although she told him she loved him countless times, according to an interview her family did in the *Daily Mail* he treated Laura very badly.

Perhaps because she'd had a baby and wanted some solidity in her life, or possibly because she wasn't thinking straight at all, she decided to tell Ashtiaq's family what was going on. So she informed his mother, who apparently went mad at her and hit her with a shoe.

Then she decided to pay Ishaq's family a visit and tell them the truth about the identity of her child's father. We now know that Ashtiaq sent a text to Ishaq very soon afterwards, telling him he was 'gonna send that bitch to hell'.

None of us could settle, knowing Laura was out there somewhere and very probably in danger. She'd been in many, many scrapes before but this felt different. Christine Brodhurst-Brown had just gone on holiday, but had asked me to update her if there was any news about Laura. All that weekend I felt odd, wondering where she was and who she was with.

A day or so later I received a visit at the project from Paul Lakin, the new council member for Children's Services. He spent a good while asking me how many cases we had, talking about the perpetrators and listening to my frustrations around reporting. We spoke about Laura and why we were so concerned about her. Then he asked me how my Paul was as he had previously been his manager at the steelworks. We also chatted about how he had once provided funding for Risky Business to rent a garage after listening to my Paul at work and realizing what was going on in his area. The conversation finished with him asking about staffing, structure and the costs of the service.

On the Monday of the following week, an officer from the PPU rang me.

'Jayne,' he said, 'we've been looking all over the place

all weekend and I have to tell you that we've found a shoe covered in blood. There's nothing else yet, but we're keeping going until there is.'

My heart sank. Could there have been an accident or could she have got into trouble somehow and be too scared to come out of hiding? All sorts of scenarios crossed my mind, including the worst one of all.

The following day my phone rang again. It was Sergeant Paul Newman. A body had been found in the canal. 'It's not been identified,' he said, 'but it's a young female. It's not looking good at all, Jayne.'

I put the phone down and felt sick. I rang Simon Perry, Christine Brodhurst-Brown's manager, and he said he'd come down to the office immediately. The staff were in pieces. Everyone was crying and wondering what more they could have done, if anything, to protect this poor, vulnerable girl who we'd known for so long. Simon Perry arrived and he hadn't been there five minutes when there was a knock at the door and in came a police officer from the Safer Neighbourhood team.

'I know you've heard,' he said, 'so I thought I'd just drop in to see you. We were worried about you.'

I asked him if there'd been any update.

'Well,' he said, 'I'm afraid that it is Laura they've found, but we're not releasing that today until she's been formally identified. There's another thing I should warn you about, too . . . we've been told that we have to take this down the honour-killing route. We can't mention anything to do with CSE in this investigation. That's what we've been told.'

My mouth dropped open. I couldn't believe it. An 'honour killing'? Like she'd somehow had a hand in her own murder? All the agencies were saying this child was being groomed for abuse from the age of ten and now here she was, dead, at just seventeen. There was no 'honour' in that. To my mind, this was the result of child sexual abuse, no question. Laura was a very needy and vulnerable girl who was taken advantage of and paid the price for her involvement with a group of abusers and their wide net of associates. Had she not been caught up with these people, she would have undoubtedly been alive today. The honour killing tag was completely inappropriate.

An emergency meeting was called that afternoon at Rotherham Borough Council's offices at Norfolk House. I attended with Simon Perry. Howard Woolfenden chaired the meeting, along with Laura's social worker and various other safeguarding people and police officers. There were a lot of grim faces around that table. As I sat there, waiting for the meeting to begin, I received a text from Sarah, who worked for Risky Business. She was forwarding a text she'd just received from Laura's mum.

'Please don't let what's happened to my baby happen to any of these other girls,' it said. 'Someone has to stop this.'

All the information we'd gathered in Laura's case file came out, and there was head-shaking all round. *How have we got to where we are?* I thought. *All this time trying to get someone to listen to what these girls are saying and finally one of our kids is dead. Not injured. Dead.*

Laura's social worker was crying through the whole meeting and when it was her turn to speak she could barely get her words out. She kept going over mistakes apparently made with Laura – things that had gone wrong when she'd moved house, when she'd had the baby. I felt for her, as she seemed to be blaming herself for everything. But it wasn't her fault. *It's this town*, I thought. *This council, this police force. They've done nothing to protect Rotherham's children. Why?* The thought echoed all round my head for the rest of the afternoon.

More information about Laura's death began to seep out that day. It appeared she'd been stabbed dozens of times in a frenzied attack and there were defence marks on her arms. She had then been thrown into the canal. We heard later that she was still alive when she entered the water and the stab wounds to her head had been inflicted to keep her under.

I was absolutely shocked and appalled by what had happened to Laura but in view of the violence and threats our girls were subjected to, I can't say I was really surprised. I'd been saying for years that it wasn't a case of 'never', but 'when'. And now that 'when' moment had finally arrived.

The day after this first meeting we were called in again. This time, Jill Holbert was there. The meeting was to decide whether there should be a Serious Case Review (SCR), which would look at everything that had happened with regard to Laura, and whether she'd been failed by any department or service involved with her. Inevitably, a SCR was found to be the only way that any such failings could be dealt with and so it was referred for approval. As we left the meeting Jill Holbert sidled up to me.

'Jayne,' she said, 'are you all right?'

'No, I'm not all right,' I said. 'One of our girls is dead. How can I be all right?'

She paused for a moment. 'You know,' she said, 'I never asked you to close Laura's case.'

I couldn't believe what I was hearing. 'Yes, you did,' I said. 'That's exactly what you said.'

'No,' she said, brazen-faced, 'I never asked you to close them all.'

'You did,' I replied, feeling myself flushing in anger, 'and I've got the email to prove it.'

'You might have misunderstood,' she said.

'I don't think so. You said that the girls, including Laura, didn't need us any more because they'd all got social workers. And you closed all the Czar cases to us.

In fact, straight afterwards I emailed Chris Brodhurst-Brown to tell her how upset I was about it.'

She turned on her heel and walked away. Nice try, Jill. When the Serious Case Review was approved, I cooperated by sending in everything we'd ever had on Laura – more than a hundred separate pieces of information. In fact, I received an email from a police officer in the murder investigation team who'd seen all this and commented to me what great information it was. This is what it said:

> Hi Jayne,
>
> I have just finished reviewing the files you provided and must say how impressed I was at the amount of information contained within them.
>
> Should this case have remained unsolved, I am sure that the information contained within your files would have provided us with positive leads to identifying the perpetrators.

Meanwhile, the girls involved in Operation Czar were so traumatized by being removed from their homes without warning that they refused to speak to the police. The whole operation was a fiasco and was abandoned. Operation Chard was also a failure. And still the abuse, violence and intimidation continued unabated.

14

The Operation Central trial began in the late autumn of 2010 at Sheffield Crown Court. Four young girls, aged between thirteen and sixteen, were pitted against eight alleged abusers who faced sexual offence charges including oral, vaginal and anal rape, among others. Each defendant had his own barrister and there was just one prosecuting barrister for all four of the girls. It would be a long trial.

We made sure our young people were supported throughout, but when we saw the lawyers crammed into their seats and the public gallery full of defendants' families our hearts sank. Granted, our girls would be giving evidence via video link but, even so, from the beginning we felt there was something of the soap opera about the whole thing.

Charlie was the first girl to take the stand. And for eight whole days she was cross-examined by the defending barristers who tried every trick in the book – legally, of course – to undermine her credibility in front of the jury. At one point there was a suggestion that Charlie was a liar, based on something written in a school report some years previously. And even more problematic was the fact that Charlie had also previously made an allegation against her stepfather, which was found to be untrue. This would have been a gift for the defence had we not been able to prove that it was her perpetrators who put her up to it in the first place. Thank God I kept comprehensive notes, which showed clearly that when Charlie's troubles were beginning and she started to go missing for hours at a time, her mum spent ages scouring the streets looking for her. Not understanding that she was being groomed by her new friends, Charlie was angry at these apparent restrictions. So her abusers told her to accuse her stepdad, so that she could 'go into a kids' home and come out whenever she wanted'. And that's what she did. Luckily we'd made clear notes to say that we didn't believe her, and that she'd been coerced into saying it.

The case was particularly difficult for Charlie as she had started to build a good relationship with her mum after years of turmoil. Because her mum was a witness, however, the two weren't allowed to communicate freely until both had given evidence. One phone call a night was permitted, with a member of staff present. And in the end, Charlie's mother wasn't even called to the stand.

I felt particularly sorry for Heather as she gave her evidence. During the time she'd been in foster care, away from Rotherham, she'd thrived. She'd started at college, had made a group of new friends and was doing really well. The day before she was due to tell the court what had happened to her, I took her to see the little room in which she would submit her evidence via video link. I wanted her to feel confident about everything, not to be nervous or intimidated, as so many child witnesses are in our country's imposing courtrooms.

'Are you OK?' I asked as she took in her surroundings.

'I'll show them,' she replied. She was made up to the nines and looked older than she was. 'I'm gonna prove to them lot that I'm not scared of them any more. I'm tougher now and they don't frighten me.'

Having known her for a while, I admired her attitude and the way she was determined to turn her life round after years of horror. Sadly, the jury didn't view it that way. All they saw when she took the stand was a hard-faced teenager who seemed to have a 'couldn't-care-less' attitude, leading them to acquit one of the accused on charges of raping her. If only they'd been there when she came back into the witness room after giving her evidence. Then they would've seen a sobbing, shaking little girl who collapsed into my arms and was subsequently sick all over the place. So much for her 'tough' demeanour. Heather had been sexually exploited from the age of just nine and this had been her chance to grab a small bit of justice for herself.

As I've said, the ripple effect of CSE tears into families like the aftershock of a bomb going off. And not just among the victims' families either. One of my abiding memories of that case is seeing an elderly Asian man in traditional clothing try to haul himself up the Crown Court steps, propped up by two walking sticks. He couldn't get his balance and people were walking around him. I was heading to my car to fetch something, so I doubled back and went up to him.

'Are you all right?' I said. 'I'll help you back down, if you want, and show you where the lift is?'

He nodded, but as I put my hand on his elbow a young woman appeared at my side.

'Thanks for helping,' she said. 'It's OK, I'll take over. It's my granddad. He struggles with walking.'

Now, I wasn't allowed to enter court because I was supporting witnesses, but I was told that this elderly man attended the courtroom every day and cried bitterly throughout the proceedings, especially when the evidence against the accused was heard in full. I presume he was either related in some way to those in the dock or was a community elder, but the point is, he should never have had to go through any of this, in the same way as the families of the girls didn't deserve what happened to them. I've always said, and I say it today, that this was never about religion. There is no religion in the world which supports child abuse. There are cultural elements involved, yes, but surely there is an opportunity to bring two damaged communities together to work to make sure such abuse never happens again? Ironically, in my present job I meet a lot of Asians who understand that it's not a race issue and are furious that the authorities never informed them of what was going on because of the fear that it would lead to community tensions.

And it has certainly done that. The publicity surrounding white girls and Asian abusers around the time of Central prompted a few unwelcome contacts with the BNP. Somehow they wormed their way into a victim's family by offering them help and support, and trumpeting this on their website. Then they started to ring us on a weekly basis, trying to find out what was going on. They used the tactic of claiming they were 'journalists', though they were always careful not to say which paper they were from. The first time they rang, I admit, they caught me on the hop . . .

'I wonder if you can tell me if it's true that you have a problem with Asian men grooming white girls in Rotherham?' said a voice when I answered the phone.

'What?'

The caller repeated his question.

'Look,' I said, 'if you're looking for a comment about Risky Business you'll have to go through the council's press office.'

'Oh, right,' he said. 'So when I print tomorrow that the manager of Risky Business refuses to admit there's a grooming problem and won't say if it's Asian men involved, that's OK, is it?'

'I didn't say that,' I said, shocked.

'So what are you saying? Are you refusing to admit there's a problem? Is there a problem or isn't there?'

'I'm saying that I'm refusing to talk to you,' I said, and put down the phone.

We soon got wind that it was the BNP, and they'd ring weekly, trying to wheedle information out of us. Of course there was a grooming problem in Rotherham involving Asian men and white girls – you'd have to be blind not to see that – but there was no way I was going to contribute to any political point-scoring on behalf of the BNP or the EDL. Sadly, from then onwards, and still today, Rotherham was the focus for far-right marches and rallies in the town centre, with people coming from all over the country to wave flags, make speeches and generally be unpleasant. So much for the council not wanting to 'damage community relations'. By their actions – or, more accurately, inaction – Rotherham has become a byword across the UK and internationally for troubled race relations.

The trial lasted eight weeks in all and, by the end of it, five men were found guilty and three acquitted. Two brothers got fifteen years between them and their cousin was given nine years for rape. One of our girls had been abused by all five of those convicted. Those who were acquitted started crying in the dock and were joined in their crocodile tears by a couple of the convicted men. The trial judge, Peter Kelson QC, wasn't impressed.

'I've listened to the backdrop of some of you sobbing – I have to say your weeping cuts no ice with me,' he said.

'All five of you were convicted of offences of sexual activity with a child. The clue is in the title, a child. This legislation concerns itself with child protection, perhaps to some extent from themselves, but particularly protection from sexual predators, like I find all five of you to be.'

We were pleased, all of us, but there was no great celebration or sense of relief. Those four girls had had to relive some of the most harrowing moments of their lives and, as one girl described it to me, felt as though their souls 'had been sucked out'. Sadly, sexual abuse is for life, and while some people deal with it more positively than others, it's always there in the background, a dark force that casts a long shadow across their lives and those of the people around them.

Ironically, it was in 2010, just after Operation Central, that I found out we'd received a police Commander's Award for contributing to its success. There was a presentation evening so I went along with Sarah, one of Risky Business's workers. A couple of Rupert Chang's officers were there, along with others.

The award citation read:

You are commended for your contribution to Operation Central. This was a very complex and sensitive multi-agency investigation into the sexual exploitation of young females within the Rotherham area. The operation has now become a beacon of proactive multi-agency working and the impact of the positive action against these groups of males has permanently transformed the lives of victims and improved the safety of young girls within the community.

So, basically, we got the award for sharing information; the kind of information we'd been trying to share with the police for years, and which had been disappearing down a bottomless rabbit hole marked 'Box Five'. Let's not forget that it was only by accident that information we were sharing about abuse in Clifton Park fell into hands that would do something about it. And that for years previously, we'd laboured under an unspoken police attitude that our girls sought trouble and were responsible for what happened to them as a result. Was I bitter? Not really, just saddened that so many girls could've also played a part in bringing their perpetrators to justice had everyone acted as they should've done. And also angry because, inexplicably, the next step had been to remove Risky Business altogether from Operation Czar. So while I was pleased to receive the Commander's Award, I have to confess that these days it sits under my bed, gathering dust.

15

In the spring of 2011, some months after the Operation Central trial, Rotherham Borough Council decided to hold a 'Lessons Learned' event at the Magna Centre to follow up on the successes of Central. So all the usual suspects came along – police officers, council officers, representatives from the various agencies involved in Central and other UK-wide agencies, plus Malcolm Stevens, author of the 'Lessons Learned' report. Other speakers included Dave Walker, from the PPU, and Joyce Thacker. I wasn't asked to speak, which I found odd. Evidently, Risky Business had played a pivotal part in Operation Central. If it hadn't been for us constantly knocking on doors, hoping someone would listen, it might never have happened at all. I wasn't the only one to wonder why we'd not been invited to say something, so I asked Christine Brodhurst-Brown. She didn't know either. However, we were asked if we would contribute something from the perspective of one of our girls so I chose Heather, the sixteen-year-old who'd been so brave in court.

Heather sat down and taped her story, part of which

we've already heard in chapter 12. Here is the rest, which begins just after I picked her up from the women's refuge in Nottingham:

I was told I could go back to Safe At Last, but we had to leave the refuge through a back door. Jayne took me down the motorway and met with Rupert and Paul and I felt safe. They then took me to Safe At Last. That night, I managed to get the first proper night's sleep I'd had in two weeks.

The next morning Jayne said social services couldn't find me anywhere to live so I'd have to stay where I was. I felt worthless. I rang my social worker but she said she had other children to worry about and I was now an adult. I stayed at Safe At Last for a few days then I was taken to a foster carer's house where I've lived ever since. My life has been up and down but I feel I have achieved so much. I went to college and did an NVQ in Health and Social Care and I passed. It wasn't easy; I had no friends and I couldn't tell anyone why I was there. Following this I joined Cat Zero (an organization delivering projects for young people) and learned plumbing, welding, team-building and even sailing.

I was asked if I wanted to sail in a clipper in a round the world yacht race. I spent six months doing intensive training and I flew to San Francisco the following year to join the boat. I spent the next four weeks sailing in Panama and on to Jamaica. I felt at this time this couldn't be happening to me, it was wonderful. Why did I deserve it? I came back and was awarded the Young Ambassador of the Year Award. This made me worried because I had no one to go with. I asked Jayne if she would come and she said yes. She found some money to get me a new dress, shoes and have my hair done.

Just when I thought everything in my life was going well, I was told I only had a 50 per cent chance of ever being a mum because I was damaged. Then I went to court and gave evidence. I was sick after being cross-examined; the tears, the nightmares and checking in the wardrobe, and believing I had done the wrong thing, wondering if he'd never really meant to hurt me.

I worked with Risky Business for three years and last year I came to understand that I was groomed and abused. No one told me how to get over him. I loved him so much and I thought he loved me. I still feel lonely. My life is OK now. I work full-time as a carer and I spent my first wage on a scooter. I still have no friends and don't socialize but I'm happy and I understand that I never asked for this to happen. None of it was my fault. When Jayne asked me to do this, she asked me to explain how it could've been different. So I say to you: look for the child who is unhappy, doesn't want to be at school, goes out an awful lot, could be driving round in cars, has more than one mobile and has an attitude and a lot of 'boyfriends' and ask yourself – is this me?

Heather's story had a powerful effect on every person who sat in that conference room. Some were in tears. After the tape had finished there was praise for Heather and also for Risky Business. In fact, every speaker that day congratulated us for the work we'd done. Simon Perry took me round the room, introducing me to everyone (which was slightly odd, as I knew most of them), and the positive reception we got made us feel very good about the work we'd been doing, the uphill struggles we'd been through and the results achieved.

Anyone who worked in local government in the UK at that time doesn't need reminding that all this congratulatory stuff was taking place against a background of severe cuts imposed by the coalition government in the middle of a recession. Jobs were going left, right and centre and everyone worried if they would be next, including us. The Youth Service was being hit hard and managers at my level were encouraged to look around for other jobs within the service. I didn't really want to go back to managing youth clubs; neither did I want to become unemployed. I'd asked Christine Brodhurst-Brown if I needed to apply for any of these and she'd said 'no'. The closing date went by, I didn't receive the jobs information pack that other managers were getting and I felt there was some kind of safety net for Risky Business – though I wasn't taking anything for granted.

In fact, after all the speakers had had their turn there was a question-and-answer session, during which someone asked Joyce Thacker whether, due to all the budget cuts and constraints, Risky Business was safe.

'In this current climate I cannot stand here and say that anyone's job is 100 per cent safe,' she said, looking directly at me, 'but I can say that for the next two years there are no issues with Risky Business.'

Well, you can't get much clearer than that, especially in front of 300 people. As far as we were concerned it was a great way to round off what had been a good day for Risky Business.

The following day, a Friday, Simon Perry strode into our office and came over to my desk.

'Have you got a minute, please?' he said. Then he asked me where Christine Brodhurst-Brown was.

'She's interviewing,' I said.

Christine had advertised the new youth work manager posts and was right in the middle of grilling the candidates.

'Well, she'll have to come out,' Simon said. 'I'll meet you both in the conference room in a couple of minutes, OK?'

And with that, he asked the receptionist to bring Christine out of the interview room before heading off down the corridor. I followed him, wondering what it could be this time. Surely we weren't in trouble again, not after the previous day's congratulations?

Simon took a seat and motioned me to sit down with a wave of his hand. A minute or so later, Christine joined us. She'd had a minor accident and was walking with a stick, and she didn't look best pleased to be brought out of an interview.

Simon leaned forward and looked directly at me.

'Right, Jayne,' he said, 'I've just come to tell you that you're fucked.'

I jumped in shock. 'What do you mean by that?' I said.

'As from today, Risky Business is no more. It's shut.'

'What?! Why? Are you telling me I've lost my job?'

'No, that's not what I'm telling you,' he said. 'As from Monday you'll be moving into Children's Social Care and you'll have a new manager, Claire Edgar. She'll be taking over the sexual exploitation team and you'll be working under her.'

I couldn't believe what I was hearing. Surely Joyce Thacker had said we were safe? Or was that just a political answer? I asked Simon what we'd done to deserve this.

'Look, Jayne,' he said, 'someone has to take the fall for Laura Wilson's murder and I'm afraid that someone is Risky Business.'

Beside me, Christine started to cry. I could also feel the tears coming but there was no way I was going to start blubbing in front of Simon Perry. Still, I just couldn't reply. There was nothing to say to a comment like that. For years we'd worked tirelessly with Laura, as we'd done with all our girls, against the odds and with very little help or support from the council or the police. To be blamed for that child's death was sickening. Risky Business is the last organization in the world that would deliberately let down the young, vulnerable people it worked with. With those words, plus his opening comment, Simon Perry told me everything I ever needed to know about Rotherham Borough Council's attitude towards us.

'What if I don't want to go into Social Care?' I asked, looking him right in the eye. He replied that I could apply for one of the youth work jobs if I wanted.

'But Christine's already interviewing for them,' I said.

'Right, well, if you want to apply for one Christine will give you an application form, you can fill it in over the weekend and she'll interview you on Monday.'

With that, he got up and walked out with barely a goodbye, leaving Christine and me rooted to the spot in shock.

'I'm really sorry, Jayne,' she said. 'I'm so, so sorry. I can't believe he told you like that. If you want to put in an application then do, I'm sure it'll be OK.'

I didn't want to work in Children's Social Care. Neither did I want to manage youth clubs. I wanted to carry on helping the victims of sexual abuse. I wanted to see more abusers go to jail. If I left, what would happen to the girls?

'I think I need to go home, Chris,' I said, 'and just try to get my head around all this.'

I'd booked a week off anyway and Christine had no problems with me going early. As I left the conference room I saw two of the project workers in the corridor. Both were in floods of tears, which finally set me off crying. Simon had obviously informed them, in his ham-fisted way, of our fate.

In a daze, I left the office and went to pick up Samuel from school. Just as I got to the school gates my phone rang. I answered, and it was Claire Edgar.

She'd been in the job for about a year and it was a position I'd been asked to apply for, but had turned down. It was a job developed to oversee CSE issues from the Children's Social Care side, but I was keen to stay within the Youth Service. I felt I had more in-dependence that way. I definitely did not want to join social services. And yet, here I was, a year later, being co-opted against my will into some new team that would neutralize what we were doing completely.

Claire said she needed to see me. 'Simon has had a chat to me,' she added, 'and he's a bit worried that the way he told you what was going to happen wasn't very tactful. So I thought we should meet up today.'

I told her I was outside school, and about to pick up my son.

'Look, there's a McDonald's nearby,' she said. 'Why don't we meet there? I really do need to see you before you go off on holiday.'

Reluctantly, I agreed. Samuel could be kept amused for five minutes while we talked. She turned up and bought me a coffee before sitting down.

'I'm so sorry,' she said, 'I didn't know this would be happening. What are you going to do?'

'I don't know,' I said. 'I'm just in shock. I need time to think about it. I want to talk it over with my husband.'

'Look, Jayne,' she said in a soft voice, 'if you want to resign, that's fine. We will accept it.'

'Oh, don't worry,' I said, 'I won't be resigning.' *No bloody chance*, I thought. *They're not pushing me out before I'm ready to go.*

I thought it over and discussed it with Paul, but I knew what the decision would be. If we had to move into Children's Social Care to keep our work going, that's what we'd do. Luckily they weren't talking about making anyone redundant so on the Monday I came back to work we all moved into our new domain.

An email went round to all Social Care staff from Christine Brodhurst-Brown. It said:

The (CYPS) Children's and Young Persons' Service are currently forming a Multi-Agency Team which will work across all aspects of Sexual Exploitation. The team will consist of police officers, social workers and also staff from the Risky Business team. The team will be managed by Claire Edgar and will be situated in Safeguarding and Corporate Parenting and will be part of Howard Woolfenden's team.

This is a major step forward in terms of the protection of young people from Sexual Exploitation and is a direct outcome of all the years of hard work that Jayne Senior and her team have undertaken.

This is to take immediate effect.

I am sure that you would wish to join me in wishing Jayne and her team all the best for the future.

Regards,

CBB

Well, we certainly needed 'all the best' for the future. I've had many, many frustrating moments – usually provoked by the council, the police, or both – during my time working in this field, but the times I've felt depressed and defeated are very few indeed. Whatever was thrown at me I knew I could take because I had a responsibility to the young people I was trying to help. But the time I spent in Children's Social Care was the most awful year I've ever had in any job. Claire Edgar made absolutely sure we knew who was boss and that, from now on, we would be doing things her way. No longer would we be submitting intelligence to the police. Her social workers would do that. We could continue to meet the girls, but not as regularly. I was stopped from delivering training and wasn't allowed to attend any meetings. They would be Claire's responsibility now. This is despite the fact that she'd told me she'd never worked with young people involved in CSE. Her background was in dealing with drug abuse, then adults with brain injuries.

Things went from bad to worse. If we did venture out of the office, Claire demanded to know where we'd been, how long we'd been out for, whether we'd filled in our time sheets. Far from creating a multi-agency CSE team, in which social workers and youth workers cooperated to protect children, it seemed that a social work model was simply being imposed on us. As I've said, we were never social workers. That wasn't how we operated. We didn't go in there, all guns blazing. We employed a more subtle approach, gaining the trust of the victims and allowing them to speak out in their own time, and in their own way. To no longer be able to do this effectively was a disaster as far as I was concerned.

Youth workers we'd known for years were horrified by what was happening to us. It affected me personally, in that the stress of the situation exacerbated bowel problems that I'd had for many years. I'd seen a consultant in Leeds who suggested I needed surgery. Claire even made attending medical appointments difficult for me, and would request meetings to discuss them. There were always issues around taking annual leave and lieu days and I was forever making calls to the head of the

HR department, trying to beg a bit of time off so that I could get myself sorted out.

Then the difficulties began at a higher level. One afternoon Claire told me that Howard Woolfenden wanted to see me. He was the senior manager who'd paid a visit to Risky Business during Operation Central and had seemed so enthusiastic – he'd spent a significant amount of time during that visit looking at our filing systems and the database and had been very impressed. With Claire, I went over to Norfolk House, where his office was. Howard waved his hand at a chair in front of him, where I sat feeling like a naughty child.

He began to talk about a girl who was working in my team at that time, and had been a victim of CSE herself. With the support of her parents she'd turned her life around and was in a normal, consensual relationship with an Asian guy.

'I've heard that she's still seeing one of her abusers,' Howard said, 'and she's still working on the project.'

I was outraged. 'How dare you?' I said. 'That guy is her boyfriend and has had nothing to do with any of this. If her dad knew you'd made a remark like that he'd hit the roof.'

The pair of them sat there and said nothing. No apology, not a word. A few weeks later I was called in again to see Howard Woolfenden, and this time he accused me of racism during a training session I'd been involved in. I'd simply spoken about the fact that the overwhelming majority of perpetrators were Asian, and that there was a problem with CSE within our Asian community. If the overwhelming majority of abusers were white, I'd have said that too.

He was also annoyed that when we'd previously shared our intelligence with the police, we'd indicated which ethnic background the perpetrator had come from. As I've said earlier, I thought that might be useful for the police to know, but Howard said the council had strict policies about the declaration of ethnicity, which I was to follow. On this occasion, he said, he'd let me off the hook . . .

Claire eventually moved her desk next to mine, which made me feel even more uncomfortable. She could hear and see everything I was doing, to the extent that if my electronic diary showed that I had a meeting, she would contact the person who'd arranged it, telling them that because she was now manager, she'd be coming instead. Life under the new regime became more and more difficult.

There was one occasion where I definitely did need to attend a meeting in person, and that was with Heather, the Operation Central victim who had just moved back to the area after living away for her own safety. The girl was struggling to adjust to life back in Rotherham, and the whole experience of being in the area again was giving her nightmares. In addition, word had got round that she was back and she'd seen various men who'd abused her hanging about her street. She'd also had her windows splattered with eggs. I tried to get her more support from another project which worked with abused women; not that I wanted to close the case on her, as far as we were concerned, but because I thought she needed intensive and specialized support. A meeting was arranged at Heather's house, and Claire Edgar agreed I could attend.

Heather was quite shy and if she wanted me to say something on her behalf she'd usually write it down. Once I'd broken the ice, she often found the courage to say something herself. So we were gathered in her front room: myself, a social worker, someone from the abused women's project and Heather herself. We were about to begin when there was a knock at the door and in came Claire Edgar. She sat on the floor and there was the usual round of introductions.

'My name's Claire Edgar,' she said when it was her turn, 'and I'm the manager of the Risky Business project.'

Well, I was shocked by that one, as it had seemed in the previous few months that the Risky Business brand had become a bit toxic, and it was barely referred to, if at all. But I wasn't prepared for what she would say next: that because Heather was eighteen she was now closing her case as far as Risky Business was concerned and it would be passed on to the voluntary sector.

Heather stared at the carpet and never said a word. I

was mortified. I promised each and every one of my girls that whenever they were ready to dump me, I would go, but until that day I would be around to help and support them. Now that promise had been broken for me, and in front of one of the girls who had done so much to bring child abusers to justice.

How I ever mended that relationship, I don't know. At the end of the meeting Heather screamed at me, telling me that I'd promised I'd always be there for her, and that I'd lied. I calmed the situation down but I felt deeply betrayed. It seemed that Claire's need to hurt and humiliate me was more important than the emotional damage such a statement would inflict on this girl.

It had got to the point where I wondered what my future would be in the council, and how I could continue to operate effectively. There was a telling and unexpected meeting out of work which confirmed how I was feeling. I'd had the afternoon off to take Samuel to the doctor and afterwards we nipped into Boots to pick up the prescription. As I collected it and made towards the exit there was a tap on my shoulder. It was Simon Perry.

I'd heard he was leaving, the victim of a restructure of senior managerial positions.

'Hello,' he said, 'what are you doing here? Not in work?'

As usual, I felt like the naughty schoolgirl. I told him

I'd taken Samuel to the doctor, and that I'd had permission to take some time off.

'I heard a rumour you're leaving,' I added.

'Yeah, it's the worst kept secret in Rotherham,' he said. 'Everyone seems to know I've lost my job.' Then he looked right at me.

'Let me give you some advice,' he said. 'The thing about Rotherham Council is that if your face doesn't fit they'll have you out – and believe me, Jayne, your face fits nowhere.'

Thanks, Simon, I thought, *that's really cheered me up*. But he was right. If I'd suspected it in the past, now I knew it was the truth.

16

Inevitably, Risky Business and its new bosses were on collision course for conflict and perhaps it is no surprise that it was triggered by the aftermath of Laura Wilson's murder. In early 2011 a panel had met to compile a Serious Case Review (SCR) into her death, as evidently there were some tough questions to be asked.

As ever, I submitted all the information I had collected on Laura's contact with Risky Business from 2004; the times we'd seen her, what we'd said, what we'd done, who we'd referred her to. The whole thing makes for upsetting reading and is the chronology of a troubled, damaged life that was to end in such a brutal way. Below are just a few extracts from across those years:

> Social worker informed project [Risky Business] that Laura and other young women have been forced to perform sex acts on a fifteen-year-old male through threats of violence. Laura now self-harming, also informed us that police are investigating the incident . . .

1–1 contact visit to cinema, very detached and without emotion today . . .

Referral to project re. missing from home, local male sexual assault on Laura, sexual favours to males in local takeaway for alcohol . . .

1–1 contact visit to Meadowhall to see lights. Laura very depressed today with situation at home . . .

Perpetrator had pointed a gun at the stomach of Laura and asked 'can I shoot your face?' [to unborn baby] . . .

Telephone call to South Yorkshire Police discussed we have serious concerns re. Laura missing . . .

Body found in canal.

I thought what we had was a very comprehensive and honest assessment which showed the level of contact with Laura and how we'd tried to help her on so many occasions.

The SCR was due to be published in May 2012 and I went into work early on the day it would be released so I could read it on the council's website. On a number of occasions I'd asked if I might look at it before it went out, but was refused every time. So I arrived at my desk to find Claire Edgar already in.

'Morning,' I said, 'you're in early.'

'Yes,' she replied. 'You know the SCR is being published today? Well, Joyce Thacker has asked that I sit with you while you read it.'

That's nice of Joyce, I thought. *She must know how upset I'll be.* It was very difficult to think about Laura's murder without getting upset. I knew I couldn't have stopped it happening but the thought of her death, and the baby she left behind, disturbed me nonetheless (as it did for everyone involved). So, with Claire by my side, I opened up the report on screen and began to read.

At first I was confused. Paragraph after paragraph was blacked out – redacted, to use the official term – so there seemed to be an awful lot of detail missing. Laura herself was referred to as 'Child S' and we appeared to be 'Project 1'. No one involved in her case from the council side was referred to by name.

As I read on, a cold chill crawled up my spine and I began to feel sick. It appeared that Risky Business was being hammered – heavily criticized for its involvement with Laura and apparent lack of care in her case. It seemed that all the information I'd sent them had been completely ignored. Instead, a very different version of events was staring me in the face. I started to cry.

'None of this is true, Claire,' I said. 'It just didn't happen this way. It's a pack of lies.'

'No, it isn't,' she replied. 'You didn't share information on the risks that Laura faced.'

'Of course we did!' I said. There was a part of the report which said that Laura had not given us the name of the father of her baby. It was complete rubbish. Not only did she share it with us, we passed it on to the police and a senior council manager.

Then there was this:

> There is evidence from [Child S's] behaviour that she did get involved in sexual exploitation, including the facts that she was vulnerable and subsequently became pregnant at 16 years of age. There were health and youth and targeted agencies, who had specialist knowledge of working with vulnerable children, involved with Child S but they were not able to encourage her to work with them.

It was nonsense. Of course Laura worked with us! How else would we have known her?

> The agencies involved in the care of Child S needed to intervene earlier.

Again, untrue. We did a dual referral when Laura was eleven years old to Social Care and the police. I knew I also had a report I sent again to a number of senior managers a couple of years later, raising our concerns.

I read on, coming across phrase after phrase that filled me with a mixture of disbelief, anger and upset.

> Child S was not really seen by any agency as the highly vulnerable child she was . . .

On a number of occasions there was a lack of effective record keeping which has created difficulty in evaluating the work of individual practitioners and agencies . . .

Child S was a vulnerable young woman whose needs were not fully assessed by any agency that had contact with her.

I felt our position and approach to Laura's case had been totally misrepresented. Simon Perry's words came back to me: 'Someone has to take the fall for Laura Wilson's murder . . .' Well, here it was, in black and white. It seemed the blame really was being pinned on Risky Business and, as manager, I was the one in the firing line. But I just couldn't accept that the untruths printed would be the official version.

'This is all rubbish,' I said to Claire, 'and I can prove it. I'll go and get Laura's file now and we'll go through it together.'

'No, you won't, Jayne,' she replied. 'It's not there any more. We've removed it for safety reasons.'

I sat at my desk and stared into the screen. At that moment, I knew I could no longer work for a council that not only denied children were being abused, but would castigate the very people who were trying to protect them and bring the issue into the public eye. I thought of Laura's mum. Much as I needed a job, could I really stay with an organization that was lying to a mother about her daughter's death in this report? I stood up and, without a word, headed straight for the loo, biting my lip the whole way. Once inside I sat in the cubicle and burst into tears. I was embarrassed and angry and hurt. To end a career this way, with fingers pointing at me from all directions, was personally humiliating. More than that, a mockery was being made of the work Risky Business had done and the girls who had so courageously told us their stories in the hope that their abuse would one day end.

As it happened the decision to leave was made for me, in part at least. Relations between myself and Claire Edgar were at rock bottom and I'd already put in complaints to HR about her attitude towards me. I'd asked for it to be logged but didn't particularly want to make a bigger issue of it than that. I just wanted to get on with my job while I looked around for another. It was then I spotted an advert on the council's website for a managerial post with a charity called Swinton Lock.

This was an activity and education centre for young people and adults by the side of the Sheffield and South Yorkshire canal near Mexborough. The work was around water-based and arts activities and although I didn't know a whole lot about either the job attracted me because it was working with young people and, being a charity, it had no links to Rotherham Borough Council.

I was mulling over applying for it, wondering

whether I'd be a good fit for it, when Claire Edgar informed me there would be a meeting later that day with all the Risky Business staff and HR. 'What now?' I wondered. So we were called in and told there would only be one position from now on at Risky Business, as social workers would be taking over most of our case-load. The job would be for a support worker on the preventative side, and we were all invited to apply for it. So this was it. I seized my chance.

'Well,' I said, 'I'd like to be considered for redun-dancy. At the end of the day I have a few health problems and I'll need major surgery, which could see me off work for a long while.'

These weren't words that came easily. Almost to the end I still held out hope that they would realize they'd made a mistake and change their mind about Risky Business. In the meantime, devastated though I was, I had to look after myself.

As I finished, another member of our staff spoke up. She too wanted to take redundancy. HR told us they'd have to take our request up higher, which they did, and a few days later we had the answer. It was a 'yes'. After all those years battling to protect children from abusers at large in the town I grew up and lived in, and con-stantly banging on doors to make someone, anyone, take seriously what was going on, it was finally time to go.

I applied for and got the job with Swinton Lock, and

officially left the council on 6 June 2012. I had an operation around this time and would officially start my new job in August. I felt awful at closing the door on the girls I'd worked with over the years, but I just couldn't stand another second at the council. Risky Business as we'd known it didn't exist any more. I expected their cases would now be closed and handed over to social services, and what would happen to them after that I couldn't say. I felt terrible for them, but was incredibly relieved to leave the council behind.

There was no great fanfare on the day I finished but a few weeks after I'd departed I received a letter with the Rotherham Borough Council postmark on it. Inside was a note and a cheque for £200. I'd forgotten that if you'd been at the council for more than twenty years (which, as a youth worker at first then a manager, I had been) you were given £200. The note was from Joyce Thacker, the one-time supporter of Risky Business, who'd gone strangely quiet in the days after we'd been co-opted into Social Care and hadn't said a word to me when I left. The note read:

Hi Jayne, I hope you are OK. Love, Joyce x

Interestingly, the day after I left a report had come out in *The Times* about Laura Wilson's Serious Case Review. I confess to not reading it – to be honest, *The Times* isn't the biggest-selling newspaper in Rotherham – but the redactions in the SCR had evidently caught the interest of the reporter, Andrew Norfolk. Although the council had attempted to use legal force to stop the paper revealing what was hidden under the thick black lines all over the report, they'd failed. And so the paper shared the news that Laura was 'one of several girls in Rotherham who were suspected of falling victim to sexual abuse by Asian men'. The paper also said that details of care professionals' involvement with her, including meetings that discussed issues around CSE, had been blocked out.

'The redactions, coupled with Rotherham's attempt to suppress the report in the courts,' Andrew Norfolk wrote, 'will lend support to the impression that child sex exploitation is not being confronted robustly by care professionals and local government.' He went on to say that, 'though the published report said that when Laura was 10, a young girl with whom she was very closely associated "is thought to have become involved in sexual exploitation", it concealed that this was "with particular reference to Asian men being involved".'

The Times had discovered that Rotherham tried to withhold the entire Laura Wilson report, a request rejected by the Department for Education. The then Education Secretary, Michael Gove, was told of differences between the review's published and unredacted versions. He saw both and 'made plain' to Alan Hazell, the SCR board chairman, his desire for the report to be published 'as fully as possible'.

When I eventually read the article, the paragraph below made me smile:

Mr Hazell said last week that 'at no stage did we have any evidence that Laura was involved in child sexual exploitation'. He suggested that her death was the story of 'a boyfriend from a relationship who callously murdered his girlfriend'. Yet the review's executive summary said: 'There is evidence from [Laura's] behaviour that she did get involved in sexual exploitation.'

Well, the SCR board either misread or mislaid her social worker's and Risky Business's reports because it was made very clear that Laura was being groomed for sexual exploitation. The unredacted report also makes this obvious.

I hadn't stopped caring – you can't just switch off so many years working with young, vulnerable people – but I was determined to make a life for myself outside of Rotherham Borough Council. I had wondered about pursuing a claim against the council for constructive dismissal but I quickly discounted this. I felt it was too late; besides, I had my redundancy and even though they'd made me feel like dirt I just wanted to walk away with my sanity and what was left of my pride intact. It wasn't much, but I hate getting angry and was determined not to let bitterness cloud everything I did. I wanted to enjoy my new job; not just for myself but for the sake of my family, who had supported me every step of the way and just wanted to see me happy. And Swinton Lock was making me very happy indeed.

When people ask me to describe it, I explain that Swinton Lock is a little piece of paradise and you don't know that until you visit it. Nobody goes there and doesn't feel that calming, supportive atmosphere. I applied for the job because I had managing skills and competency in drawing down funding, but when I went for the interview my first thought was, *What am I supposed to do with two boats?* – the canal barges that the charity uses as activity centres. Today, I still don't know anything about boats and don't particularly want to learn, but I see how being on the water or by the water has an almost miraculous calming effect on the young people and adults who come through our gates. We have young people who come as part of a re-engagement programme – they tend to be the ones who have been permanently excluded from school or are struggling to attend education for lots of reasons. They've given up on school, and vice versa – and I'm not judging schools here. If you have twenty-five kids in a class and one of them is refusing to let the others learn, there has to be something in place outside the classroom for that one person. So they come to us and we do lots of alternative

and therapeutic arts education, and it's very successful. In 2014 we had a 97 per cent attendance rate and
that's from young people whose school attendance is
appalling.

From day one I was determined to implement the
youth work model, in that we offered a wide range of
activities which led to young people gaining practical
skills but also finding the space in those activities to
open up about their lives and understand themselves on
a deeper level. It wasn't easy to start with because the
staff weren't youth workers, but gradually they understood what I was trying to bring to Swinton Lock and
gave me their full support. One of the things I've
changed is that when we do reports on young people
for schools – which cover everything from attendance
to whatever they're working on with us – no matter
what that person is going through, we look for the
positives first. We might imply a negative, but we make
sure it's based on making changes. So, for example, if
David comes in swearing his head off, we don't say
that; instead, we say that he is 'a well-mannered young
man who's keen to engage with others, we just need
to work on his choice of language occasionally when
around staff'. Believe me, our young people truly appreciate that. 'You haven't said owt horrible about me!'
they'll say. And because we're positive about them, the
positivity comes back to us and most times we do notice
a change in their behaviour.

We're not a secure unit and we make it clear to the young people that if they do go missing off site we are going to have to report that. Very rarely does anyone go missing, and I believe it's because of that open-door policy. If we locked the gates the challenge for the kids would be to climb over and escape.

When I first started I was keen for the young people to have some kind of CSE training, not only because they were vulnerable but because I'd seen how any young person, regardless of background, could get ensnared in grooming. Now that there was a dedicated CSE team in Rotherham I hoped they might come along and impart their knowledge, so I contacted Claire Edgar, my former boss. After several phone calls and emails she finally came out to see us and I explained that we needed a couple of youth workers to come along and raise CSE awareness among our young people. She said she'd send out someone – a former colleague of mine, as it happened – but no one ever turned up and I just thought, *Here we go again – no support for Rotherham's forgotten kids*. In response, I trained up a couple of my own staff in CSE issues and, as usual, we did it our way.

Back then, the name of Risky Business was mud, and mine wasn't far behind it. A councillor connected with Swinton Lock asked me what I'd done before and when I told him his reply was: 'I'd keep that quiet if I were you.'

Still, we've now got a management committee at Swinton Lock who are incredibly supportive of all the work we do there, and of me personally. They know who I am and what I've tried to do, and I've never had a word of criticism from any of them. Instead of trying to suppress me, which has been the story of the past sixteen years, they've encouraged me to speak out about my experiences. 'Take as much time as you need,' one of them said when news of the abuse finally started to come out, 'you can't let this go ignored any longer.'

Today, when I sit in my office overlooking the canal and see the young people gardening or working on the barges, I consider myself very lucky to be working here. Swinton Lock is a fine example of a supportive and caring working environment that every organization should aspire to. I owe them a lot.

17

Although I was settling into my new job and looked forward to a time when I no longer felt stressed or under siege, I was aware through friends within the council that girls were continuing to be abused in Rotherham with very little being done to prevent it.

A number of chance meetings with girls that I'd tried to help kept reminding me that real action needed to be taken. One afternoon I was due to attend a meeting on behalf of Swinton Lock when I bumped into Paula, a girl I'd known since she was a carefree eleven-year-old. I've already written about her grooming by various taxi drivers and her subsequent relationship with an Asian man who forced her to convert to Islam and became violent towards her. There was incident after incident involving Paula, but as hard as we tried we couldn't break the cycle of abuse she was suffering. It was difficult to even make her see that she was being abused – despite everything, she seemed in thrall to this man.

As I walked across the car park that summer's afternoon, en route to the meeting, I saw a young woman approaching me from the other direction. She was wearing full Muslim dress, including a hijab, and was pushing a pram. I took little notice of her until she was almost in front of me.

'Hiya, Jayne!' she said. 'How are you?' It was only then that I recognized her.

'Hello, you,' I said. 'Long time no see. How are you? I see you've got your hands full.'

I nodded at the pram and she smiled.

'I've got two now,' she said proudly.

I knew she'd had one child by her abuser and I wondered who might be the father of the other one. Maybe she guessed what I was thinking, because she immediately confirmed that she was still in a relationship with this man, describing him as her 'boyfriend'.

'So everything's OK?' I asked, wondering if her home life had improved at all.

'It's fine,' she said, 'as long as I'm a good Muslim and I do what is right. He respects me then.'

'And what if you do something wrong?' I asked.

'Well,' she replied, not looking me in the eye, 'you know how it is with blokes. You have your ups and downs like anyone else.'

I thought about her so-called 'boyfriend': the beatings he'd given her, the number of times he'd humiliated her in front of his friends, and the countless affairs with other women that she'd had to put up with. Her relationship was definitely more 'down' than 'up' and by the sound of things little had changed since I last saw her.

I looked at my watch. My meeting was in five minutes and I had to go. But I didn't want to just walk away with a 'see you around'.

'Listen,' I said, 'do you fancy going for a coffee some time? It'd be really nice to catch up properly. That's if you're not busy with anything else?'

Her face clouded over. 'Oh, I'm not sure, Jayne,' she said. 'I'd have to ask his permission. He's not very keen on me going out on my own, or meeting up with people. I don't know whether he'd allow it, to be honest . . .'

'Oh well,' I said. 'If you get the chance, give me a call. You've got my number.'

We smiled and said goodbye. As I walked to the meeting I recalled that when I had last seen Paula, she was about fifteen or sixteen and in a real mess. And even though she now seemed outwardly calm, it was clear to me that she was still very much trapped in the abuse that had started in her childhood. My heart sank when I thought about all the girls like Paula; the ones I'd tried to help and were still out there, caught up in their own turmoil and unable to break the awful cycle of abuse, past and present. *Something has to be done*, I thought. *Something really has to be done.*

Later that summer, I received a phone call from a family whose daughter had been the victim of sexual abuse. The girl's dad told me the family had recently been talking to a reporter from *The Times* who was trying to uncover issues around CSE in Rotherham. Andrew Norfolk had already published one story about the redacted report. He'd also been very involved in reporting the abuse scandals in Rochdale and other towns. Apparently he had good sources and interesting information about Rotherham, but a lot of it couldn't be corroborated.

'He's not some typical tabloid journalist, Jayne,' her dad said. 'He's been very helpful with us and I know he really wants to do something about this issue. I trust him. I was wondering if you would take some time to speak to him?'

I told him I'd think about it. To put it mildly, I was wary. So many times people from all walks of life had expressed interest in 'doing something' for the Rotherham victims, but so few had been as good as their word. What could possibly lead me to believe that this Andrew Norfolk would be any different? But he had been highly recommended by a man who knew how hard we'd worked to try to stop CSE from spreading in the town, and who also realized what barriers we faced in trying to do so.

I said that while I wouldn't give Andrew Norfolk my address, I would meet him at the girl's family home. 'That's fine,' said her dad. 'I think you'll find it very interesting.'

A week or so later I travelled out to where the girl's parents now lived to be met by them and a balding, grey-haired man wearing round John Lennon-style glasses who looked more like the headmaster of a primary school than a *Times* journalist. I liked Andrew Norfolk immediately. He was clearly taking the issues around CSE very seriously. He'd spent time sensitively interviewing the girl and her parents and seemed shocked by what he'd heard.

And yes, he seemed to have information that was obviously confidential and, in terms of what it revealed about CSE in Rotherham over the years, potential dynamite. I wondered where he'd obtained it, but didn't ask. It was very good information too – confidential police and council reports, research papers and case files – and chimed completely with what I knew of CSE in Rotherham, plus the council's and police's attitude towards victims in the years I'd worked at Risky Business. Tentatively, I'd taken along a copy of the 'Lessons Learned' review and a couple of reports, just to see how the ground lay and whether he would be shocked by what I had. I then told him I could produce the Serious Case Review and numerous other documents.

I must have spoken to him for a couple of hours and I answered his questions in complete honesty. Apart from the BNP, who were just pretending to be journalists, I'd never had dealings with the press and I was particularly nervous talking to someone from a national newspaper. But Andrew assured me that in no circumstances would he divulge his contacts and sources, and told me I wasn't the only one he was talking to. From that day to this he has been as good as his word.

I came away thinking there was a volcano about to erupt. And yet, in a way, I felt it was time that it did. As I've said, I held no bitterness. I just wanted to get on with my life and luckily I could. There were many others who could never step away from the trauma of abuse they'd suffered as children. If nothing else, an article in the national press might give them some vindication.

A couple of weeks later Andrew asked to meet me again. He told me that he was almost ready to put out his first story, and asked for more information. I showed him some of the reports I'd done in the very early stages of my time with Risky Business. He told me he'd been in touch with a couple of the victims and that they'd shared their stories with him. This, he said, would help back up what he was saying in his main article – that there was systematic sexual abuse of children in and around Rotherham that was known about but had never been publicly acknowledged. He said he'd text me the day before the story was due to break. He was as good as his word, and on 23 September 2012 I received that message from him.

The next day I diverted to a newsagent's on the way to Swinton Lock and picked up a copy of *The Times*. 'Police files reveal vast child protection scandal,' went the headline. I sat in my car and read the rest of the article. There it was, in black and white: for years, council staff and police officers had known the scale of the problem but had been worried about 'culturally sensitive' issues. One paragraph in particular, based on a police intelligence report in 2010, stood out for me:

'Possibly the most shocking threat is the existence of substantial and organised offender networks that groom and exploit victims on a worrying scale,' the report says. 'Practitioners throughout the force state there is a problem with networks of Asian offenders both locally and nationally. This was particularly stressed in Sheffield and even more so in Rotherham, where there appears to be a significant problem with networks of Asian males exploiting young white females.' Such groups are said to have trafficked South Yorkshire child victims 'to many other cities, including Bristol, Manchester, Birmingham, Bradford and Dover.'

Then there was this:

Another confidential 2010 report, for the Rotherham Safeguarding Children Board, noted that such crimes had 'cultural characteristics ... which are locally sensitive in terms of diversity'.

It said: 'There are sensitivities of ethnicity with potential to endanger the harmony of community relationships. Great care will be taken in drafting . . . this report to ensure that its findings embrace Rotherham's qualities of diversity. It is imperative that suggestions of a wider cultural phenomenon are avoided.'

I was staggered. I shouldn't have been, knowing what I'd known over all those years, but it was still extraordinary seeing it all in print. There had been times, in the past, when I'd thought I was going mad. Was it just me who was seeing all this abuse? And if it wasn't, why was nothing being done about it? Finally, after years of false hopes and new dawns that came to nothing, we had found someone who would expose the truth and allow the voices of victims to be heard. I drove into work and read the rest at my desk. Andrew had done a very good job indeed. I wondered what Rotherham Borough Council and the local police would be thinking at this moment . . .

The following day *The Times* published one girl's account of what happened to her – her grooming, the abuse and what she told the police. No one was ever charged in connection with any sexual offence against her, the article said.

I knew the story well but, again, it was still shocking to see it there in print. I left the paper on the desk and it was lying there when a Rotherham Borough councillor connected with Swinton Lock came in for a meeting. He pointed to the newspaper.

'I reckon she's only saying all that because she's been paid to,' he said.

'Oh, do you?' I replied. 'And after all she's gone through, would you begrudge her a bit of money? Anyway, I'm told *The Times* doesn't pay for stories.'

'Yeah, right,' he said. 'That's what they tell you.'

I smiled and said nothing. There was definitely no cheque waiting for me from *The Times*, and there never has been.

Andrew then followed up his original story with several others. There was one about calls for an independent public inquiry, and another asking Rotherham people what they thought about the whole thing. One of those asked replied: 'It's not news. This has been happening all over the country.' Well, yes, but try telling Rotherham Borough Council that . . . As a result of *The Times* reporting, David Crompton, South Yorkshire's Chief Constable, was in the news as well after he was asked to appear at the Home Affairs Select Committee in October 2012. He admitted that 'until recently' the force had not given a high enough priority to the sexual exploitation of children. Keith Vaz MP, the select committee chairman, said: 'You don't need forensic training to know that there's something wrong.'

One day during all this I went into the office to be told by the receptionist that 'a Joyce Thacker' had rung, and could I call her back? By this time, Joyce was the head of Children's Services in Rotherham, a very powerful position to hold. I hadn't heard from her since I received my £200 cheque and the note, so I decided to call her back. I'd no illusions as to the context of the conversation I was about to have.

'Oh, hello, Jayne,' she said, all bright and breezy, 'how are you?'

'Fine,' I said. 'Busy.'

After a bit of small talk about my family she moved on to the main event. 'I expect you've seen all these stories in *The Times*? Well, I was just wondering where the reporter might have got his information from?'

'No idea,' I replied.

It was partly the truth. I'd no idea who'd leaked the police intelligence document and I didn't want to know.

'Have you still got any information relating to Risky Business?' she said.

'I've still got my timesheets and annual leave forms. Why?'

'Well,' she said, sounding serious, 'you do know that whoever it is that has shared this information could be looking at a prison sentence? It was confidential information. It shouldn't have been leaked.'

I felt panic rising in my throat. I hadn't leaked the police report but I had helped Andrew with his questions, drip-fed him information and shared reports of my own with him, including all the police operations and the Laura Wilson saga. *I can't do right for doing bloody wrong*, I thought. I fobbed off Joyce, telling her I'd no idea who'd shared what with whom, and as soon as I put the phone down to her I picked it up and rang Andrew. He told me not to worry, and that he'd be over to see me as soon as he could.

I was worried. It wasn't about me being arrested or even sent to prison. If you're sent to jail for telling the truth, so be it. Hopefully the truth will come out one day and you'll be freed. But I was in a right state, and all because of the effect I knew it would have on our Samuel. I spoke to a solicitor friend who told me that because 'they' were embarrassed by what had been written about them in *The Times*, they might come for me publicly. I had visions of a squad of police banging on the door at 6 a.m., camera crews and photographers in tow, and taking me away in full view of Samuel. There was no way I could put him through that.

After a couple of nail-biting days Andrew came over. 'I've spoken to *The Times*' lawyers in London and if you are arrested they will represent you for free,' he said.

'But what I do suggest is that if you are arrested, go quietly, don't say a word and make sure you give me your husband's number before I leave today. If they come for you, Paul will ring me and I guarantee I'll have every newspaper in the country outside Rotherham police station within two hours. I'll tell them that the police have just arrested the Rotherham whistle-blower.'

I didn't know whether to feel relieved or start crying. There were no guarantees I wouldn't be arrested, but Andrew had promised to help me if I was. *Here we are*, I thought, *no new charges against any child abusers but there's talk of arresting the whistle-blower*. Typical, really.

So Christmas 2012 came and went without me having to eat my turkey in a prison cell. I did receive another phone call from Joyce Thacker, who asked if I knew that Andrew Norfolk was 'talking to someone' about files that had been removed from Risky Business, and did I know anything about that?

I didn't know who he was talking to (though I could take an educated guess), but I did know that Joyce was aware of the files that had gone missing in 2002 because it had been shared with her in a steering group meeting when she arrived at Risky Business. That said, it was a while ago, so I gave her the benefit of the doubt and told her what had happened. She wondered if I still had a copy of the report that Adele, the Home Office researcher, had compiled at the time, and whether I could give her Adele's contact details? I didn't have the full report, only chapter four, and no way was I about to give Adele's details to Rotherham Borough Council. I did say, however, that I would ring her and pass on the message that they wanted to get in touch.

Joyce told me that the council had employed a solicitor to examine how effective the council was at storing information, and asked would I meet him to offer any advice on how information at Risky Business was stored? I said I would, because I was too worried that if I said no they would think it was because I had something to hide. So he came out to meet me, taking notes as I told him about our database and how it worked. Then he went away and produced a statement which bore little resemblance to what I'd told him. I was fuming. I showed it to Adele's solicitor husband, who said it looked like 'a set-up'. I refused to sign the statement, despite some pressure, and therefore refused to agree to anything in it.

Much later, I discovered the council had spent a considerable amount of money engaging a firm of solicitors to look into who had shared information with Andrew Norfolk. I was only told after the event that this was at a cost of £20,000 and the solicitors were told from the outset the council believed it was me. And they were right. If I hadn't, where would we be now, given that so much information has gone missing from or been mislaid by the police and council? I'm glad I kept what I did, and I kept a lot.

18

By early 2013 the position at Swinton Lock was going well, I was enjoying working with young people again and I felt in a much better place. I didn't really know what else would happen as far as CSE in Rotherham was concerned. I guessed the council might recognize that there had been a serious issue, put their hands up to it and invest funds in supporting the victims. Maybe there would be some prosecutions too. Or maybe not. At least Andrew's articles had provided some recognition for what our girls had been through, and a strong sense that the wrongs done to them should be righted.

The start of the year was, however, a very tricky one for Rotherham Borough Council. In January Joyce Thacker and Martin Kimber, the council's chief executive, appeared in front of the Home Affairs Select Committee (HASC), again chaired by Keith Vaz MP. The HASC had evidently taken a very bleak view of Rotherham's attitude to the abuse of its children and had summoned Joyce and Martin to explain themselves.

During the hearing Joyce was asked by Keith Vaz to explain why the council 'has failed so dismally to deal with the issue of child grooming?' Joyce didn't agree that the failure was dismal. Keith Vaz then had this to say:

'Let us look at the evidence. We have received evidence that the council identified 600 victims during the previous ten years. In terms of what the police have done, only eight men have been arrested for offences against four children. In 2002 the Home Office research project found the fact that there were hundreds of girls who risked exploitation, and in 2010 an independent report described the localized grooming offences prosecuted in Rotherham as being at the top end of seriousness. We are talking about hundreds of victims, of vulnerable young girls who have not been protected because, at the end of the day, what people are looking for are prosecutions, are they not?'

Joyce replied that prosecutions were 'the icing on the cake' but that 'prevention' was the 'key issue' for her. Then why effectively neutralize the one organization in Rotherham that was doing preventative work with young people?

When asked why more people hadn't been prosecuted for CSE in Rotherham, Joyce pinned the blame squarely on the Crown Prosecution Service for not taking the Operation Czar evidence any further. I was annoyed by this; as far as I was concerned, Czar fell to pieces because social workers uprooted the girls from their homes and put them into care with barely any warning, leading them to refuse to speak to police. And if your key witnesses won't tell you anything, you haven't got much of a case.

Martin Kimber was questioned about the role taxi drivers played in CSE, i.e. picking up girls and driving them to places – takeaways, flats, parks, waste ground – where they would be abused. He was asked if the council had taken any action to remove the licences of those suspected of being involved.

To my astonishment, Martin Kimber said the council had only been aware this was 'one of the features of grooming' from 2010 onwards. If I'd been in that room I'd have laughed in his face at that remark. Almost from the beginning we were sharing information about Rotherham minicab firms and their drivers who were ferrying girls all over the place and sometimes actively taking part in their abuse. Martin Kimber said he didn't know how many firms had had their licences removed. The whole thing was becoming a joke.

Martin Kimber apologized for 'letting down' the girls and their families, and added that everyone was now trying to 'learn lessons'. In conclusion, Keith Vaz had this to say:

'The committee is very concerned about the record of Rotherham as far as child grooming is concerned. We are very disappointed to have heard some of the evidence we have today and previously about Rotherham. We look forward to receiving those internal reports and indeed we look forward to receiving your vision for the future as to how you are working now as opposed to five years ago, because we accept that some of this is historic, but what is not historic is the fact that last year there were absolutely no prosecutions in South York-shire for child grooming whereas, as Ms Blackwood [Nicola Blackwood MP] has said, there were 100 in Lancashire, and we can see good practice in terms of the evidence we have received so far. I will be writing to you again, and we may well be calling other witnesses from your council.'

Later that day, the HASC heard from one of the victims, who told the committee:

'The Asian community in Rotherham know this is happening, and they are absolutely appalled by it. They want these people out of their community like anybody else would. They do not want their children around these people. But I think also what has happened – and not just with the Asian community but with everybody in Rotherham who is a young person or in their early twenties – is it is spoken about and it is almost accepted in a way because it has been going on that long. It is just normal. It has been going on that long, and been left to go on, that we have normalized it. That is just part of growing up; that is what happens.'

The committee must have been appalled by that, as anyone would be. But would the HASC actually do anything to make sure the council was properly taken to task for the years of neglect? I did wonder, especially as time ticked by and everything appeared to go strangely quiet on the Rotherham front.

Then in June 2013 the HASC issued its report into child sexual abuse, focusing specifically on Rotherham and Rochdale. To put it mildly, they didn't seem at all impressed by what Joyce Thacker and Martin Kimber had told them. The report acknowledged there was a problem of grooming between Asian men and young white girls, which appeared to have been ignored, and stressed that those trying to prevent CSE should be able to raise concerns without being labelled 'racist'. The report also called for better support for CSE victims during court trials and criticized both councils for failing in their duty of care to victims.

Part of the report stated:

Both Rochdale and Rotherham Councils were inexcusably slow to realise that the widespread, organised sexual abuse of children, many of them in the care of the local authority, was taking place on their doorstep. This is due in large part to a woeful lack of professional curiosity or indifference, from the council Chief Executive who claims to have known nothing about the problem during his first decade in post, to the Director of Children's Services who saw prosecution of sex offenders as a desirable but ancillary goal, through the Local Safeguarding Children's

Board which tried to suppress criticisms in a Serious Case Review, to the individual practitioners who, in a chilling confirmation of the abusers' blackmail and threats, dismissed the victims – children as young as 12 – as 'prostitutes'.

That it took so long for anybody, at any level from the Chief Executive downward, to look at reports of young girls with multiple, middle-aged 'boyfriends', hanging around takeaways, drinking and taking drugs, and to think that it might be worth investigating further, is shocking.

Interestingly, Shaun Wright – who was, by this time, the Police and Crime Commissioner for South Yorkshire – was singled out for his 'reluctance to engage with victims'. Previously, he had been asked whether he had met with any victims of child sexual exploitation in his former role as Rotherham Council's Cabinet Member for Children and Young People's services between May 2005 and May 2010. His reply to them was: 'I do not believe it would have been appropriate for me to request to meet victims of child sexual exploitation as this would have been an invasion of the privacy of these vulnerable young victims.'

As we know, Shaun Wright *had* met victims of CSE. If he didn't remember it, they certainly did. Neither did he appear to have any idea that the abuse was 'on an industrial scale', despite the very detailed report about sixty-seven girls that I'd put together which was passed to him.

Now, he had his own reasons for denying he spoke to one of our girls, and for not realizing just how many kids were being abused under his nose, but to make such denials – especially where it concerns an abused child – is, to me, nothing short of wicked. After he made this denial in public, the girl contacted me.

'My story horrifies people when I tell them,' she said, 'and yet he says he can't remember any of it. Does that mean that no one else takes me seriously?'

How do you explain this to a girl who's been through so much? That she's told her story to someone she trusted, who then went on record to say that he couldn't remember a word of it. Victims of abuse deserve far better treatment than this. Even if I'd only ever met one abused child, that memory would stay with me forever.

The report added: 'Considering the lack of prosecutions for offences relating to child sexual exploitation in South Yorkshire, despite evidence that it is still occurring, we suggest Mr Wright may wish to take more of an interest in the victims then he has done previously.'

A whole list of recommendations was made for both councils and, ultimately, for any other council with a CSE problem on its patch. As expected, Andrew Norfolk covered this report and kept his eagle eye on what was going on in Rotherham, and other towns. We'd kept in touch after his first article was published and I continued to assist him where I could. He was particularly interested in the story about the raid on Risky Business's offices in 2003 and I was able to help him with my account of that, which I've detailed earlier in this book.

The summer went by and, apart from the occasional call or email from Andrew, plus a story about a Rotherham councillor, Jahangir Akhtar, resigning after claims (which he denied) that he acted as a go-between in the recovery of a pregnant fourteen-year-old from the clutches of a member of his family, there seemed to be another lull in the whole sorry saga until September, when the council commissioned an independent review of their handling of CSE issues. There was the usual expression of regret, this time from Roger Stone, the leader of the council, who apologized 'to those young people who have been let down by our safeguarding services, which prior to 2009 simply weren't good enough'.

I'll admit, I was very sceptical about this review. It claimed to be 'independent', but it had been commissioned and paid for by Rotherham Borough Council. I expected that it would be simply another stitch-up of Risky Business, another excuse to lay the blame elsewhere, even though the HASC had made it quite clear they would no longer tolerate such passing of the buck, and had urged Rotherham to take responsibility for its actions. Even so, I wanted nothing to do with it. I was done with the council and its workings. I'd just about got back a sense of self-worth and I didn't want to lose that again.

But, as ever, this thing just refused to go away. In the late autumn of that year I took a call from a friend of mine at the council – who must remain nameless – to talk about a potential CSE case we were both involved with; my friend from the council's side and me as manager of Swinton Lock. Then he asked if Alexis Jay had been in touch with me. This was the person who was leading the council-commissioned inquiry. I knew she was a senior social work inspector with an OBE, and an adviser to the Scottish government. Despite all that, I still had no intentions of meeting her.

'Look,' he said, 'I've met her once and I'm due to see her again. When I saw her, I asked if she was coming to see you. And she said she'd not been given your details.'

Well, there's a surprise, I thought.

'If you haven't seen her,' he continued, 'I'd suggest you do. Just saying . . . I'll pass on your details to her if you want.'

No, I didn't want. Not really. Why would I put myself up for a kicking all over again? But I trusted this friend. If he thought I should see her, then perhaps I should?

'Oh, all right then,' I said, wondering if this would ever leave my doorstep. 'I'll wait to hear from her – if she's interested.'

Well, she did get in touch and arranged to see me at Swinton Lock. She'd booked a thirty-minute slot with me and had arranged for a taxi to pick her up as soon as our appointment was over. Evidently, she was a very busy woman.

As I'd never met her and wasn't at all sure of her intentions I decided that I wouldn't offer up a lot of information voluntarily. If she asked me questions I would answer them factually and honestly. She seemed a nice enough person – but there again, so did many others who'd visited Risky Business over the years, promising the earth. She asked me questions and as I answered she took notes. I stuck to my strategy of not volunteering much until a point came when she asked me about the case of a fourteen-year-old who'd been doused in petrol. Her abuser had threatened to set her alight. This incident had also been mentioned in Angie Heal's 2003 report and was a tactic that had been used by abusers more than once since then.

'Is that really true?' she asked, open-mouthed.

I said it was, and went on to describe the case in a little more detail. The girl had been groomed by an older man who'd trafficked her out to other parts of Yorkshire. The authorities got involved and she was threatened and beaten by her abuser to stop her identifying him. Not only that, but one of her siblings was attacked and hospitalized with serious injuries and another was threatened and had to go into hiding.

Although she tried to break away from this man, he stalked her, poured petrol over her and told her she would be burned alive if she went to the police. Not that she would've done, as she and her family had by this time lost faith in the police to protect them. The poor girl then took several overdoses and by the time she was eighteen her family situation had broken down and she was homeless.

As I spoke I stared out of the window, trying to remember all the details. It was a terrible case, of course, but by no means unique. I'd heard many stories like this one. I came to the end and turned to look at Alexis Jay. Her face was a picture of horror and shock and emotion. I thought she was going to cry.

Then it struck me. *Whoever this woman is*, I thought, *deep down she truly cares about kids*. No one could look like that if they were simply employed to disprove all the evidence around them, or in it for the money. From that moment on I sensed that my fears of a witch-hunt against Risky Business might be unfounded.

Our thirty minutes was soon up but Alexis was reluctant to leave. However, the taxi was waiting outside. She asked if she could see me again in the presence of her assistant, Kathy Somers, who was reading documents connected with CSE going back years. I said it was fine, and we arranged another meeting.

Kathy, it turned out, was reading a lot of the Risky Business files which were being held in the council's headquarters for 'safekeeping'. When we met again, and on several occasions afterwards, I was asked to confirm details of or elaborate on some of the cases they were reading about in our files.

These included:

- A twelve-year-old who was groomed and had sex with five men. A case conference agreed that the girl should be placed on the child protection register, but a CID officer argued against the category of 'sexual abuse', saying that she had been '100 per cent consensual in every incident'.

- A fourteen-year-old who was being sexually exploited and whose social worker considered that the child's mother was not able to accept that what her daughter was going through was just 'part of her growing up'.

- A twelve-year-old girl who had been sexually assaulted and had indecent pictures taken of her. Her case was closed by a social-work manager because she wasn't considered to be at risk of sexual exploitation. Later she was found in a house with a group of older males and was arrested for being drunk and disorderly. None of the males were arrested.

- A thirteen-year-old who was raped, trafficked and threatened. Although Risky Business worked very

hard with her and her parents, a social-care
assessment said she 'placed herself at risk of
sexual exploitation and danger'.

These were just a few of the cases discussed with Alexis
Jay and on each occasion she never failed to express
shock and concern that this had been going on, seemingly unchecked, for so many years. I knew she was
speaking to a lot of people and I assisted her in finding
others who had left the council but might still be useful
for her to talk to.

I never put myself or Risky Business up to Alexis Jay
as plaster saints, and I never have to anyone. We are all
human and we all have our faults. I said that if Risky
Business warranted any constructive criticism, that was
fine. She asked me what sort of criticism I thought
Risky Business might deserve.

'Going over and above what we should've been
doing,' I said. 'It was never in my job description to
sit all night with pregnant girls giving birth to their
abusers' children, or to chase down girls who had taken
an overdose then phoned me to say goodbye. All that
was really someone else's job. So perhaps we stepped
out of that box and brought trouble on ourselves. But if
I had to do it all again, I wouldn't do it any differently.'

All the time we were together, Alexis Jay was wholly
professional in that she never let slip a word of what
her report would contain or who it might criticize. She

wouldn't tell me when it was coming out, but promised to drop me a line the day before. Somewhere around 25 August 2014 I heard that it was imminent so I rang Alexis Jay to see if she could confirm it.

'I can't tell you anything, Jayne,' she said, 'but if you wait until two p.m. tomorrow you'll find what you're looking for.'

'Oh God,' I said, feeling my stomach turn over and over.

'Like I said, I can't tell you anything,' she said, 'but I will say one thing – that you don't need to worry.'

And that's all she would say. I put down the phone and stared out of the window. *Perhaps we're not going to get the blame for this after all*, I thought. *Maybe we won't have to take the fall*. But how could I be sure? Reassurance or not, I was still in for a restless night ahead.

19

26 August 2014

I'd tried to access Rotherham Borough Council's website all afternoon, and every time I was greeted with an error message, something about 'abnormal traffic to the site'.

What would Alexis Jay say about us, and everyone else? So far she had played her cards close to her chest, and now I was about to punch my laptop in frustration. After an hour, an email came from Andrew Norfolk with the report attached, and at the same time I managed to get onto the council's intranet site. I double-clicked the PDF file and saw that it was a lengthy report, almost 150 pages long. I hoped I had enough printer paper and ink. I don't like reading documents on the screen and invariably I print everything out. Perhaps that's why I have copies of so many documents that would otherwise have gone missing. I turned the pages, past the title page and the preface which set out the reasons she'd been asked to write the report. Then I came to the Executive Summary, and read the first paragraph:

No one knows the true scale of child sexual exploitation (CSE) in Rotherham over the years. Our conservative estimate is that approximately 1,400 children were sexually exploited over the full inquiry period, from 1997 to 2013.

I read the paragraph again and again. Did it really say 1,400 children? I knew there were a lot, because of the reports I'd prepared and the referrals I'd handled but . . . 1,400? Really? In all the years I'd worked for Risky Business I'd never actually totted up the total. Now I did a quick calculation. *Yes*, I thought, *that figure is probably true. And yes, she's right to describe it as conservative.* Now, I believe the figure is closer to 1,700. Almost 2,000 children in a population of around 250,000 people. That is a very high, very unacceptable proportion of a town being abused and exploited.

I read on.

The collective failures of political and officer leadership were blatant . . . the scale and seriousness of the problem was underplayed by senior managers . . . the Police gave no priority to CSE . . . reports effectively suppressed . . . suggestions of cover-up . . . fear of being thought racist . . .

Oh my God. It was all there. Everything I'd seen and experienced over the years, everything I'd suspected or been told to shut up about. In the second paragraph, Alexis said she found it 'hard to describe the appalling nature of the abuse that child victims suffered', before telling of rape, trafficking, beatings, threats of violence and multiple sexual assaults. There was a direct reference to the story of the child soaked in petrol and threatened with burning alive that I'd told her about. So my gut feeling about Alexis Jay, formed from the moment I first met her, was right.

But what had she actually said about us? I flicked quickly to the section on Risky Business. We either stood or fell on the verdict of this four-page chapter.

> From 2007, the project worked effectively with the police on Operation Central. But it was too often seen as something of a nuisance, particularly by children's Social Care, and there were many tensions between the two. There were allegations of exaggeration and unprofessional approaches by the project, **none of which have been substantiated by the inquiry.**

Throughout my entire time with Risky Business I'd only cried twice – when we were told we had to 'take the fall' for Laura Wilson's murder and would be effectively closed down, and when I read Laura's Serious Case Review. Now, having read the final part of the last sentence in the paragraph above, the tears came again. We'd been exonerated, all of us who worked on that project and tried to make a difference to the lives of the girls we had contact with. There had been times when I'd doubted myself and the truth that was staring me in the face.

I read on. Alexis Jay went through the history of Risky Business and appeared to understand that we were not social workers, we did not 'prescribe or direct'. She identified how senior managers saw us as 'a group of youth workers treading on their territories' and what we presented was considered nothing more than 'professional gossip'. And yet, when she investigated our record-keeping, which had long been criticized, she found what we had to be 'detailed and well-kept'. I was particularly grateful to hear her say that because so much depends on the accuracy and general good order of records. If you don't do this you let everyone down, particularly those you're meant to be caring for.

The report said the council's management 'failed to understand and resolve' the difficulties between us and there had been a 'running flaw' in the development of child protection in relation to CSE. Furthermore, the reasons for the council effectively closing the project by bringing it into Social Care failed 'to recognize the quality of their work with individual children, and their distinctively different professional role, and entirely misses the point'.

As I finished reading the Risky Business section, I cried again. I was pleased that we'd come out of the report so well, but so sad and sorry that this had had to happen in the first place. If we'd been listened to and if we'd been taken seriously from the start, so many of these 1,400 victims would never have been victims at all. They'd have been normal little girls, allowed to live their lives in peace and without fear or threat. Risky Business had been badly let down, yes, but we were grown-ups. It was, and still remains, the victims of Rotherham who were failed most terribly and, crucially, the Jay Report recognized that right from the beginning.

Work finished and I drove home to find Paul watching the news on the TV in the kitchen.

'Have you seen this?' he said, shaking his head. 'Fourteen hundred? Is that right? I can't believe it's that many.'

'I've never added it up,' I said, 'but yeah, I think it probably is. And possibly more than that.'

Paul knows more than most about the story of trying and mostly failing to get anything done about Rotherham's abused children but even he was shocked by the scale of the problem and the systematic failures of both council and police. And then you think, 'How many others has this affected?' Families and communities pulled apart, innocent lives wrecked. To this day I wonder if Rotherham will ever recover from it.

We watched the rolling news bulletins for hours. Even as it looped and looped, I still couldn't believe what I was hearing, and the impact it was having. 'Horrific', 'appalling', 'disgusting', 'scandalous', 'shocking' – on and on it went, with commentators lining up to lambast the authorities for failing to protect the innocent. I was getting text after text and dozens of emails from girls I'd worked with over the years. They were in shock. Some rang up in tears, hysterical that the news had brought all their trauma back and angry because they now knew for sure that they weren't the only ones. Then, later on in the evening, I started to get emails and texts from journalists. 'Is this all true?' 'What are your feelings about it?' 'Can we have an interview?' 'What should happen next?'

I was so angry; deeply angry and upset. I felt absolutely winded. As I watched the story unfold on the news I burst into tears, thinking that maybe if I had done more or worked longer hours I could have helped more girls. But I also thought about the numbers we'd saved or steered away from abuse, either early in the grooming process or through the preventative work we did.

'I think you'd better turn that off and go to bed, Jayne,' Paul said. 'I've got a feeling that tomorrow will be bonkers.'

The following day, Paul's prediction came true. I could not have anticipated the level of media interest in this story, and Risky Business's part in it. I'm not exaggerating, and certainly not blowing my own trumpet, when I say that every media organization in this country and a whole lot of others from abroad wanted to interview me. There were phone calls, texts, knocks on the door. I answered them all, and as politely as I could I said that I wouldn't be making any statement that day. I hadn't had any media training and I could hardly expect Rotherham Borough Council's press office to help me this time. So I felt the best course of action was to say 'thanks, but no thanks', as nicely as I could. I felt that if I did say something – and there was plenty I could've said – it might have put the funding for Swinton Lock at risk. Schools send children for activities at Swinton Lock, and most schools sit within the council's education service. So I had to be very careful.

Obviously, being the press, they weren't going to give up that easily. Reporters tried all sorts of verbal tricks to get me to talk, but I wouldn't. I was also offered money, which I wouldn't take. But although they were persistent, I have to say that every journalist I fielded calls from or spoke to on my doorstep was polite and respectful. Then again, I wasn't the one facing the hostile questioning and several journalists said that I was 'the only person' who was coming out of this in a positive light.

One thing did get to me a little bit that day, and that was when I had a couple of press phone calls telling me that I was 'Rotherham's Erin Brockovich' and what did I think of that? At first I laughed, not really knowing much about this person, other than it was something to do with a film about a campaigner. Then I began to feel annoyed. We were talking about abused children here. It didn't seem right to tie up the experiences we'd had in Rotherham with some Hollywood thing. There is no making light of CSE and it upset me that people were going on about a film I hadn't even seen.

The calls kept coming. The *Chicago Tribune*. The *Sydney Morning Herald*. The *New York Times*. The BBC. Channel Four. Film companies. Documentary people. It had gone ballistic. My neighbours must've been wondering what I'd done. And in the middle of all this, I had to explain to a nine-year-old boy why journalists wanted to speak to his mum. Actually, Paul did this. I was too caught up in the whole thing to think out a proper way of telling him. Paul told Samuel that 'Mum has done a good thing and has tried to keep children safe, and that's why people want to speak to her about it'. And, thank goodness, he was OK with that.

The one phone call which made me sit up and think, *Should I go public?* was one from the German news magazine *Der Spiegel*. In perfect English, the reporter introduced himself as 'Christoph' and explained that the magazine – which I'd never heard of – published in-depth features and wasn't interested in scandal. This was interesting because so far most of those who'd been in touch wanted me to dish the dirt.

'We want to look at this from a different angle,' he

said. 'To see it from the victims' point of view and describe how grooming can happen so easily, warning parents about the signs.'

This was music to my ears. If I was going to do anything, it had to be of some practical use. I took Christoph's number and promised that I would contact him in the future, albeit I could barely see further than a few hours ahead. And then it was on to the rest of the day. We learned that Roger Stone, the leader of Rotherham Borough Council, had resigned 'with immediate effect'. In his resignation statement he apologized (again) to the victims and their families who, he said, had been 'badly let down' by the council. Martin Kimber, the council's chief executive, also apologized but did not appear to be resigning. Instead, he said: 'The report confirms that our services have improved significantly over the last five years and are stronger today than ever before.' He went on to say that there was 'not enough evidence' to discipline anyone at the council, and those who were in senior positions 'during critical periods' were now working elsewhere.

Well, I smiled at that last one but, for me, his words sounded eerily familiar. Although Alexis had described the council as 'bullying' and 'macho', and said that its failings were 'blatant', suddenly we appeared to be seeing the usual head-in-the-sand behaviour which, personally, was my experience of dealing with the council. Martin said he would not be resigning because he felt he was 'part of the solution' which would somehow cure the council of all its ills. It was, I felt, a typical response, even in the face of what was now blowing into a big crisis for Rotherham Borough Council.

The fallout continued to blow over Rotherham and the rest of the UK days and weeks after the initial explosion of the Jay Report. Andrew Norfolk and *The Times* reported that Joyce Thacker had, just five months previously, told a meeting that agencies needed to keep a 'sense of proportionality' about CSE in Rotherham because it 'only accounted for 2.3 per cent of the council's safeguarding work'. She'd said that 'although it is a very important issue, child neglect is a much more significant problem'. There were also calls for Shaun Wright, the Police and Crime Commissioner, to resign, though for the moment he seemed very well dug in even though the Home Secretary said he should go.

Denis MacShane, the town's former MP who had by now served a spell in prison for parliamentary expenses fraud, denied that anyone had ever approached him about CSE issues, even though we know he attended an event about it, and said he wouldn't have pushed hard to raise issues that might cause ethnic tension because, in his own words, he was 'a *Guardian* reader and liberal leftie'. Which, I imagine, does a great disservice to *Guardian* readers.

Andrew Norfolk also broke the story of the raid on Risky Business in 2002, and the removal of Adele's

Home Office files. The council and police told Andrew they had no knowledge of any raid on the Risky Business office but that 'they were prepared to investigate the matter'. That was an interesting response because Joyce definitely knew what had happened – it was me who'd told her. Andrew also published the story about Shaun Wright meeting one of the girls we'd worked with, even though he told *The Times* and the Home Affairs Select Committee that he had no recollection of doing so. The culture of denial, it seemed, was still firmly in place at the council.

August rolled into September and early on in that month I was due to attend a scheduled meeting at the council. Joyce Thacker would be there. After the meeting which, although routine, was a very strange affair, given the circumstances, Joyce came up to me and caught me by the arm. It was the first time we'd spoken face-to-face in ages. She looked drawn and tired, and although I was aware of everything she'd said and done, I didn't have the heart to hate her.

'Hello, Jayne,' she said, 'and how are you?'

'I'm fine,' I replied.

'You've come out of all this very well, you know,' she said.

'I know,' I said. 'But how else should we have come out of it, Joyce?'

She smiled. 'Jayne,' she said, 'have you been asked to

attend the Home Affairs Select Committee? Because you don't have to go if you don't want to, you know . . .'

I paused before answering. A couple of days previously I'd been contacted by the HASC's clerk, asking me if I would attend a hearing on 9 September. They would be interviewing Joyce Thacker, Martin Kimber and Shaun Wright, the secretary said, and they would very much like to hear from me and Adele. Again, I wondered if there would be repercussions for Swinton Lock if I attended and gave my evidence, which would no doubt be thrown at Joyce, Shaun and Martin.

'Do I have to come?' I said to the clerk.

'We can't compel you to come, no,' she replied.

'Can I be summoned to come?'

'Not unless you've done something wrong,' she said.

'Look,' I said, 'I want to come but for various reasons you'll have to summon me. It's the only way I will do it.'

So that's what we did. Which is why, when Joyce wondered if I'd been 'asked' to attend the committee, I could truthfully say, 'No. I've been summoned.'

She looked a touch disappointed. 'Listen,' she said, 'why don't you pop in again on Friday? Perhaps we can talk about this *Times* report about the missing files? I think Martin [Kimber] wants to know more about it too.'

I was unsure, but agreed to the meeting anyway. When I got back to Swinton Lock the receptionist told me the council had been on the phone, and a time for the meeting, plus a parking space, was already booked. Talk about being 'summoned' . . . Something really didn't feel right so I rang Andrew Norfolk and asked his advice.

'Don't go anywhere near it,' he said. 'The select committee might very well be asking about those missing files next week and it wouldn't be right if they're asking you for information beforehand.'

He was right, but just to double-check I rang the HASC clerk. She hit the roof. 'The council has been told they will have to answer questions about those files and if you're giving evidence too there is no way they should be asking you for a meeting. So the answer is no. Do not go.'

I took the advice and cancelled the meeting. I had enough to think about, being summoned (voluntarily) to the House of Commons to be questioned by a panel of influential MPs, annoyed that their previous appeal for Rotherham Borough Council to clean up its act hadn't been acted upon. Still, I was glad I wasn't in Joyce Thacker's or Shaun Wright's shoes . . .

20

I could have screamed. Today of all days, the car park at Meadowhall train station was closed. I was already frazzled from a near-sleepless night full of anticipation and apprehension. Disruption of our travel plans was the last thing on my mind. I was due to meet the train to London at Wakefield station. I had to think. Quickly, I called Adele.

'Now don't worry,' she said – the same words Ian Austin MP had said to me the previous evening, as he tried and failed to reassure me that my appearance at the feared Home Affairs Select Committee wouldn't be the interrogation I fully expected. Adele, Angie Heal (the researcher who compiled the Home Office reports in 2003 and 2006) and I would be giving evidence in private ahead of the main event – the public appearance of Joyce Thacker, Martin Kimber and Shaun Wright, plus two senior South Yorkshire police officers, Chief Constable David Crompton and Meredydd Hughes, the former Chief Constable.

'Stay calm,' said Adele, 'just drive to my house now and we'll go in my car to Wakefield. It'll be OK.'

I took a deep breath and pointed the car in the direction of Adele's place. We just couldn't be late for this meeting/interview/interrogation; whatever you might call it. It was a serious business.

The previous evening I'd arrived home from work and was sat in the dining room going through my paperwork when the phone rang. 'Good evening,' said a male voice, 'I do apologize for ringing. It's Ian Austin MP, from the select committee.'

'Oh, hello,' I said, somewhat nervously. I still wasn't 100 per cent sure that we wouldn't be somehow blamed for what had gone on in Rotherham and I was wary. The MP told me he wanted to clarify a couple of points relating to whether Shaun Wright did or did not meet any victims when he was in charge of Children's Services. I said that he came to Risky Business and met victims, and that he'd had reports about the project.

'Hang on,' said Ian Austin, 'are you saying Shaun Wright knew about this?'

'Yes,' I said, 'I'm just having a look now at a report I did for him.'

'Will you be bringing this?' he asked.

'Yes,' I said, 'if you want me to.'

'I do want you to,' he replied, 'and I'd just like to tell you not to worry. We're just asking for your help. We're really looking forward to seeing you.'

'I am a bit worried,' I said. 'I'm not sure how I'll sleep tonight.'

'Please don't worry,' he repeated, 'it will be fine.'

On the passenger seat of my car was a battered grey file of information I'd prepared over the previous few days: examples of the intelligence we'd supplied to the police, records of meetings with council officers, case studies of girls we'd helped. All sorts of information I thought the committee might find helpful, and which I hoped would help me to answer their questions, including the report I did for Shaun Wright.

The file itself had been borrowed from Swinton Lock. It was actually our signing-in book. I should've bought a new file, but the previous couple of weeks had been so manic, with the press on my tail, that I'd just not had time to get to the shops. It was scruffy, but it would have to do.

We got to Wakefield by the skin of our teeth. Adele's employers had agreed to upgrade her to First Class, and she'd asked them if I could travel in similar style. They'd said yes and I wasn't arguing; it was probably the first and last time I'd ever travel this way and if there was ever a day we needed a little bit of pampering, it was this one. The free coffee and pastries were very welcome, as was the complimentary copy of *The Times*. The paper's reporters and the rest of Fleet Street would be at the Commons today because, although I was giving my evidence in private, the appearance of senior

Rotherham council and police officers was very big news.

The countryside swept past as I looked out of the train window, the industry of the North and Midlands giving way to the softer, wealthier pastures of the South. I thought of the girls we'd helped over the years who would never travel down to London, never visit the corridors of power, never imagine a life beyond their own troubled existence in and around Rotherham. I thought about fifteen-year-old Mandy, who had been ordered by her abusers to perform sex acts on men in seedy hotels, and told that if she refused she was 'one bullet' away from death. I thought about Julie, who at twelve years old had a so-called 'boyfriend' (aged twenty-four) and whose own mother had invited her abusers into their home, enabling them to force her into giving oral sex in her bedroom for the price of ten cigarettes. I also thought about Kate, whose abuser slashed her across the face with a knife and went on to murder a young woman in a nightclub.

These, and the hundreds of girls I'd seen over fifteen years, were the reason I was on this train. Not for myself. The Jay Report had already exonerated Risky Business and I was happy with that. But for all those years the girls had, at best, been ignored; at worst, they'd been looked down upon as little sluts – 'undesirables' as the Jay Report put it – making a 'choice' about the people they were seeing and the lives they were living. The point is, they were just children – some as young as twelve – who were certainly not making a choice about being raped, beaten, tortured, threatened with death and pimped out to men all over the country. First and last, they were victims.

My phone rang, and as it did the door opened at the end of the carriage and the ticket inspector walked through it. I nudged Adele, who had the tickets, and pressed my phone's 'Answer' button. The number was unfamiliar.

'Hello, Jayne, it's Ian Austin MP. Hope you got the train OK? I'm looking through a few documents here,' he said, 'and I wanted to ask you a couple of questions about how you shared intelligence with the police.'

'That's fine,' I said, 'in fact I've got some samples here to show you.' Ian was a calm, well-spoken man and I had no problem talking to him. He had been very supportive so far and I'd no reason to believe he'd be anything other than that when we finally met. So when he asked, I told him, matter-of-factly, about collecting car registrations, dates of birth, nicknames, mobile numbers—

'STOP!' he shouted. I was stunned. He sounded like a grizzly bear roaring down the phone.

'Are you telling me,' he yelled, 'that you had this level of detail?!'

'Yes,' I replied, wondering where this was going. Meanwhile, the ticket collector had asked to see our tickets and a bit of an argument was breaking out between him and Adele – something about not having the right upgrade tickets and a fine. Trying to listen to each conversation, I seemed to be getting the worst of both: the collector insisting on an immediate payment and Ian Austin yelling about the intelligence.

'Never mind what questions we'll ask you,' he ranted, 'what do you want us to ask them?!' On he went, and you could clearly hear every word he was saying. Then we went into a tunnel and for a minute Ian was cut off in full flow, giving me a chance to find out what was going on across the table.

'I'm sorry,' the ticket man said, 'but you've only upgraded for one person and I'm going to have to impose a £250 fine.'

'Can't we just pay now?' Adele pleaded.

'I'm sorry, we can't do it that way as you've already had the breakfast and coffee. I'll have to fine you now and you can take it up with the train company later.'

Great, I thought, *that's the most expensive breakfast I'll ever have*. Then we came out of the tunnel and my phone rang again. To my surprise and relief, grizzly bear had been replaced by panda bear.

'I'm sorry for shouting,' Ian said, 'but I just can't believe you've got all this information and no one's done a thing about it.'

'It's true,' I replied.

'Like I said last night: don't worry, you're just coming

down to help us, and I'm really looking forward to meeting you. Make sure you bring that file in with you. See you later.'

He rang off. The ticket collector looked at Adele and me quizzically. 'Are you going to London about all that Rotherham stuff?' he said.

We nodded.

'In that case, forget the fine. Just give me the extra for the upgrade and we'll call it quits. And good luck to you down there.'

We arrived and made our way to Parliament Square, where we met a member of the House of Commons staff who would escort us in. This bloke was an odd character; his limbs moved like they weren't put together quite right and he walked at high speed, leaving me and Adele trying to keep up. I shouted for him to slow down, and as he did he tripped on the kerb, just avoiding falling flat on his face. We could hardly keep ourselves from bursting out laughing. Looking back, I think it was hysteria; we were both as nervous as hell, especially when we saw the amount of armed police officers around the place. Bags checked and security photographs taken, we were shown into a waiting room. Then the escort asked if we'd like to see the Home Affairs Select Committee room, 'so you'll feel better when you go in to give evidence'. We took him up on it. Mistake. It looked like a courtroom, with a semicircle of chairs for the MPs facing those we would be sitting on.

'How many MPs are we expecting?' I asked.

'Oh,' he replied, 'it's usually about six but on this occasion we've got all eleven in.'

I felt queasy with fear and needed to go to the loo. Adele joined me. We shut the door behind us and giggled like two schoolgirls.

'How did I end up here?' I said, trying to stop myself from bursting out laughing. 'I mean, me? Why am I sitting in a room guarded by armed police, telling a load of MPs what I did when I worked for Rotherham Borough Council?'

It was hard to believe, but there it was. In ten minutes' time I'd be telling them all about my days trying to persuade those in charge that children were being abused all over Rotherham and failing to get almost anyone interested. I'd no problem with that. But I did have difficulty with one more request, relayed to us by our minder for the day: that Rotherham's MP, Sarah Champion, would like to sit in on the hearing.

'No way,' I said. 'I don't want anyone from Rotherham there when I give my evidence.' I still didn't know whether Risky Business was for the high jump (again) and I didn't want anyone from Rotherham chipping in and trying to cover things up. But having made a snap decision, I sat down and thought about it. I'd seen coverage in the *Rotherham Advertiser* of what Sarah Champion was doing for the town and I'd been impressed by what she was saying. She seemed genuine enough. Almost as quickly as I'd said 'no', I changed my mind, and told our escort she could come in as long as she didn't ask any questions of me.

Just before we went in, a bloke who was sitting outside had spotted me. Because I hadn't given an interview or consented to photographs, despite scores of requests, I thought no one would recognize me. But this young man obviously did, mouthing 'good luck' to me as I walked by. I'd no idea who he was, and I'd no time to ponder, because my name had been called and I was due in the firing line. As I took my seat, my heart thudded in my mouth. I barely looked at the MPs, headed by chairman Keith Vaz, in a semicircle opposite me. To my left, Sarah Champion took a seat in the press bench. She was so close we could've shaken hands, but I completely avoided eye contact with her.

It was a stormy gathering. Adele, Angie and I faced a barrage of questions. They asked Adele about her report and the Home Office files that had been taken from the Risky Business offices. She told them that our manager, Christine Brodhurst-Brown, had said we needn't report the matter to the police. They demanded to know of me if the authorities – police, councillors, council officers and the CPS – knew about grooming in Rotherham.

'Categorically, yes,' I answered, telling them about all the intelligence gathered from the beginning that had been passed to the highest levels of South Yorkshire Police. To howls of outrage, Adele described how she had been subjected to bullying during her time with Rotherham Borough Council, and outright intimidation at the hands of the police.

Then, as promised during that grizzly bear moment on the train down, Ian Austin asked me what I would like the committee to ask Joyce, Martin and Shaun, along with the two senior South Yorkshire police officers.

'For me,' I said, 'I would like to ask the question why the information and the intelligence that was shared monthly and sometimes weekly was never enough to be used to go out there and hunt these people down, so maybe half of these children would have not been harmed. I have information here on perpetrators in 2006 who were still active in 2011 and 2012.'

At last, I'd said it to a group of powerful people who might actually be able to do something about it. I told them that I'd raised concerns, again and again, with all the key players, including Christine, Joyce and Shaun Wright. Then Keith Vaz asked me if the committee might take my file, the battered old grey thing that I'd used to carry my notes, case studies and examples, because I'd said there were reports in there that both Joyce and Shaun had previously seen. Keith Vaz said the committee would copy it and post it back to me. I handed it over; there was nothing in there they shouldn't see, and everything that they really should have a look at.

After the committee questioned Angie at length, the spotlight was turned on me again. Keith Vaz asked me if there was a 'reluctance' to take on the Pakistani community over allegations of CSE.

'For me,' I said, 'through speaking to managers and speaking to people that worked on the ground, the social workers, the police officers, I was always given three reasons [for this reluctance] over the whole of the period. I was told quite categorically that I could not mention the race or ethnicity in any training that I delivered and was told that was it. I used to get a lot of comments – especially by the police – that these girls made a choice; it was a lifestyle, the way that they lived. Obviously we would challenge that, and that was said in open meetings sometimes with others. We also used to get told on numerous occasions, "Where is your evidence? Where is your evidence?" We were project workers, we were youth workers, we were not police officers, and we believed that we gave enough information for them to get the evidence.'

Adele also answered the same question from the chairman. Then Michael Ellis, Conservative MP for Northampton North, piped up. 'If I can say at the outset, I am full of admiration for all three of you and thank you for what you did and tried to do,' he said. 'I am absolutely convinced that Risky Business must have saved lives, frankly, with some of the women that you were dealing with. So I very much want to say that.'

I could hardly believe what I was hearing. Apart from the girls we'd worked with, and Sergeant Rupert Chang, no one ever had anything good to say about Risky Business, and certainly no one in authority. To hear this from an MP was astonishing, and as heads nodded in agreement I knew we had the full weight of the committee on our side. And it was nowhere near the end; the MPs asked us in detail about who knew what and when, and why we thought so little had been done.

That warm September afternoon, emotions were running high. I thought Nicola Blackwood, Conservative MP for Oxford West and Abingdon, might burst into tears at any moment. That made me want to cry too, and as I turned away from her I looked directly at Sarah Champion. 'I'm so sorry,' she whispered – to this day, the only apology I've ever received from anyone, and from someone who wasn't even involved in any of this.

Finally, Keith Vaz brought the session to a close. He thanked us for coming and invited us to stay for the remainder of the session. It was a kind offer, but I didn't think I'd gain much from hearing Joyce Thacker et al giving evidence. Then he added this:

'I think you all have very worthwhile evidence to give and we are at a loss to know why these matters were not progressed earlier, but we are very grateful to you for coming in here and we promise you this: the committee will be producing a short report based on what we have seen over the last two weeks and that we will continue to monitor this until Parliament rises in March of next year.

'We will not leave it for some time in the future. We will come back to this issue again and again and again until we see progress and you get the justice that you deserve also, as people who have watched what is happening but have not been able to see a conclusion to what you have done.'

We stood up to go, then suddenly I felt the overwhelming urge to get something off my chest, something I'd been dying to say for a long time to anyone who wanted to listen. I indicated that I wanted to speak, so Keith Vaz ordered that everyone resume their seats. A hush descended around the committee room and I noticed people leaning forward in their seats.

'Can I say one last thing to all of us, really?' I said. 'Unless you have experienced what these children have experienced none of us will ever walk in their shoes, but maybe what we all now need to do is walk alongside them and recognize that these kids deserve a life.'

I felt like Oliver Twist, who asked for 'more'. But instead of being shouted at for speaking my mind, the committee replied with a chorus of 'Hear! Hear!' just like you'd get in the Commons. I couldn't believe it. What a day this had been. Surreal, scary, moving and empowering. Never again would I feel that we weren't being listened to. We'd expressed ourselves truthfully in the House of Commons, and I only wished we could've had every one of those girls we'd tried to help in that room with us, just so they'd know that someone had finally taken notice.

As we left, the two senior police officers were about to enter the committee room, and the press kerfuffle around them was so intense that we slipped away unnoticed, much to my relief. We left the House of Commons as we'd entered it, total strangers, and for that I was glad. We thought about going for a drink or some food, but I think we were all too shell-shocked by what had happened inside that grand building to make any rational decision. In our hearts, we just wanted to go home and return to those we loved. It had been that kind of day.

Once again, we availed ourselves of the First Class facilities aboard the train. I had a text from Christoph, the reporter at *Der Spiegel*. He said he'd seen me going into the committee room that afternoon. Then it clicked – he was the bloke sitting outside who'd wished me good luck. But how did he know it was me? Intrigued, I rang him.

'Your picture is on Twitter,' he said. 'You're standing on a canal boat with some other people.'

Of course. I'd had my picture taken with a councillor who'd come to visit Swinton Lock just after I'd started. It had been in the *Rotherham Advertiser* and must have been picked up. Oh well, these things happen, especially with social media. Christoph told me he'd just nipped out of the hearing with Joyce Thacker and Martin

0

Kimber. 'The committee are hammering them,' he said. 'I'll go back and text you some updates.'

Christoph kept us informed all the way home. Apparently, the book was being thrown at Joyce and Martin, and later Shaun Wright, who seemed to be getting a particularly heavy kicking. At that point, only Martin had resigned (although he wasn't due to go until December 2014). Joyce had said nothing and Shaun was openly refusing to fall on his sword. The committee were angry, and rightly so. In his position, Shaun should've done the decent thing as soon as the Jay Report was published.

It was gone 10 p.m. by the time I got home. I was keen to see what had happened in the committee room after we'd left, so I switched on the laptop and headed for the HASC website. Paul had poured me a large glass of wine.

'I can't drink all that, love,' I said, putting the brimming glass on the coffee table. I'm not a drinker; in fact, if the truth's told, I'm a very cheap night out.

'Relax,' he said, 'you've had a very stressful day. Anyway, when you see the footage I think you're going to need a drink.'

He must have seen the news. I watched in disbelief, not knowing whether to laugh or cry. In fact, I did both. Keith Vaz had made Joyce and the others swear to tell the truth on oath, apparently the first time the select committee had ever insisted on this formality. Then, as he started to question them, Keith Vaz began waving my file at them; the battered grey signing-in book that I'd borrowed from work. I was mortified, and I instinctively knew that Joyce would've known whose file it was, because only I could've presented such important documents to a powerful committee in a tatty old file. If I'd known they'd be waving it in their faces, I'd have at least made it presentable.

Martin looked very uncomfortable indeed, particularly when Keith Vaz was talking about 'industrial' scales of abuse, and why Martin had publicly declared that no one in the council would be disciplined for what had happened. And when Martin said that he didn't know Joyce had chaired the steering group of Risky Business – and therefore knew what we were all shouting about – I thought, *It's all up for Joyce now*, especially when Martin said: 'You can be reassured if that additional information tells me that I need to do anything, I will do it. I have evidence in place that I have taken such decisions in the past and I will do so in the future if I need to.'

Then they turned to Joyce. She admitted she knew about CSE in Rotherham, but not the scale of it. Keith Vaz waved the file again, and said the contents of it showed she knew what was going on much earlier than she'd indicated, and therefore why hadn't she resigned 'in all decency and honesty'? She fought back, passing the buck to Shaun Wright by telling the committee that 'he knew' about CSE as far back as 2008 when he received our report. But Nicola Blackwood tore into her, again and again, and she was finally told her evidence was 'unimpressive'. I thought that was bad enough, but when Shaun Wright sat down the committee made mincemeat of him. Paul Flynn, Labour MP for Newport West, told him he was ashamed to be in the same party as him and that he was 'the least credible witness' he had ever come across.

'Wouldn't you agree that you are a busted flush, you are a dead PCC walking?' he said. 'No one will take you seriously in future. You will have no influence. What is the point of continuing?'

And yet, as I watched Shaun Wright's world implode on screen, I felt a small amount of pity for him. I felt some sympathy for Martin Kimber, and Joyce too, even though they hadn't had a shred of any for me. I struggle to hate anybody, apart from those who abuse children, even if it's people who ignored me, threatened me and forced me out of a job I loved. *What I am doing*, I thought, as I watched the committee verbally batter the living daylights out of them, *trying to find good in people who did that to me?*

Joyce eventually resigned, and Shaun too, though shame on him, he took a good few days before he finally accepted he was finished. Even then, it wasn't quite over. A day or so after Joyce resigned I had a message from a friend still working at Rotherham Council.

'They're blaming you for Joyce losing her job, you know, Jayne . . .'

I was stung by this. 'Go back and tell them,' I replied, 'that next time anything happens and I'm called back to the House of Commons to give evidence, I will tell lies, lose my job and my credibility and never work in Rotherham again, I won't be able to pay my mortgage and my kids will suffer, but all that will be fine as long as senior managers keep their jobs. I am where I am today because I told the truth and if I get summoned down every week for a year I'll continue to tell the truth.'

'OK, Jayne,' came the reply, 'don't shoot the messenger . . .'

21

Joyce Thacker resigned in mid September, as did Martin Kimber. In a statement, Paul Lakin, the leader of the council, apologized on behalf of everyone to the people of Rotherham for letting them down so badly.

He said: 'The Jay Report makes clear that the scale of the problem was far greater than anyone imagined, except those who were actually suffering its effects of course.

'But it was happening, and some people knew it was happening, and some of them were in a position to do something about it, but did not.

'We need to ensure that they are called to account.'

I assume he was including himself here. As we know, he'd visited the project around the time of Laura Wilson's murder and had listened to me telling him everything about Risky Business and its work.

Shaun Wright took most of the flak for hanging on. He was heckled at a meeting in Rotherham by victims and their families, and although Prime Minister David Cameron publicly said he should go, he seemed determined to stay put. If only he'd fought so stubbornly for the hundreds of girls abused while he was in the top job. Eventually he had no choice but to relinquish his well-paid post. John Mann, a Labour MP on the HASC, said: 'Shaun Wright has finally done the decent thing and resigned, but for many people it's too little too late. He failed the people of Rotherham and to try and remain in his post as Police and Crime Commissioner was an insult to the victims and their families.'

I had to agree. As I've said, I don't like seeing anyone get a hammering, especially so publicly, but Shaun Wright's reluctance to accept the inevitable was shameful. I still felt some sympathy for Joyce, despite everything, and although she resigned she was still facing questions about the redacted Serious Case Review into Laura Wilson's murder.

As for me, I was still fielding calls from the press about the whole affair but was keeping to my rule, which was that I would take a number and if and when I had something to say, I would call the journalist back. I did contact Rotherham Borough Council's communications team on at least four occasions asking for help with this, stating that I had worked for them for twenty-two years and was struggling to deal with this on my own and could they help me write a press statement? The answer was a categorical 'no' – they did not do press statements for anyone out of the council. However, some days later I was in a meeting and another voluntary organization mentioned to everyone there that the council had just done them a press release. In the end Andrew Norfolk and a firm of solicitors helped me to do one.

A couple of weeks after the select committee meeting I arranged to meet Sarah Champion, Rotherham's MP, who had slipped in to listen to the select committee evidence. Her whispered apology to me – which she needn't have given, as she was only elected in 2012 and therefore wasn't connected with any of this – made me intrigued. There hadn't been time to speak to her after the HASC hearing so I arranged to see her at Swinton Lock. I didn't want to meet her publicly as I didn't yet know if I could trust her.

We have a canal barge at the charity which we use as a pleasure boat and as it was a pleasant day we decided to take a trip down the canal while we talked. Sarah wanted to know as much background as possible to the sexual abuse scandal (as it was now being termed) and so I went over it again. She said she'd make further enquiries about the more serious allegations aimed at council officials and police officers.

'What are you planning to do now, Jayne?' she said. 'You've told the truth, the report has exonerated you and everyone wants to know who you are. A lot of people have huge respect for you now.'

I wasn't quite sure where this was going, so I said I hadn't really made up my mind but would probably carry on with what I was doing at Swinton Lock. Then she said something that completely stunned me into silence – and that doesn't happen very often.

'How would you feel,' she said, 'if I put you forward to run for the Police and Crime Commissioner's job, as the Labour candidate, now that Shaun Wright has gone?'

Shocked, I stared at her for a few moments. Had I heard that right?

'Well, I . . . don't know,' I spluttered. 'It's, erm, not something I'd have considered, to be honest.'

Me? In charge of South Yorkshire Police? Was I dreaming this?

'I just think you're a person people would respect for your honesty, and the fact that you continue to fight for victims,' Sarah said. 'So can I give your name to the director of the local Labour Party so he can chat to you about it?'

'I suppose so,' I said, still astounded. We carried on with the rest of the meeting but, if I'm honest, I didn't take in much else after that. When Sarah had gone I sneaked into the garden at Swinton Lock to phone Paul in private. He didn't pick up, so I sat there on my own, staring into space. Sharon, the receptionist, must have seen me and came out to ask if I was all right.

'I just need five minutes,' I said.

Then my phone rang. It was Andrew Norfolk, wanting to see if I was OK and to ask if I needed any additional support regarding the press.

'You're not going to believe what I've just been offered,' I said, then told him about the meeting with Sarah Champion. He cracked up laughing.

'You're kidding,' he said. '. . . No, you're not kidding, are you? I'll tell you what, you'd make a bloody good PCC, but would you really want to do it?'

I couldn't answer that one. It seemed such a bizarre idea, and yet it was an intriguing one. What did you need to have to qualify? What was the job description? I had many questions, so I thought the best way would be to see the Labour Party guy and find out.

A day or so later, Paul Nicholson, Regional Director of the Yorkshire and Humber Labour Party, found himself in the unlikely setting of Ponds Forge swimming centre in Sheffield, talking to me while our Samuel was diving.

Just to put this into context: Samuel was always a good swimmer, right from being a little kid, and we were looking for an activity for him that would suit his abilities. He's not a boisterous type so it wouldn't be contact sports or anything like that. Paul suggested diving as he'd enjoyed it when he was young. So we took him to lessons in Maltby and within a short space of time the instructors said he had a talent for it, and would he be interested in trying out for the Ponds Forge squad? We thought it wouldn't do him any harm so he joined the squad and within a few months he'd won a Silver at a national championships in Plymouth. His confidence, which had taken such a hit when he was little because of the various tragedies in our family, really soared, with the result that Paul and I now spend a fair amount of our time by various poolsides. And if I have to hold meetings in such venues, so be it.

So we were sat in the poolside cafe and Paul Nicholson was telling me about the job and how I might be a good fit for it. I had reservations, but when the meeting ended I found myself agreeing to put in an application, which I did. Thankfully, perhaps, I wasn't selected as Labour Party candidate for the post. The reason was that I didn't have a political background and I thought that was absolutely fair enough. Since I'd handed in the application my doubts about my suitability had only increased. I knew about child sexual exploitation, but what did I know about burglary, car crime, mugging, shoplifting and all the rest? I also wondered why anyone would really want that job, given all the hassle around Shaun Wright refusing to resign. Finally, I thought it was too much money. I was appalled that anyone could demand £85,000 for a job like that.

Following this, I had another meeting with Sarah Champion. She had passed on further information I held and the Independent Police Complaints Commission were keen to meet her, and would I also come along? I said I would – I was happy to talk to any official body who might be able to help. So we jointly met the IPCC and afterwards went for a coffee in Rother-ham town centre.

I was warming to Sarah. Because she is a sensitive and emotional person it is easy to forget she is an MP and, strangely, that's what made me like her. I don't have a political background and, to me, most MPs just make a lot of noise in Parliament. If they're making noise about the things I agree with, I vote for them. If not, I switch off. Sarah is different. She never made me feel that I had to watch what I said in front of her. In fact, when we met for coffee I had a feta cheese and pesto sandwich, which isn't the usual fare you'd find in Rotherham. I bit into it and the cheese flew out and straight into my coffee. I was mortified, but luckily Sarah didn't make me feel like I was having tea with the Queen and needed to have better table manners! We have since laughed about this . . .

During the lunch Sarah asked me would I consider working for her, if she could get the funding? She wasn't quite sure what the job would entail but it would involve supporting Rotherham's victims and holding the council and police to task around policies and good practice. Was I interested? Yes, I was. But I had Swinton Lock to think about. They'd given me a job when I was a pariah in Rotherham and the management committee had been very supportive ever since. The only solution would be to split my time between working for Sarah and keeping some hours at Swinton Lock. Although

Sarah warned me that my two part-time jobs would feel like two full-time positions (and she was right), I decided I would give it a try until Christmas and then see how it was going.

In the aftermath of the Jay Report victims were coming forward in the hope that finally they would be listened to. It would be my job to support them, plus assist the police with the knowledge they required to understand the needs of victims as they carried out their investigations. Since the Jay Report the pressure was on to get results, but to do this they needed the cooperation of the victims – which meant they needed to treat them with respect and sensitivity.

As ever, I logged all the hours I worked for Sarah, keeping records of the meetings I'd attended and the people I'd seen. This was second nature to me, and I was used to such information being scrutinized by the various bosses I'd had. Sarah, however, was of a different mindset. After six weeks I went to her and told her that she'd been paying me but didn't know if I was doing any work or not as she'd never once asked to look at my timesheets.

She laughed. 'Why would I ask?' she said. 'I trust you to do the job properly. Why wouldn't I? At the end of the day I base things on results, not on how long it's taken you or where you've been.'

I respected her for the trust she put in me, but I also knew she was no pushover. She's a warm, friendly woman with an emotional, caring side but if she's not happy about something and wants to change it, you can hear people's knees knocking from a mile off! The fact that she isn't on a box-ticking exercise doesn't mean that she is not to be taken seriously. I wouldn't want her job, or that of any MP. It's a twenty-four-hour-a-day job, with very little time to switch off and enjoy a social life. And yet with Sarah it's sometimes easy to forget she's an MP. She doesn't couch things in political language – she says it how it is, and I think people from all political persuasions like her for that.

So we had girls coming forward, preparing to make statements to the police, and after a short while it was obvious that the Jay Report had not only empowered the victims in Rotherham. Abused people from all over the country were starting to speak out and it was clear that some kind of strategy had to be devised to tackle child sexual exploitation on a national level. After some thought and consultation with those affected we put together a five-point plan which Sarah drove upwards. This was:

- To establish a national task force to combat organized CSE.
- Mandatory Personal, Social and Health Education (PSHE) to Key Stage 1 children (aged five–seven years old), teaching them about healthy relationships.

- To make it mandatory that anyone employed to work with children has training in spotting the signs of child abuse and how to report concerns.
- For the government to make it clear that there will be penalties if health, education, local authorities and the police do not share information to prevent child abuse.
- To create a culture where victims of child abuse are believed.

We felt these points covered everything that had been neglected in Rotherham, and while our town is unique in the sheer numbers of its children that were abused, the five points could apply to any part of the UK, any local authority and any police force.

I feel the point about a specialist national task force is particularly important. If you have a disaster, say at a football match, specialist teams looking for evidence or providing help and support to victims are always on hand to step in at a moment's notice. But not so with child sexual exploitation, especially on the scale we've seen in Rotherham. Such a team would have the skills, expertise, knowledge and understanding of victims that you wouldn't or shouldn't expect your local police to have, at least not to the highest standards required. Police in Rotherham, and elsewhere, are about investigating criminals and that's great, we want that, but there needs to be a layer below that and that means understanding the needs of victims: why they don't turn up, why they're sometimes unreliable, why they struggle to remember what happened, why they often refuse counselling. Where victims are concerned, one size doesn't fit all, and that has to be remembered during the course of an investigation.

As time went on, just under 200 victims came forward, with accompanying families, siblings and parents. And we started calling them 'survivors' from the early days because there were those who told us they didn't want to be known as victims. One girl said, 'I was a victim when police and social services ignored me. Now I've gone on to survive, so I'm a survivor.'

On the other hand, there were those who still saw themselves as victims, and hadn't yet found what they needed to move to the next stage. For many, that is a long road ahead.

I did most of my work for Sarah Champion either at home or at Swinton Lock or in the homes of those who had come forward. I did try using her constituency office, but it was a nightmare. Anyone who claims to be able to work peacefully in an MP's office has an MP who doesn't do anything. I'd go into Sarah's office and the phones would be ringing constantly. The staff answered every call, but the volume was incredible. There was no way I could concentrate, so when I needed to catch up on the admin I'd hide away at Swinton Lock, where the only disturbance was the quacking of ducks on the canal.

Hard on the heels of the Jay Report came another detailed investigation into the workings of Rotherham Borough Council and its attitude towards CSE. Eric Pickles, the then Secretary of State for Communities and Local Government, appointed Louise Casey, a social welfare specialist at national level, to carry out the inspection. She would be looking at whether the council had covered up information, had taken action against staff guilty of gross misconduct and was addressing previous failures, among other areas. She arrived in Rotherham in October 2014 and I was asked if I would meet her soon after. I was the first person she wanted to see, so that I might give her an overview of the whole thing.

Like a fool I looked her up on the internet and discovered that she had a reputation for being scary and was also a government official so I was nervous the day I arrived at her hotel suite in Rotherham, which she was using as a base. On top of that, I was still worried that sharing information would lead to me receiving a prison sentence. With hindsight, there was a lot more I could've told Alexis Jay if I hadn't been so concerned. I was sick of having this fear constantly on my mind.

That first day, a Friday, Louise and I worked from 9 a.m. to almost 7 p.m. with barely a break. Far from being scary, she was actually one of the warmest people I'd ever met. She was very huggy and kept saying she was 'so sorry' that I had been treated so badly. I trusted her within minutes of meeting her, and at lunchtime I told her I was the whistle-blower.

'We thought it would be you,' she said, with a smile.

She wanted to know everything: every detail, every person involved, every incident, every encounter I'd had with council officials and police officers. As is usual whenever I tell my story there were several occasions when a look of sheer disbelief crossed her face and at one point she asked: 'Can you prove any of this? Do you have any evidence to back it all up?'

'Yes I can,' I said. 'Would you like me to bring in the evidence?'

She asked if I could bring it all in the following Monday, so I spent the weekend photocopying everything I had. It was a good job I'd kept copies of it all because Rotherham Borough Council had by now admitted it had lost various important pieces of information. I copied everything on to paper that was a sickly peach colour. Unfortunately I'd run out of white and this was the only shade I could get hold of in time. On the Monday I arrived at the hotel carrying a large cardboard box stuffed full of photocopying.

'Wow,' said one of Louise's assistants when she saw me struggling at reception, 'this looks like a lot of paperwork.'

'I can't carry the rest,' I said. 'I've got two more box-loads of this stuff in the car . . .'

So Louise had everything, and whenever the team was looking for something to corroborate what Louise had been told, the saying was: 'Refer to the peach papers.' Louise Casey was utterly determined to sort out the problems with local government in Rotherham. I was under no illusion that she would demand complete root-and-branch reform and I sometimes wondered if our complacent, forever-in-denial council knew what a tsunami was heading its way.

During the course of her inspection she held more than 200 meetings with victims, their families, councillors and council officers, senior managers, former staff, representatives from the police, community leaders, health workers and education representatives. To their credit, everyone she asked to speak to agreed to her request – all except former council leader Roger Stone, who gave a written statement, and our old friend Shaun Wright.

Louise Casey's report was due out on 5 February 2015. By now I'd met her on several occasions, helping her with more questions and information as she began to lift the lid on the past sixteen years. She was always friendly and encouraging, telling me to keep going and hold my head up because one day Risky Business might open again as a self-funding project and not necessarily on a local scale only.

That day, I'd gone to Lincoln with Jessica and Sally, the mother of another victim. Both were prepared to tell their stories and were excellent ambassadors for the kind of work we were doing with other survivors and their families. We'd gone to see a project called InMind Children's Services, a national organization run by a woman called Charu Kashyap whom I'd met through Sarah Champion and who initially wanted to help out in Rotherham. Sarah set up a meeting with her in London and when we spoke I knew she was serious about wanting to help. She came up to Rotherham a couple of times and I'd promised to have a look at one of InMind's centres, offering alternative education to vulnerable young people – not dissimilar to what Swinton Lock was doing, but with a residential element. So we were invited to Lincoln, where Charu had arranged a tour of the facilities and a lunch in our honour.

Looking back, I wish we'd had more time to concentrate on what we'd been invited down for, but when news broke of Louise Casey's report being released, the purpose of the visit went somewhat astray. All of us, visitors and staff, ended up gathered round a TV, watching events unfold. I kept apologizing, saying we'd spoiled the visit, but they told us they were honoured to meet the people from Rotherham on the day this report was published.

And as I watched, I didn't know whether to laugh or cry. I had no idea the report would be so hard-hitting. I knew Louise Casey was a tough cookie, but she had spared no one and nothing in her quest for the truth.

The report's opening line – 'Rotherham Metropolitan Borough Council is not fit for purpose' – set the tone for everything else that was to follow. Louise said that it was failing in its duties to protect vulnerable children and young people from harm. She went on:

> The Council's culture is unhealthy: bullying, sexism, suppression and misplaced 'political correctness' have cemented its failures. The Council is currently incapable of tackling its weaknesses without a sustained intervention.

She went further, saying the council was 'in denial':

> They denied that there had been a problem [of abuse] or if there had been, that it was as big as was said. If there was a problem they were certainly not told – it was someone else's job. They were no worse than anyone else. They had won awards. The media were out to get them ... both today and in the past, Rotherham has at times taken more care of its reputation than it has of its most needy ...
>
> Terrible things happened in Rotherham. On a significant scale, kids were sexually exploited by men who largely came from the Pakistani community. Not enough was done to acknowledge this was happening.

Not enough was done to protect children and apprehend the perpetrators.

Victims were denied justice. Decent individuals – social workers, police officers, taxi drivers and the many law-abiding members of the Pakistani community – were all let down and hurt by association because people didn't want to face up to an uncomfortable truth.

In her opening statement Louise referred directly to Risky Business when she said that although we repeatedly told the council what was happening, they chose 'not only not to act, but to close that service down'.

The report went on to explore issues of bullying, a macho culture and race. The latter was interesting. In interviews, anonymous council employees told how they'd had their 'knuckles rapped', as I did, for mentioning ethnic origins. Even talking about 'Asian taxi drivers' was too controversial, it seemed. One social worker remembered a meeting in which Asian taxi drivers had to be referred to as 'men of a certain ethnicity, engaged in a particular occupation'. And yet, as the report clearly found, not mentioning race or ethnicity just made the problem worse, as it played straight into the hands of the BNP and EDL.

Then there was the Risky Business issue. Louise Casey had this to say about us:

The strengths of Risky Business were actually considered weaknesses within RMBC [Rotherham Metropolitan Borough Council]. The contribution that the youth workers made was not properly appreciated or valued. They were not accorded the professional respect given to social workers. Too often, the information they gleaned was ignored and not acted upon. They spoke uncomfortable truths no one wanted to hear . . . the critical work they undertook is now missing from RMBC.

In addition, the report found an 'ongoing imperative to suppress, keep quiet or cover up issues relating to CSE which stretched across the years'.

So there it was. The cover-up that we all suspected was going on, but could never draw anyone's attention to. Louise Casey was very clear that not only had Rotherham not done anything to protect its young people, it had covered up attempts to do something about those failings.

On and on the report went, hammering the council for its incompetence. The treatment of victims in Rotherham was 'historically poor in the extreme'. The attitude of Children's Social Care was a 'tendency to blame the victims' for the abuse they'd experienced. Perpetrators were not pursued – 'often they were believed over victims and their families'. The council as a whole 'does not have the capacity to address past weaknesses'.

Louise Casey also addressed the issue of the redactions in Laura Wilson's Serious Case Review, saying that the review 'minimised her involvement in CSE' and that instead of actually finding out what was going on, the council chose to launch a legal action against *The Times* to stop it publishing the unredacted report. 'Staff,' said the report, 'told Inspectors of a culture where bad news was not welcome and difficult matters were taken off agendas'. This part also addressed how Risky Business was treated in the case review, describing how social work methodology was used to assess what we, as a youth service, had done, disregarding all the information we'd collected and using this as an excuse to bring us into Social Care. The report stated:

Inspectors consider that the SCR was used to justify this decision, which appears to have resolved the traditional tension between youth work and social work models by removing youth work – and the invaluable outreach work which it enabled – from the council's response to child sexual exploitation in Rotherham.

'Damning' was the word I most frequently heard in relation to the Casey Report and within hours of its publication the entire leadership of Rotherham Borough Council resigned en masse. Given the circumstances, I don't think they had much choice about those resignations. The only person I felt sympathy for was Emma Hoddinott: she had only just joined the cabinet and was actually making some good decisions around moving forward in the fight against CSE in the town. Eric Pickles told Parliament they would be replaced by government commissioners. As with the publication of the Jay Report, I watched the rolling news coverage of Louise Casey's investigation with a kind of disbelieving satisfaction. Had it really taken this long to be taken seriously? I watched as the grim-faced council leaders paraded out of Riverside, heads down, not wanting to answer questions from the pursuing press pack.

I knew that Louise Casey would be honest. She had the integrity to do the right thing, and would look at it completely objectively. It wasn't a report that would just claim that 'Risky Business saved the day'. And neither should it have been. Everybody needs criticism – if you don't get that you can't change and learn.

So I expected it to be a thorough report on everything that had gone wrong in the past. But when I actually read the report, I was most shocked by the criticisms of what was happening in the present. The biggest shock was the complete denial of the Jay Report. Louise discovered that, far from accepting the findings of Alexis Jay and putting its house in order, the council was denying that what she'd said was the truth. Instead of doing something positive, officers were still challenging the facts, describing the report as 'flawed' and 'inaccurate'.

To continue bleating about a report which they'd commissioned and which had led to high-profile resignations just didn't make sense. One interviewee from the council side claimed it was 'difficult to read'. I would argue that's because it makes for difficult reading.

I was shocked, but possibly not surprised. A few days after the Jay Report was released I had spoken to a police officer, and during the course of our conversation he said the one thing the police 'couldn't get their heads around' was the number of abused children; the 1,400 that Alexis Jay had estimated, which had been the focus of such media scrutiny.

'We just can't be sure this is a true number,' he said. 'What do you think?'

'No,' I said, 'I don't think it's correct either.'

'I knew we were right,' he replied triumphantly. 'I thought that figure was wrong. We've gone through every bit of paperwork and we can only find 1,100 victims.'

I took a breath, then replied very calmly: 'So if it's *only* 1,100 children, we can now say, "Oh, is that all?"'

'Well,' he said, 'you've just said it was wrong anyway.'

'Yes,' I replied. 'That's because I've identified at least 1,700 victims from my paperwork, and there could well be more. And let's not forget all the families caught up in this too.'

Personally, I believe that there could be up to 2,000 victims of child sexual abuse in Rotherham. I think there are those who haven't come forward and are unable to explain what happened to them, for whatever reason. Perhaps we'll never know the true figure. But Alexis Jay always said that the 1,400 she quoted was a 'conservative number'; sadly, I can only agree.

I drove back from the meeting in Lincoln and didn't get home until late. Paul, bless him, had recorded every local news channel for me. I remember watching the Channel 4 News, and seeing one of the Rotherham councillors being interviewed. They asked him what he thought and he replied by saying that there ought to be 'a review of this latest report'. And I thought: *You've had Alexis Jay, you've had Louise Casey, you've had a terrible Ofsted. So what are you waiting for? A report that will tell you how brilliant you are? Will you accept that one?*

Would anything change now, I wondered? Would kids continue to be raped, abused, neglected, ignored? Would council officials and police officers finally pull out their fingers and take this seriously? I hoped they would. More importantly, I hoped that all the talk and the investigations and reports and pledges to do something would lead to some arrests and convictions. There can never be 'closure' for most of the girls and young women I've worked with over the years, but jail terms for those men who stole their childhoods and turned them into vulnerable, damaged women will go some way to redressing the balance.

22

Christmas 2014 came, and I made the decision to continue working for Sarah Champion. So many survivors had now come forward that it was impossible to say, 'Well, that's it, I'm going back to my old job full-time. Goodbye.' I spent the whole of the Christmas break going through every report I'd ever written to compile a list of names of all the girls we'd worked with between 1999 and 2011 – a list which Louise Casey and Sarah Champion saw, but no one else seemed interested in, not least Rotherham Borough Council.

Girls continued to get in touch, disclosing years of post-abuse self-harming, eating disorders, domestic violence and broken relationships. The vast majority now had children of their own. I took one of these girls, Liz, to meet Louise Casey. She told her of the abuse she'd suffered from the age of nine. When she was sixteen a young white boy who was a drug runner for the main group of abusers became close to her, telling her that his masters had found her a job in another northern town, and so off she went, without me knowing until about three days later.

She found herself living in a homeless hostel where she was abused by numerous men. I spent the next six months ringing Social Care who constantly told me she was now sixteen and could make her own choices. Then I heard a rumour about where she was working and tried the local police, who couldn't understand why I was ringing them, but I think I got on their nerves so much that they offered to look for her.

Lo and behold, I then received a telephone call from Liz. She was hysterical, saying she needed to get home because things had turned out badly. She couldn't get any help from anywhere so I arranged for tickets for her to get to Sheffield. I met her at the station and then took her to a hostel in Sheffield. She never told me what had happened to her – I can only presume that she was being raped and abused regularly by gangs of men visiting from Rotherham and quite possibly by other sets of abusers from across the north of England.

That hostel also helped out another girl I was involved with. I received a telephone call from Social Care saying that a girl had been found doused in petrol at a motorway station and was refusing to speak. Could I go down to Norfolk House (Rotherham Borough Council's HQ at the time), pick her up and find her somewhere to live? I found her in an absolutely filthy state, stinking to high heaven of petrol and with a head full of lice. I took her to a hostel where she remained, although she was mute for weeks. When she began to open up she told how she was gang-raped nightly and when her main abuser had tired of her he had poured petrol all over her (a tactic used against a number of girls I worked with) and told her he was driving her to her death in Rotherham, before leaving her at a motorway services.

While visiting this young woman I began to notice she always had blood around the crotch of her trousers. Eventually she disclosed that she self-harmed by cutting her vagina with a razor blade, as that way no male would ever show interest in her again.

Such cases shocked those I was working with to bring the whole thing together, but at least now I had people on my side. Important, powerful people who would stop at nothing to make the voices of survivors heard, and at the highest level. In late February Louise Casey phoned me to say that Eric Pickles, having replaced Rotherham Borough Council's senior management with a panel of commissioners, would now put £250,000 into an outreach programme that would help CSE victims in Rotherham. There was talk of reinstating the Risky Business programme but I wasn't so sure that was a good idea. Things had moved on hugely since the founding of Risky Business and I felt that any organization working on similar lines had to have a fresh start.

Still, the pledge of money was a very welcome boost and it proved we were finally being taken seriously. And if any more confirmation were needed, it came towards the end of February in a phone call from Sarah Tatham, a colleague of Louise Casey. We were watching TV at the time and I'll never forget the look on Paul's face as he realized what was unfolding over the phone.

To cut a long story short, Sarah told me that David Cameron had requested to meet me at 10 Downing Street, ahead of a summit being held there about CSE. This would be in early March. He also wanted to meet some survivors, as it was important he heard their stories first-hand. I knew about the summit, as Sarah Champion was going along, so I asked if Sarah could come with me to the reception beforehand. Sarah Tatham said she'd check it out with Downing Street, but she was sure it would be OK. Alexis Jay would also be there. Louise Casey couldn't go as she was on leave.

I decided to invite Sally, the mother of a survivor, and Jessica; the same women who'd come down to Lincoln with me on the day the Casey Report was released. I phoned Jessica and asked if she was sitting down.

'Why?' she said.

'Well, we've been invited to another meeting,' I said.

'Oh,' she said, sounding a bit flat. 'Where this time?'

'10 Downing Street. With David Cameron.'

'Jayne, shurrup,' she said, 'you're having me on . . .'

I had to laugh. I could hardly believe it myself. And I'd been invited as 'the whistle-blower'. So even David Cameron knew . . . obviously this wasn't much of a secret any more. It would only be a matter of time before I'd have to go public.

The three of us travelled down on the train, resisting the temptation to have a glass of wine en route to calm our nerves. But I wasn't going to shout and scream and stamp my foot about Rotherham. By now, the whole country knew what had gone on there and how all those victims had been so badly let down. As ever, I just wanted to speak honestly about it, and definitely not in any kind of political way.

David Cameron listened very carefully to the three of us and I think he was as shocked as anyone by what he heard. It was an informal meeting – perhaps a bit too informal for me, as I completely forgot any protocol and, instead of addressing him as 'Prime Minister', kept calling him 'Dave'. He didn't appear to mind, even as I was being nudged by all and sundry whenever I mentioned his name. Before the meeting I'd been asked to write three short biographies of ourselves so that he could be briefed and as he spoke it was obvious he'd done his homework. He didn't make any promises to us, but he certainly made a lot of the right noises when we talked about the Five Point Plan and the need for a national agency to look after CSE issues. Now he is Prime Minister again I do hope that he will take the whole field of CSE as seriously as he appeared to do that day at 10 Downing Street.

We'd also been asked previously if we wanted to

meet 'Larry'. I wasn't sure who this Larry was and, not wanting to make a fool of myself, didn't like to ask. I assumed he was some kind of government minister, so I agreed anyway. Wrong. Larry turned out to be the Downing Street cat, who had come from Battersea Dogs and Cats Home and was now living at the most famous address in the UK. Suppressing giggles, we were taken to a downstairs kitchen where Larry resided. Sadly, he was asleep and wouldn't come out so we never got to pet him, but we were given a souvenir postcard of him. It was a slightly surreal end to what had been a quite incredible day.

I was invited to attend the summit but I made the choice to stay with the two survivors instead. Afterwards, we were due to give an interview to Sky News so we went along to their HQ. I remember thinking about the whistle-blower tag. I'd never felt like that; just someone who felt they should speak the truth. Which I guess is the definition of a whistle-blower, but I'd never done it for myself, only as a way of bringing what I thought was a very important issue to public attention.

Inevitably, perhaps, I was starting to become the 'face' of the Rotherham child abuse scandal, like it or not. I was interviewed by Sky News ahead of the Louise Casey Report and again after we'd seen the Prime Minister. The *Wall Street Journal* got in touch and asked if I would contribute a video interview for their website.

I was amazed that a New York-based newspaper would take an interest in something happening in South Yorkshire, but there it was. I was also approached by *The Times* to do a short interview about Andrew Norfolk, and his winning of the Reporter of the Year award for what he had done in Rotherham. I had to laugh when an editor rang me and said he had been given my name by Andrew, but didn't know why. I told him who I was and that it was me who had met with Andrew Norfolk and given him the information.

'Andrew never told me that,' he said, shocked.

I smiled. Andrew had obviously kept his word and never revealed his source. Eventually I did the interview, thinking, *Oh well, if David Cameron knows I might as well out myself on camera!*

In fact I was getting fed up of having the whole issue hanging over my head and worrying about Samuel and what impact it would have on him if I was arrested. The final straw came after I visited the council's offices and someone 'jokingly' said to me, 'I'm surprised to see you here – I thought you would be behind bars by now.' It might have been a joke but I took it seriously because the council were well within their rights to call in the police if they suspected I'd whistleblown. I rang Andrew Norfolk and told him I'd had enough and needed to go public but wanted to give him a heads up. He asked if I would do it with *The Times* and I said yes.

I also rang the National Crime Agency and told them

that if I had to be detained for questioning I wanted to get it over with sooner rather than later, and I needed notice so I could make arrangements for someone to look after my son. The officer I spoke to was quite shocked and rang me back saying he had informed his superiors, to be told that I would never be arrested for whistleblowing as it would never be in the public interest to do so.

That was a huge relief but I got het up again the following week when our local paper came out with the headline JAYNE WAS TIMES' DEEP THROAT SOURCE. I was absolutely livid. How dare they link me to the notorious 1970s porn film and why would they do such a thing? I rang Andrew Norfolk and was ranting down the phone, expecting him to be similarly outraged, when I was stunned to realize he was actually giggling.

'Jayne, do you know what deep throat really means?' he asked.

'Yes, I do know what it means. I'm not naive!' I said huffily.

'No, no, it's actually a term of respect in a journalistic context,' he said. 'It was the name given to the source in the Watergate scandal who brought down US President Richard Nixon.'

'It might be a term of respect in America but not in bloody Rotherham!' I said.

In the end no one mentioned the title of the article to

me, but I did get a lot of hugs and 'well dones' when it all came out. I can't really imagine anyone being surprised to hear that it was me who passed on all the information. But I didn't do it all. I gave Andrew the information he needed to do what a good journalist should do, and dig for more. And after he did his first story it gave people confidence to come forward with more information. I hope what I did was positive; having a secret like that felt like a cloud over my head, and I was always worried about the threat of arrest. But telling Andrew started a chain of events which mean that I will never need to blow the whistle to a newspaper again. Back then, I had no option because no one was listening. Now I have five commissioners at Rotherham Borough Council, the Police and Crime Commissioner, the local MP and many a few friendly senior police officers, all of whom I can talk to if I feel there is a wrong which needs righting. Now, people are listening and if blowing the whistle has achieved anything, it is that.

Before the commissioners came into Rotherham, I had a meeting with the then council leader, Paul Lakin, at which I asked for some help and support with the practical issues surrounding the women and girls who were coming forward. The police were keen for me to get as many girls in for interviews as I could, but putting a victim through a police interview requires support both before and afterwards. Some needed to move house for their own safety, some needed the help of social services, some needed counselling. Everyone had a raft of issues, but I was just one person.

'No,' Paul Lakin said, 'we can't give you any support. We can't be seen to be giving money to the local MP' – a reference to the fact that I was working for Sarah Champion, of course. I understood that, but even when I suggested they could put money into Swinton Lock, it being a charity, which would enable me to employ someone to help with post-abuse support, the answer was one of deafening silence. Evidently I was still toxic in the eyes of the council – never mind the victims, blame the whistle-blower. And yet at every meeting I had with the council post-Jay Report I emphasized that I was not the problem, but part of the solution. A youth worker I hadn't seen for a long time had been sitting with a group of people, including managers, when I was attending a meeting with the council during this time, and according to her one of the managers said, 'What's she doing here? Come to spread more lies?' So that was the prevailing attitude, unchanged in years.

I decided that the only way I could get Rotherham Borough Council to see me in a different light was to stand as a councillor and join their ranks. I thought that if I got in there, my reputation for telling the truth would stand me in good stead and I would be in a position to carry on the fight for victims and survivors, i.e. from the inside. I applied to be a Labour councillor and passed two interviews. The next step would be to find a ward to stand for in the forthcoming May 2015 elections but, after long and careful thought, it seemed a step too far. I'm good at giving 100 per cent to everything I put my mind to, but when I stopped to think, I realized that I had one job with an MP and another with a charity. I also had a family who needed me. A campaign to run as a councillor would have taken up so much time, effort and energy, and a great deal of commitment. I realized I just couldn't do it all, and decided not to proceed any further. That said, the whole of the council faces re-election in 2016, so who knows, I may find I have the time and energy to run then. In the meantime, though, I feel I made the right decision at the right time.

In the run-up to the election I helped Sarah on the campaign trail. Although I'm not a political person as such, it was fascinating to get a glimpse into what canvassing entails – and it's an awful lot more than just knocking on doors. Paperwork, charts, tick-boxes, graphs, plans – I'm amazed we actually had time to talk to the voters! But we did and it was good. We had very few doors slammed in our faces, and most people seemed keen to meet Sarah and hear about the work she was doing. There was a threat from UKIP to take the seat, and although I was always sure Sarah would get back in, there were one or two wobbly moments. UKIP unveiled a poster: '1,400 reasons not to trust Labour', a direct reference to the town's victims. It was a disgraceful attempt to make political gain out of an appalling situation involving children and it backfired spectacularly. Nigel Farage came up to Rotherham and Sarah accused him of 'rubbernecking', which caused another great storm. I guess it's all the usual stuff you'd expect at an election, but UKIP's was a dirty tactic and it really didn't go down too well among the people it referred to – the victims themselves.

I'm glad Sarah got back in, and I think the town as a whole was too. When the campaign was going on there was a knock on my door one afternoon. I wasn't feeling too well, but I got up to answer it. Standing in front of me were two blokes from the Conservative Party, asking if I'd sign something so they'd have enough support to stand as candidates. I laughed and said that I couldn't as I was working for Sarah Champion MP.

'Are you Jayne Senior?' said one of the men. 'I'm very pleased to meet you. In fact, let me tell you something in confidence. I actually hope Sarah Champion gets back in because I like her and I think she's doing a good job.'

And with that, they walked back down my drive. I thought, *Why can't UKIP have that attitude, instead of feeling the need to play dirty?* Politics, eh?

23

Quite often I find myself apologizing to people I've promised to catch up with or do something for, and haven't quite had the time to see. 'I'm sorry,' I say, 'it's just me and my mad life . . .' And when I look back on my story, with all its twists and turns, all the setbacks and tragedies – and the achievements too – I think, *How the hell did this happen to me?*

I certainly didn't set out to be a campaigner. I got a job in a youth club because I liked kids and the hours fitted my life as a young mum. It was no more complicated than that. I didn't intend to be a manager and I certainly had no aspirations to shake things up or cause trouble for anyone.

And yet, when trouble came my way – in the form of naive young girls telling me about their much older 'boyfriends' and how badly they were being treated by them – I didn't ignore it. I didn't treat the girls' stories as 'silly' and didn't assume that they'd 'grow out of it'. I took what they were saying seriously, and when we looked under the surface we soon realized how right we were to do so.

Even now, when I look back, I don't think I've done anything that special. I couldn't – and still can't – understand why anyone would think that the grooming and sexual exploitation of a child is something to be ignored or covered up. As I've said, it doesn't matter who the abuser is and where they are from – child abuse is child abuse. I was brought up to know the difference between right and wrong and I've kept to this all my life. It's to Rotherham's shame – and many other places besides – that the boundaries between right and wrong have been blurred for many reasons, leading to the most appalling abuse of the most vulnerable members of our society.

I hope I don't sound sanctimonious. All I've ever wanted to do is make people understand that sexual abuse of children is wrong, and that it must be tackled before it spreads like a fire. That is what happened in Rotherham. And it certainly wasn't just me who was shouting about it. As we've seen, respected researchers like Adele Weir (now Gladman) and Angie Heal recognized what was going on and tried to make others aware. They were ignored, and they weren't the only ones. Last week, I discovered in my files a letter from CROP (The Coalition for the Removal of Pimping), who worked with Risky Business in the early days. The letter was about two girls being sexually exploited, around whom there was a high level of intelligence. An all-agencies meeting was held, but CROP did not feel that the girls' cases were being handled in any way properly.

> My purpose in writing this letter [it says] is to advise you, as a person in Rotherham responsible for child protection, that children under your care are not, in this instance, being protected from violent sexual abuse. Furthermore [the girl], who is nearly sixteen, appears to be receiving no effective support what-soever. As you are no doubt aware social care have an obligation to work to protect children up to the age of eighteen; my sense is that as she is nearing the age of sixteen, and therefore the age of consent, 'feet are being dragged' regarding the response she is getting . . . I would appreciate your speedy response to this letter and more importantly your speedy and effective intervention on this case before one of these children, or another, gets seriously hurt.

The letter went to senior managers at the council, senior police officers and other agency representatives. It was dated September 2009 – a full five years before the publication of the Jay Report and the council's admission that, yes, they had failed the children of Rotherham.

By their actions or, more accurately, inaction, the council and police allowed Rotherham's sexual preda-tors to believe they were untouchable; that nothing would happen to them as long as they didn't cause too much trouble. In that climate, the abuse of children flourished. That, to me, is criminal and I hope that eventually the weight of the law recognizes that and deals appropriately with those who chose not to listen to Rotherham's victims.

At the same time, the many, many good people who work for the council and the police should be supported 100 per cent in their efforts to root out CSE. We all know that public servants have busy and complicated working lives, and don't always have the time to focus intensively on one aspect of their jobs. Any reform that frees up public sector employees from the weight of paperwork and encourages them to once again work with people on the ground should be encouraged. At the same time, I think there should be compulsory training for anyone who works with children around the issues of CSE and grooming. If people don't have the knowledge they can hardly be expected to have the empathy required to understand and deal with those who have been subjected to CSE. Education is everything; if a professional is able to use his or her judgement about grooming and can intervene early, we may avoid the horrendous escalation of abuse that we have seen in my town. I also think there needs to be a complete overhaul of the laws relating to child witnesses in adult courts, and better training for judges, solicitors and barristers who come into contact with young people this way. I fail to understand why a child who says she has been raped and abused has to be cross-examined by eight barristers over eight days, as happened with Charlie. The law is the law and the rule must always be 'innocent until proven guilty', but equally there should be better consideration given to young victims and witnesses giving evidence in adult courts.

I'm often asked what I think the Muslim community should do about abusers in their midst. My reply would be that every community in this country needs to look at itself closely to see who among it might be abusing children. That said, if the Muslim community has a problem with abusers – and clearly it does – then people inside those communities need to accept that and have the confidence to report matters to the authorities. It's no use us keep saying, 'Oh well, it's only a problem between white girls and Asian men,' as that isn't always the case. The problem is that Asian girls and women will not, in the main, come forward and report what is happening to them. They need to find equality and be empowered to speak out. Risky Business once worked with a little Asian girl who was being exploited by Asian men. They were raping her anally, telling her the reason they were doing it that way was that she'd still be a virgin when she got married. The twisted logic in that is beyond belief. What person in any community in this country would be pleased to know that their sons, fathers, cousins or brothers were anally raping a ten-year-old child? What could possibly justify that to anyone?

Despite advances in equality and understanding what that means in all areas, we still seem to treat women of all backgrounds as second-class citizens and sexual objects. And if you argue otherwise you're accused of being a feminist (like it's a term of abuse!) or a trouble-maker. Women today seem far more sexualized than they ever have been and I do think the easy accessibility of porn on the internet is really fuelling that. Sexual images that were once the preserve of the over-eighteens are now an everyday fact of life for children and it gives them a very false image of sexual behaviour that can stay with them for life. Some pornography sets out to glamorize prostitution – but when did anyone last see Richard Gere charging through Rotherham on a white horse to rescue Julia Roberts?

Aside from all the recommendations in the Jay and Casey reports, what is needed in Rotherham now is an open and frank discussion between all sections of the community about how we move forward. I would hope that members of the Asian community would understand how important this is, and that if we work together we will get somewhere. Especially the women. If women from all over Rotherham come out to say how wrong and unacceptable CSE is, we will be stronger. I appreciate that some women might feel threatened by the community they live in and I know I would feel dreadful if this was happening under my nose and I was too frightened to do anything about it. However, in Rotherham we now have the opportunity to change that. The same must apply in all the towns and cities where CSE is a problem.

The truth – and it's an important truth – is that abusers of CSE and domestic violence are all-powerful when it comes to screwing with the minds of children, but when they take on a strong woman we see a very different set of adult men. I will never allow myself to live in fear of any man who abuses children because to do so gives them power and allows them to win. It's there in the old playground wisdom – if you stand up to the bully you may encounter unpleasantness and hostility, but while you do you are helping to diminish his power. If I was ever fearful of an abuser I would not back down. I would ring the police and demand something was done. Not request – demand.

As for wanting something for myself, well . . . I don't really know. My job with Sarah Champion finished after the May 2015 election, as we'd agreed, and at the time of writing I'm back full-time at Swinton Lock. However, victims are still coming forward and need what support I can give them. Will this work become something which rolls out on a national basis? I don't know, but I'd like to think that others in the UK take CSE as seriously as I do, and that one day we can join forces to make sure none of our children ever get abused on such a scale again. I know these people are out there because they contact me from across the UK, and occasionally from the USA and Canada. Some are in the position I was in just a few years ago: ignored, preventing from speaking out and not believed. With help and support such people can come forward with the confidence that they will be listened to and their warnings acted upon. I doubt whether I will be ignored again, and I hope my story will give people the confidence to go to managers and say 'this is not working'. I hope and pray that managers will think twice before they ignore vital information or put it through the shredder.

Meanwhile, I have been seeking support from Rotherham Borough Council and its new commissioners, put in to replace the council's highest tier of management and get the borough back on a better footing. As I mentioned, I've been trying to support as many victims as possible, especially those who might form part of a police investigation into their abusers. Charges have been laid against certain individuals and it has been my role to help and advise those who might have to face these men in the witness box. Malcolm Newsam, the commissioner for Children's Social Care, and Mary Ney, a supporting commissioner, have both offered support. Both know that I have been struggling to cope with the sheer numbers of victims coming forward, and that previously the council has ignored or rejected any requests for help. It all came to a head as this book was being written, when one of the victims I've worked with for years said she would organize a charity 'bag pack' at a local supermarket to raise funds to keep the support going, as she realized she and many others were putting pressure on me just because they needed to be heard.

I appreciated the thought, but equally considered it ridiculous that she and others would have to take part in a charity event for Rotherham victims. At the very least, the council needed to take this seriously. At the same time, a friend inside the council working on CSE helped me out with a case I wasn't getting anywhere with. She took it directly to Malcom Newsam and within a week I was attending a strategy meeting – just like the old days except this time I was confident something positive would happen as a result.

And it did. Not only was my case assisted, two weeks later I was told that the commissioners had agreed to put £60,000 into Swinton Lock, which was enough for me to pay for a full-time CSE support worker to manage our ever-increasing caseload of victims of historical abuse. I was assured I would get this money but old habits die hard and I was sceptical right up to the moment I received official confirmation. It was excellent news and indicative, I hope, of the way Rotherham Borough Council is turning the corner.

I feel our local police still have some way to go before

they treat the victims of CSE with the understanding and respect they deserve. However, I've been helping the National Crime Agency (NCA) with the investigation into CSE in Rotherham, and while I can't say much more about it at this point, it has been a very interesting period of time.

Rotherham itself now has the opportunity to become a beacon of good practice around issues of CSE. I'd love nothing better than to see other local authorities coming to us for advice or training because we in Rotherham are getting it right. If nothing else, I hope that will be my legacy; that, and seeing the victims of this terrible situation living happy, fulfilling lives free from the shadow of child sexual exploitation that has haunted them for so long.

Epilogue

I'm sitting alongside a thirty-year-old woman at Swinton Lock, working our way through a pile of official papers, reports and statements as we try to fathom ways of making sure that the child abuse scandal which has blighted our town never happens here again, or anywhere else for that matter. As always, Jessica is very well turned-out today. Her hair is cut fashionably and her clothes flatter her figure. The woman she is now reminds me of the little girl she once was: confident, attractive, keen to please. She has a ready smile and handles herself well in many different and often challenging situations.

Yet Jessica has more experience than most of child sexual abuse. From a young age she was groomed by a man much older than her, then lured into sexual and physical abuse which lasted well into her twenties. This man had a grip of iron over her, and she and her family went through hell. Some of her experiences have already been recounted in this book – you'll remember she was the woman I first met as a child at a youth club I was running; a lively little girl with huge eyes who loved to dance. A few short years later I held her in my arms as she sobbed and sobbed, fearing she would never break free of the man who cast a deep shadow over every aspect of her life.

Even today, those shadows still loom large, and there are aspects of her own story that she can't remember, so deep is the damage. I know what they are and one day soon, when the time is right, I will sit her down and tell her these stories.

One of the ways she has dealt with the trauma of such horrific exploitation is to throw herself into the work we are now doing to highlight the grooming and abuse of children as a national issue. We are part of a steering group working on more effective and tighter licensing for taxis, better training for and checks on staff working in takeaways and a more integral approach to CSE awareness in all schools. We want to see these proposals put into place now in order to reduce the likelihood of others experiencing such horrific crimes. CSE is a nationwide problem that needs to be tackled robustly from all angles and this can only be achieved if we all unite.

I watch as Jessica reads over the details and suggests initiatives and ideas that could only come from long and painful personal experience. There was always something about this girl that I liked very much, even from a young age and before the darkness descended on her, and now I see how, despite everything, she has blossomed into a person of great maturity and wisdom.

I discussed Jessica with my colleagues many times during my period at Risky Business but she was so deeply involved with her abuser that it was extremely hard to engage with her. I knew her life was falling into chaos and occasionally I would hear stories about her that would upset me terribly. One day I was in a newsagent's shop when I heard a total stranger telling the woman at the till that she was buying a particular paper or a magazine as Jessica was in it, topless modelling. She claimed to know her, and went into a tirade of horrible comments.

I leaned forward. 'Excuse me,' I said, 'but is your life so boring you don't have anything better to do than spit out jealous comments about someone?'

'Oi!' shouted the woman. 'Who asked for your opinion, you nosy bitch!?'

'You don't know what you're talking about,' I said. 'You don't know anything about her life.'

'I know she's a little slag,' she replied, and with that we descended into bickering that was so nasty the manager was called and we were both asked to leave.

Although I knew Jessica was around, I didn't hear any more about her until a connection was made through a member of her family. This was around the same time that information about Rotherham and its children was leaking into the national press. I passed my number to the family member and asked that Jessica call me. She didn't and a year went by before she finally made contact.

At the time I was working with Andrew Norfolk, very much on the quiet, and I wanted him to meet Jessica. But first, I wanted her to meet Adele, who was working with solicitors involved in the various cases coming forward. I asked Adele to make Jessica a priority and offered a room at Swinton Lock for them to meet. I was in reception when Jessica arrived and I wanted to cry when she walked in. The poor girl was thin and quiet; a shadow of the vibrant child she once was. I rang Andrew and said, 'There is one victim you really need to speak to.' Every time I shared some information with him I thought of her as a little girl and it made me ever more determined that the truth about Rotherham should come out. He did speak to her, and her story eventually appeared in *The Times*.

Then the Jay Report came out and in its aftermath Jessica was so angry, trying to understand what had happened. I knew I needed to help this girl who was in such trouble: drinking, self-harming, not eating, trying to be a mother and trying to understand the mess her life was in.

And now I am so proud to say that in a short space of time Jessica has gone from being a bewildered victim to writing national plans, speaking out, helping others and becoming a role model for young people in her situation. She is my hero, and she is Rotherham's hero too.

Although this has been my story, there would be no story at all if there hadn't been sexual abuse of children in Rotherham. I wish that had been the case. Sadly, it wasn't, which is why I want one of those victims to end this book. For many years their stories were ignored or dismissed because the truth of what was happening didn't suit those in authority. Now that situation is reversed, and our lost children in Rotherham are being heard loud and clear. Here, then, is what Jessica has to say.

26 August 2014; a normal day for most people but not for me. As I turned on the TV every channel was covering the headlines, '1,400 children abused in Rotherham.' I was one of those children.

I remembered working with the Risky Business Project when I was fourteen years old; now I was in my late twenties, a mother of two beautiful boys, trying to cope with the realization that I had been living under a cloud until now. Today that cloud was about to be lifted . . .

Twelve months earlier I'd talked to Andrew Norfolk about my experiences of being a child raped and abused by gangs. My story horrified those who had read it in The Times. *For me, I still thought I was to blame as neither the police nor social services had believed me and had always told me what happened had been my fault. Even my abusers had convinced me no one could help me and I was worthless.*

Alexis Jay changed my life forever. My phone was red hot with reporters from all over the world wanting to listen to what I had to say. I always knew it wasn't only me, but 1,400 children? I was shocked, disgusted and angry. The findings said the abuse had gone on between 1997 and 2013. My abuse had been in the early 2000s. Why had it continued, and why were so many other children left to go through what I went through? Around lunchtime on the day the Jay Report was published I got a text from Jayne, who had just heard me on the radio. 'I am so proud of you,' she said.

I felt I needed to get my experiences out there. At long last I felt like I was believed and I hoped that by doing this others would come forward. I now felt I had a purpose and a path to travel down – never again would anyone say I lied or 'was up for it'.

However, I knew that I needed to do more than just talk about my experience. I started a petition almost immediately asking for more support for those survivors in Rotherham and other areas in the UK. What shocked me then was that for the next six months nothing seemed to happen for us survivors; instead we seemed to have a council more fixated on disputing the number 1,400. Why?

Jayne continued to offer me support and introduced me to a woman whose daughter had gone through what I had ten years later. We began a friendship that was like a breath of fresh air; at long last, someone else knows what I feel inside, understands why I have bad days and on those dark days when I feel I cannot even get out of bed comes along and makes me carry on. In December 2014 Jayne asked if I would meet with someone called Louise Casey and once again share my experiences. 'Here we go again,' I thought, 'another report and what will actually change? Will the council even believe this one?'

One cold morning in February 2015, I sat with my friend and Jayne to listen to the news, as we knew Louise Casey's report was to be published. You could have heard a pin drop when the report said that 'Rotherham Metropolitan Borough Council is not fit for purpose'. Elected members stood down, and the press descended on our town once again.

By then, I was attending numerous support groups at Swinton Lock that Jayne had set up. We mainly participated in art therapy but sometimes we just had a coffee and became angry at all our failings. This group grew and one day Jayne said, 'Why don't we put all this anger to some use and become part of the solution for Rotherham? No one can change the past and what happened but let's use all these experiences to shape the future.'

I now co-lead a CSE post-abuse steering group and during the last few months we have worked together to develop a national plan, written to the education minister to develop a mandatory education package, delivered training in Nottingham and Doncaster, assisted the Rotherham Commissioners in needs analysis data, participated in amending the licensing regulations for taxi drivers, met with David Cameron and local MP Sarah Champion, developed a video for the NHS and attended consultations with Barnardo's and KPMG to ensure that funding comes into Rotherham.

So has Rotherham got it sorted? 'No' is the answer. Are we on the right path? Yes, I honestly think we are. Some services are now in place and work is continuing to find out what those survivors of CSE need, not what those professionals think we need.

People regularly ask me where I see my future heading. I can't answer that – no one can – but I have spent the last fourteen years of my life afraid of anyone judging me for being a child involved in CSE. Today I feel strong. I have been given a purpose and I want to change things for the better and assist in making Rotherham somewhere safe for children and young people to grow and play.

I am not ready yet to give my real identity as I need to think carefully of my safety and that of my children's, but next time you visit Tesco or Asda or walk around Rotherham town centre, look out for me – I am the one with my head held high and a smile on my face, because I have a reason to get up in the mornings now and a destiny to fulfil.

Acknowledgements

I'd like to thank: my husband for giving me the support to keep going; my sons for putting up with me, and my family for being there; Andrew Norfolk for being the first person to believe this incredible story; Sarah Champion, Alexis Jay and Louise Casey – three strong women who gave me the courage to continue; the Post-Abuse Steering Group – you know who you are – for having the strength and courage to work with me in moving Rotherham forward; Adele Gladman – a friend, and for being my voice of reason; Tom Henry for his editorial support; John for believing me; Sharon Cooke, who answered every press call for me after the Jay Report and is always full of good ideas; Marg, my mother-in-law, baby-sitter and dog-sitter at the drop of a hat; Maxine, who's been there from the beginning and helped me through some of my darkest moments; Amanda, who is the only person I know who can talk more than me; the staff of Risky Business for their tireless contributions; those 1,400-plus children who touched my life and made me who I am today; Sgt Rupert Chang, the first police officer who didn't ask me for evidence but used the intelligence: an unsung hero.

extracts reading groups
competitions books new
discounts extracts
competitions
books new
events books
extracts new reading groups
interviews
discounts
new books events
events new
discounts extracts discounts
www.panmacmillan.com
extracts events reading groups
competitions books extracts new